PRAISE FOR THE 7E

M000159934

"By the end of the introduction, I realized for the first time that my long-time lethargy and dissatisfaction were the result of burnout!

Dr. Grossman's approach is firm and compassionate. She walks the reader through the causes and symptoms of burnout and offers a broad range of specific solutions that address the physical, emotional, and spiritual."

– Michael Palladino, Co-founder, Let Blu

"Dr. Sharon's book is transformative and compassionate. With her help you can see burnout as just the reason for personal transformation when life shows that it is time to adjust your course. If you have a job, family and a side hustle or you are an entrepreneur, this book is essential for your survival and strive."

– Bence Agosthazi, MBA, Business Transformation Professional, First Republic Bank

"In *The 7E Solution to Burnout*, Sharon Grossman takes a rational and research-based approach to keep you from burnout. The pages share how to move beyond self-judgments, fears, and the tendency to be an unbalanced high achiever. Full of examples and stories of how our perceptions affect our efforts, she lays out a compelling argument that our minds shape our successes."

– Ryan Foland, Speaker and Author of *Ditch the Act*, Reveal the Surprising Power of the Real You For Greater Success.

"Dr. Grossman's book is a must read for mental health care professionals and their patients. Filled with cutting edge research and much wisdom, Dr. Grossman points the way forward for all of us to regain a healthier work/life balance."

– John Schick, PhD, CEO and Founder, Psychiatric Alternatives and Wellness Center.

"Comprehensive, meaningful and practical are the words that come to mind after reading *The 7E Solution to Burnout*. Dr. Sharon has struck a delightful and effective balance of information, stories, and practical suggestions. The reader walks away with a deep understanding of the psychological factors affecting burnout, a sense of how burnout plays itself out in real lives, and practical steps every person can take to better care for themselves in their work life. A must read for anyone struggling with stress at work as well as for managers looking for ways to support their employees and increase enthusiasm and investment in the workplace."

– Paul T. Haefner, PhD Clinical and Sport Performance Psychologist

"Dr. Sharon shares an encyclopedia of information on how to alleviate burnout. I could tell this has been a labor of love. What I enjoyed the most was her elaboration on compassion, heartfulness, and selflessness as modalities in thriving and reducing burnout."

– Vy Le, Mindfulness Instructor, CMT-P (Certified Mindfulness Teacher - Professional) from the International Mindfulness Teachers Association (IMTA)

"Each year that goes by leaves us with more things to do, have and become and everyone around us reinforces this compulsion to go, go, go. Dr. Sharon's book is a technical workbook on how to reclaim our lives, find our focus and create something so rare in our modern times—balance and happiness."

– Chris Fellows, VP of Customer Solutions at 10Pearls

TRANSFORMING HIGH ACHIEVERS
FROM EXHAUSTED TO EXTRAORDINARY

THE 7E
SOLUTION TO
BURNOUT

SHARON GROSSMAN, PHD

WARRIOR
PUBLISHING

ISBN: 978-1-952437-00-7

Front cover image by Una Salimovic
Book design by Gaudencio Jr. Canta

First printing edition, September, 2020

www.7ESolution.com

FREE GIFT FOR MY READERS

As a way of saying thank you for purchasing my book, I want to gift you my **7 Day Burnout to Your Best Life Bootcamp** to help you bounce back!

This 7 Day Challenge includes:

1. Daily burnout solutions delivered through short videos!

2. A burnout assessment to see how burnout is affecting YOU!

3. Empowerment exercises so you can customize the solutions to your situation!

4. A guided meditation.

Join the 7 Day Burnout to Your Best Life Bootcamp NOW at:
www.7DayBurnoutChallenge.com

If you find this book helpful in transforming you out of burnout, consider gifting it to 3, 6, or 12 of your colleagues. To reward your generosity, I will gift you free monthly coaching videos.

Purchase 3 books - receive 3 months of coaching videos and learn how to:

- Develop Adaptability
- Communicate Effectively
- Conquer Your Fears

Purchase 6 books - receive everything in the 3-month package plus learn how to:

- Create Killer Focus
- Overcome Procrastination
- Alter Perfectionism

Purchase 12 or more books - receive everything in the 6-month package plus learn how to:

- Delegate with Ease
- Turn Helplessness to Optimism
- Love Yourself
- Cultivate Inner Balance
- Build Up Resilience
- Attain Mastery

Simply email your purchase receipt to 7ereceipts@gmail.com

DEDICATION

To Ariella and Ben

May you find your calling, be immersed in work that inspires and challenges you, and create a life filled with vigor and joy.

CONTENTS

INTRODUCTION

The Story Behind This Book

MOST PEOPLE WANT to feel fulfilled by their career. The problem is that they often do not. This is because they lack control over aspects of their work and their mind gets in the way. But with the right mindset, they can create a positive outcome.

When your job asks you to do too much, you become overwhelmed and think, "I can't do this." When your job asks you to do too little, you become bored at work and feel frustrated that you are not tapping into your full potential. Having too much control can feel scary and create anxiety while having too little control can feel stifling and aggravating.

If you are experiencing this, you are not alone.

Most people want to be successful. Success is often defined as making more money, having more physical goods, enjoying higher status, and feeling that you have "made it." People think that more success will bring more happiness. But more often than not, the opposite happens.

I have been working with high achievers for two decades and have found that they either settle for, "it's never going to get better" and accept that happiness is not in the cards for them or, in attempts to achieve happiness, they switch jobs or even change careers and still end up in the same miserable state of mind.

If this is you, I've got you covered.

After all my years of working with burned-out professionals as a psychologist and coach, I recognize it takes an internal transformation to attain success and feel happy in your job. It is when your mind is in alignment with your needs, strengths, and actions that you become unstoppable.

Wherever you are in your career, it is crucial to stay in the game. Even if you are highly energized and living with purpose, you may find that it becomes increasingly hard to keep your fire alive. And, if you are doing your best without passion, you might find that no matter how hard you try, your environment slows you down. Working with the wrong mindset can wreak havoc on your inner resources and lead you to burn out.

Several years ago, I found myself in such a situation. I wanted to transition out of nonprofit work. As I considered my options, I recognized an opportunity to start a private practice. I had heard so much about other psychologists who had gone into private practice and burned out. That put me on a mission: I was going to do it smarter.

To ensure I would not burn out, I created a schedule that included breaks, healthy lunches, and exercising mid-day. I kept my office hours reasonable: not working early mornings, nights, or weekends. My excitement about having a successful private practice kept me feeling positive about my career. For a while.

Over time, I noticed that even with my mission to do it smarter, I had fallen into the "grind." I ended up doing the bare minimum. I was having session after session with clients and stopped feeling very engaged. Although I was paying attention during the sessions and really cared about my clients, I had stopped doing anything above and beyond.

I was brought to this place of relative burnout because I had lost touch with my purpose. When I realized this, I sat down and asked myself, "Why am I doing this work?" I connected to what drove my passion for wanting to help people live better lives, and because I knew I had what it takes to help them achieve happiness in their work, I got reconnected to my purpose in my own career.

With this renewed sense of purpose, I started to prepare for my sessions. I came up with resources and exercises to challenge my clients and help them move beyond their "stuck points" and conflicts. I gave them ideas about what they can do in-between sessions so they can continue to grow and learn.

Having had that experience, I am now enjoying my work and feeling energized seeing my clients overcome their own obstacles and reach their potential. Whitney, a physician from San Francisco says, "Years of negative thinking had gotten me into a technically good place in life where I was miserable—a scary place of burnout, fatigue, demoralization, and finally depression despite doing yoga, meditation, seeking help from friends, family and other therapists. I was and continue to be (happily) shocked at the change in perspective that working with Dr. Sharon helped me to take, and by the impact that it has had on my life. Most significant is my awareness of negative thinking and how it's not helpful—so I am able to let it go. And a shift toward self-compassion and trusting my own wisdom, as opposed to second-guessing myself and the world constantly. This shift has had a dramatic impact on my moment-to-moment contentedness, which has made me a more present, happy, and effective mother, doctor, mentor, friend, colleague, and wife."

I want to share the lessons of burnout and how to overcome it so you too can rediscover the reason you got started in your career. I spent ten years studying to become a licensed psychologist. You, like me, probably spent years of your life learning, specializing, training, and gaining experience.

I wrote this book and created the Exhausted to Extraordinary Program that accompanies it to help professionals like you best utilize your years of preparation, enjoy the work you do, and benefit from the results of your work and from the way you choose to live your life. I want to provide you with a fresh perspective on an age-old problem, to give you the tools to achieve fulfillment in your career, and to encourage you to take small steps that have a big impact.

Book a call now to discuss whether you will be a good fit for my program by going to: www.drsharongrossman.com and filling out the application.

Why You Should Read This Book

When I was growing up in the 1980s, kids played M.A.S.H., a fortune-telling game that showed, amongst other things, in what kind of a dwelling you would end up. You could get a Mansion, Apartment, Shack, or House. Other categories included your life partner, the number of kids you would have, what kind of car you would drive, and in what career you would work.

Everyone wanted to work in either the entertainment industry as an actor or singer or the lucrative sectors requiring higher education (e.g., a doctor or a lawyer). While being famous was a definite draw, the more practical solution was to be rich, and there was a clear line between certain careers and which ones guaranteed financial success.

Fast forward by about three decades. I ironically ended up working with many people in the medical and legal fields and money aside, these careers also more demanding and challenging. Consequently, doctors and lawyers were more likely to burn out.

Most people do not realize that they are burning out until it is too late. Burnout is not something that happens overnight. It is something that happens gradually. Even when you are aware of the symptoms, you likely will not label yourself as "burned out." When my clients described what was going on with them, I would suggest, "it sounds like you may be burning out." Only then did it hit them.

Because the signs of stress and burnout are sometimes subtle, you need to become aware of what to look out for in advance. Once you can identify burnout for yourself, it is imperative that you have effective solutions to help you recover.

Ultimately, the ideal situation is that you can design a life that prevents burnout. Helping you avoid burnout or move past the point of burnout is why I wrote this book.

The 7E Solution to Burnout

I put together a comprehensive guide you can follow to help you effectively reorganize how you engage with your work so that you can remain vibrant, passionate, and thrive. As part of this guide, I have compiled the most relevant research findings on the topic. During my research process, I realized that experts in this field focus primarily on the environment. While it is true that the environment can have a strong impact on your well-being and on how you feel at work, this angle leaves you feeling victimized by circumstances outside of your control.

To truly empower you, I have expanded the toolkit for overcoming burnout to include strategies that strengthen you from the inside. In this way, you can tackle any situation you come across without feeling overwhelmed, fearful, or stuck.

This book is divided into three parts.

In Part I:

- I share with you everything you need to know about the stress-burn-out continuum, including what you can do to become stress-hardy.

- I describe what leads to burnout so you can identify stressors that contribute to your burnout experience.

- Finally, I explain all the ways burnout manifests so you can correctly diagnose it as it is happening and intervene in its midst.

I also organized this book around seven distinct solutions to burnout. Part II of the book incorporates the first four solutions. These solutions build on each other and are about *doing* things to make a difference in your experience. They include:

- **Emotional Intelligence**. To implement any sort of change, you first have to be aware of what is happening to you. Part of Emotional Intelligence (EQ) involves self-awareness. It follows, then, that EQ would be the first solution to burnout. As part of this solution, we explore ways to increase not only awareness but also self-mastery and relationship-related skills. The knowledge imparted as part of this solution will serve you in many ways that will augment your on-the-job experiences.

- **Empowerment.** Once you are aware and masterful over your reactions to stress, you are ready to tune into your personal power. As a second solution to burnout, Empowerment helps you identify where you gain and where you lose power. Distinguishing between the two can make a massive impact on your energy and overall well-being.

- **Engagement.** Building on your personal power, we delve into how to engage in your work in a meaningful way. As part of the Engagement solution to burnout, you will learn how you can diminish poor engagement habits, optimize your overall engagement and, thus, your performance.

- **Efficacy**. To be truly successful, you have to believe in yourself. If you lack confidence in your ability, you will be less likely to take risks or push yourself to grow. When you become more efficacious, you can be more daring and, as a result, take more action.

Part III of the book incorporates the final three solutions. These solutions focus on *non-doing* and are less hierarchical than the *doing* solutions. They help you align with your purpose, and rely on momentum to make the most of your efforts. They include:

- **Energy.** While I address Energy throughout the book, this topic is so pivotal to recovering from burnout because it is the antithesis to burnout's primary symptom: exhaustion. Being smart about how you protect and recover your energy will allow you to stay productive long-term.

- **Effort.** Here we examine the dynamics between motivation (rewards) and effort with a focus on working smarter, not harder. As we explore more deeply the notion of non-doing, I highlight certain actions to avoid that are not serving you, as well as how to take positive action with increased awareness.

- **Enlightenment.** In the seventh and final solution to burnout you have an opportunity to investigate your values for creating a balanced, happy, and easy life, and where you learn highly effective tools to help you go beyond limitation and attain transformation.

This book will teach you the application of techniques and mindset shifts that focus on your inner self. These seven solutions will empower you to feel confident when faced with challenges, strengthen your ability to cope with difficult emotions and situations, and elevate you to think in a new way so you can align with your true purpose.

A Burnout Story

Eddy[1] was a nurse working overtime to save money to buy a house and start a family. He did not mind sacrificing himself in pursuit of his long-term goals. He was on track financially when he hit a stumbling block.

One of his coworkers harassed Eddy in an attempt to assert control over the hierarchy at work. He did not like that Eddy was taking a leadership role during many of his overtime shifts.

His behavior caused Eddy to have tremendous anxiety while at work, and especially around this coworker, which manifested in Eddy having debilitating knee pain. Following doctors' orders, Eddy proceeded to have knee surgery.

At the end of his medical leave, Eddy returned to work consumed with anxiety about what was to come. In his mind, he tended to perseverate on his problems. Eddy noticed he did not have as much energy or motivation. He found it impossible to relax. At night, the anxiety would not allow him to sleep. All this resulted in Eddy feeling absolutely drained.

At work, it was hard to get going and even when he did, Eddy found it impossible to focus. He became less productive and, to Eddy, productivity was a large part of his self-worth. With energy levels waning, he began to see himself in a negative light. He labeled himself as "lazy," "pathetic," and "a loser." He became irritable with his wife and knew, "this isn't me."

I worked with Eddy to build up his self-worth and self-efficacy so he could trust himself to deal with any situation he comes across. His strengthened belief in his abilities allowed him to let go of the need for

---

[1] In this book, I use case studies based on some of the clients I have worked with in my clinical and coaching practices. Client names and other identifying information have been changed to protect their identity.

control. He reestablished a self-care routine and started practicing grounding techniques to overcome his anxiety regarding his job. He engaged in fun activities, which allowed him to play, not just focus on responsibilities. Lastly, it was about changing his negative core belief that he is only valuable when he is productive. Consequently, Eddy was able to see that he has value for who he is as a person, not merely for his productivity. He was then able to have self-compassion, start loving himself, and listen to his needs rather than focus outwardly on everyone else.

By implementing some of the same solutions mentioned in this book, Eddy transformed not only his energy, confidence, and mental state, but also his relationship with himself.

It is my belief that burnout can be resolved mainly from the inside out. The tools I share with you in this book have been proven to create positive, long-lasting results that will strengthen, encourage, and enliven you without needing to change your environment. In fact, I promise that if you implement the tools of the 7E Solution to Burnout, you will get more done with less stress, boost your confidence and trust in yourself to be resilient, exchange negative thinking for optimism, and create a balanced, happy, and easy life. The rewards are well worth it.

Do not let burnout happen to you because you get overwhelmed by the demands of your life or the negativity of your own mind. Be the kind of person who has control over their thoughts, feelings, and behaviors. Be the kind of person who gets things done and still has time and energy for themselves. Be the kind of person who trusts themselves to make decisions and takes immediate action to achieve their goals.

Come take this journey with me. Embrace a Beginner's Mind. Forget your limitations. Leave your stories and excuses behind, and give yourself an opportunity for a fresh start. I will help you get your spark back. All you have to do is keep reading.

How to Use This Book

To reap maximum benefit, I advise against reading this book like a novel. It is not a tool merely to inspire you. Instead, it is a book and workbook in one. It provides a comprehensive account of the research on burnout and tools that I believe can help you thrive.

I have broken the content into smaller chunks by inserting exercises after each critical segment. It is essential that you engage in these exercises and apply them to your situation before you move on to the next section. Keep in mind, it is not a race to complete the book, but a process where I am coaching you through a transformation.

I have left space in the book for you to write in your responses to the exercises. That said, I recommend that you also use a notebook where you can write more thorough answers to the questions. This will serve as a place to examine your transformation from the book's entirety. I have also compiled the exercises into a digital workbook which you can download and print out. To access the workbook and other bonus materials including several guided meditations, visit www.BurnoutToResilience.com.

There are plenty of opportunities for reflection within the myriad of exercises. Feel free to complete as many or as few of these practices and checklists as you like. As with anything else, the more you put into this process, the more you will get out of it.

Before you can implement any solution, you need to be clear on the problem. One of the biggest obstacles to overcoming burnout is a lack of understanding of what it's all about. In the Stress-Burnout Continuum, we will unearth the relationship between stress and burnout, what personal and environmental stressors contribute to the problem, and how burnout results so you can identify its symptoms. Correct diagnosis is the first step toward finding a matching remedy.

PART I: ABOUT BURNOUT

The Stress-Burnout Continuum

"Stress arises when individuals perceive that they cannot adequately cope with the demands being made on them or with threats to their well-being."

– R. S. Lazarus

STRESS IS THE arousal you experience when demands are placed on you if you perceive those demands to exceed your resources. Performance increases with stress to a point. The Human Function Curve, as displayed in Figure 1.1, depicts the point where this relationship peaks. As stress levels go up, you begin to experience tension. Once you pass your comfort zone, you reach the apex, named "The Hump."[1] This is the point where you have exceeded your resources and where fatigue sets in. If stress continues to climb, this is when productivity starts to decline due to exhaustion and ill health. Ultimately, you will experience a breakdown. This breakdown is your burnout point.

Each of us has a different set point for where good stress turns into distress. According to research from the City University of New York, three characteristics define people who are stress hardy.[2] The first characteristic correlates with how much *perceived* control a person thinks they have over a situation in front of them. To reduce the effects of a stressor, one needs to find ways to feel more in control. Faulty perceptions may cause you to see yourself as having less control than you have, so changing such perceptions can positively impact your resilience, thus also improving your performance.

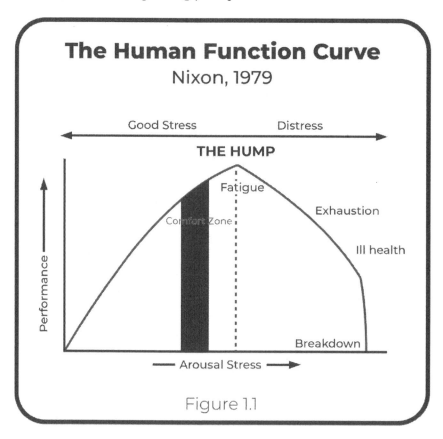

Figure 1.1

The second characteristic explains that stress hardy individuals tend to be highly committed to and engaged in their tasks. By giving your work your full attention, you are changing the way you behave rather than having to change any external circumstances. Engagement, in turn, gives you more control over the situation so that you can focus on maximizing your returns.

The third and final characteristic is when individuals are flexible in their thinking, they embrace change by seeing it as a *challenge* rather than a threat. Recognize that what worked for you in the past may not work now. It would be best if you found new ways to interact, adapt, and re-prioritize as change occurs.

By shifting your perspective about what you have control over, how committed you are to your work, and what represents a challenge rather than a threat, you can increase your stress hardiness.

TURN YOUR STRESS AROUND

1. Consider a work situation that currently feels highly stressful to you. In one sentence, write down what the situation is about:

   _____

   _____

2. Identify what makes it so stressful (too many demands, too many stressful episodes, too little time to recover):

   _____

   _____

Pick one or more stress-hardy strategies (control, commitment, challenge) to turn your situation around.

   a. How much control do you think you have in this instance? How did you come to that perception? If you could look at the situation from the perspective that you have more control, what would that look like?

   _____

   _____

   _____

   b. How committed and engaged have you been in your tasks? Is something preventing you from being more fully committed? Identify what the obstacles are. Then come up with a strategy to remove them and increase your commitment.

   _____

   _____

   _____

c. If the stress you feel is due to a change you are facing, identify what thoughts are going through your mind about the change:

_____

_____

_____

Notice if you perceive the change as a threat. Then come up with a new way of thinking about the situation where you see it, instead, as a challenge:

_____

_____

_____

_____

There are also three common ways people become overly stressed. Keep these three critical aspects in mind as you learn to avoid burnout.

Imagine that you are a frog jumping from rock to rock across a pond (Figure 1.2). To be effective, each rock should be big enough for you to easily land on but not so big that you become stuck there. Similarly, the first aspect to keep in mind at work is that your tasks should induce enough stress to motivate you, but not be overly taxing on your resources so that you experience an unhealthy degree of stress.

Figure 1.2

Each of the rocks symbolizes a stressful episode. The number of jumps you have to take will impact your total energy level. When it comes to your work, the second aspect to remember is you want to get through the day without too many stressful episodes.

Lastly, before jumping to the next rock, you need time to recover your energy from the last jump. While it might be tempting to push yourself from one stressful episode to the next, the third aspect reminds you to take time to de-stress and regain your energy before moving forward. Doing so will enable you to have the energy you need to complete your journey.

You might have incredibly high demands in any given task. Your job responsibilities might include too many stressful episodes that lead to overwhelm. Or, you might not have enough time to recover before moving on to the next challenge. Indeed, these circumstances can lead to burnout over time.

Conclusion

Stress can help or hinder your performance. To avoid burnout, you must pay attention to your energy levels and notice where fatigue sets in. When demands are incredibly high, when your job responsibilities are too many, or when you do not have enough time to recover between tasks, over time you can burn out. On the flip side, when you perceive yourself as having control, when you are committed to your work and see it as challenging rather than threatening, you will become more stress-hardy.

What Leads to Burnout?

IN THE SAME WAY that you and your neighbor might experience depression or happiness for different reasons, burnout can also result differently in each person. In this section, we will uncover three main stressors that contribute to burnout: your work environment, your personality, and the interaction between the two.

Environmental Stressors

When it comes to burnout stressors, it is easiest to start looking for the problems outside of yourself and then investigate personal contributing factors. To start, let's examine how your work environment can lead you to feel stressed. Consider three main work-related stressors: demands, resources, and control.

DEMANDS

Job demands are defined as "aspects of the job that require sustained physical or mental effort and are therefore associated with certain physiological and psychological costs."[1] When you have too much on your plate, have sudden conflicts with coworkers, or prolonged worry about your job security, amongst many other aspects, you can become drained.

Demands can be emotional, mental, physical, or a work-home conflict. You might feel overwhelmed when there are excessive demands on your internal resources (e.g., time and energy), when the pace of change is too quick, when there are expectations of working long hours, or when deadlines become tighter. These high expectations can quickly deplete your energy reserves. Intense demands can also be nonverbal as in work cultures where workers pride themselves on working overtime and not taking a lunch break. Adverse change, bureaucracy, harassment, role or interpersonal conflicts are additional organizational factors that can feel taxing.

According to a 2014 analytics and advisory company poll (Gallup), nearly 40 percent of Americans work over 50 hours per week, and almost 20 percent put in over 60 hours per week.[2] This is likely because of high demands and the desire to get ahead. Research from Stanford indicates that the heavy investment of time and energy does not pay off.[3] This is because productivity steeply declines after 55 hours. All that results from that extra personal investment is stress.

It is not just the demands of work that are eating people up. There is also life outside the office. There are people you care about, and to cultivate these relationships, whether they are friends, family members, a spouse, or children, you need time and energy after work. If your home life is also demanding, you just are not getting a break. You might soon realize this is not sustainable.

In an attempt to stay afloat on the work front, maybe you have sacrificed your personal time. You stopped going to the gym. You get home after the kids are already in bed. You have no time to unwind from work because you get home with barely enough time to eat, shower, and get to bed. You might even be taking work home. You keep coming back to the notion that "there's got to be a better way."

JOB RESOURCES

According to burnout researchers, there are various types of job resources whose purpose is to support the worker to achieve job-related goals, increase learning and personal growth, and reduce stress.[4]

Autonomy is one such resource. Self-Determination Theory (SDT) states that autonomy is an innate psychological need that, when satisfied, allows the person to function more optimally. When we are given the freedom to act in harmony with our needs, we feel more in control, more respected, and more motivated.[5] When working autonomously under stress, we cope more adaptively because we feel like we have more choice in how and when to respond.

Social support is a resource that allows you to get more done in less time through high-quality relationships with colleagues and supervisors. It can include both instrumental support such as help with technical difficulties or advice about how to deal with a difficult client, and emotional support that helps you feel understood and validated.

Through constructive feedback, employees increase their work effectiveness. When you are recognized for good performance, your motivation soars. And, when feedback focuses on problem areas, you can improve and overcome challenges more easily rather than remain stuck.

I often hear from my clients that their work lacks opportunities for growth. Once you have mastered the demands of your job, you seek to grow and be challenged anew. Autonomy can help you stay engaged and promote leadership and other critical skills that escalate your professional career.

Consider what resources your job provides that keep you motivated, engaged, and performing optimally. Then, consider what resources might be missing that, if you could access them, would make your job less stressful. The Engagement section provides a more in depth look at additional types of job resources.

DEMANDS AND RESOURCES

Stress does not result merely by being faced with excessive demands. There is more to it. Researchers Bakker and Demerouti proposed a visual model that exemplifies how the combination of demands and resources affects employee well-being (Figure 2.1).[6] Of the four possible combinations, three are unsustainable. Only one promotes wellness. This book looks, in particular, at the intersection of high job demands with low resources, which brings about burnout, and its polar opposite of high demands coupled with adequate resources which leads to work engagement.

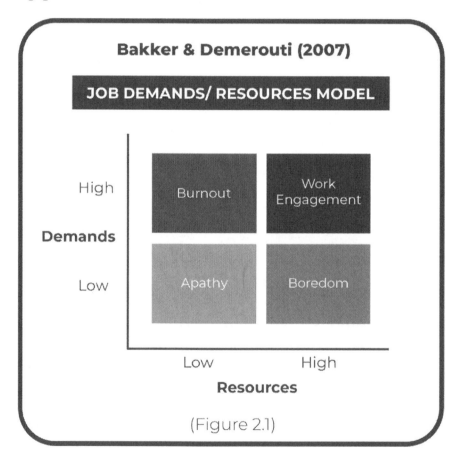

(Figure 2.1)

24

As the model notes, the answer is not necessarily about lowering work demands. It is about looking at the interaction between demands and resources. When demands are low but resources are high, employees are prone to boredom. When demands and resources are both low, employees feel apathetic. Optimal performance results when demands and resources are in proper balance.

That said, we can further delve into how to distinguish between two different types of high demands.[7] The authors looked at the amount of effort and energy tasks required and their respective outcomes.

Together, these factors helped determine whether a demand is a challenge or a hindrance. *Challenge demands* are when you use your energy efficiently while investing effort into tasks and when these tasks result in learning, goal attainment, competence, or mastery. *Hindrance demands*, which can include interpersonal conflicts, require a considerable amount of effort and energy but lack positive outcomes related to growth. As such, high demands can have different results depending on the rewards you get for your efforts.

CONTROL

"We're never in control, not of anything but the monologue in our head and the actions we choose to take. Everything else, if we're lucky, is a matter of influence. If we do our work and invest our energy, perhaps we can influence events, perhaps we can contribute to things turning out in a way we're pleased with. When the illusion of control collides with the reality of influence, it highlights the fable the entire illusion is based on. You're responsible for what you do, but you don't have authority and control over the outcome. We can hide from that, or we can embrace it."

– Seth Godin

Too little or too much control can wreak havoc on your experience at work. Lack of control is one of the main reasons why people burn out, especially if the control you feel on the job does not match your desire for control.[8]

If you find yourself reporting to a boss who is a micromanager, you will likely want to have greater autonomy. We all aspire to have accountability and recognition for our efforts rather than have someone standing over us watching our every move. We feel micromanaging bosses don't trust us to get the job done right, similar to a parent who watches their kid like a hawk to make sure they do not hurt themselves or break something, always ready with a critique of how the child needs to be more careful.

Alternatively, Type A personalities, or those who are highly competitive and who have control, often do not delegate responsibility. Their work keeps piling up, but they want to do it all themselves, which leads to a sense of overwhelm.

Your relationship with control is not only based on your personality, but it is also related to where on the burnout spectrum you are. If you already feel worn out, making decisions will be difficult. To protect your energy, you will be more likely to avoid additional responsibilities.

There are many upsides to having control including "more intrinsic motivation, greater interest, less pressure and tension, more creativity, more cognitive flexibility, better conceptual learning, a more positive emotional tone, higher self-esteem, more trust, greater persistence of behavior change, and better physical and psychological health."[9]

When we feel most out of control within, we focus on controlling the world without. Low control leads to lower levels of satisfaction and inner reward, which leads workers to demand more external rewards, including higher pay. And regardless of the truth of your situation, your perception of control is what matters. When you feel you have control, you feel less stressed and more capable of making good decisions.

26

DEMANDS AND CONTROL

While demands and control are both stress-related factors, it is the interaction between them that can lead to burnout. This interaction is the Job Demands-Control Model (Figure 2.2).[10]

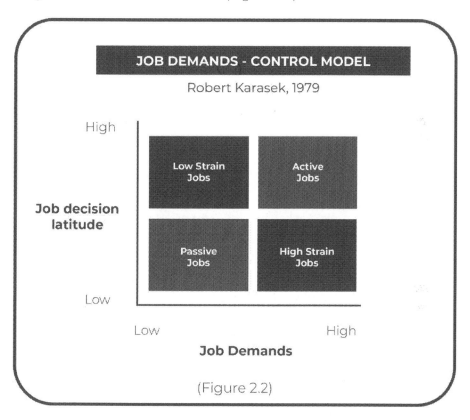

(Figure 2.2)

High strain jobs are those where demands are high and autonomy is low. While these types of jobs may suit a person who is motivated by challenges, it can still lead that person to work at a frenetic pace and subsequently feel exhausted.

Low strain jobs are at the opposite end of the spectrum with low demands and high autonomy. This may be the product of leadership that empowers workers to participate in decision-making and to take owner-ship of tasks. Aspects of this may be ideal, especially if there is a sense of community and a culture of teamwork that make workers feel supported and significant. However, these types of jobs may also lack the necessary level of challenge for growth and result in dissatisfaction over time.

Active jobs contain high demands and high autonomy. When you get to call the shots, you have less fear of change and are more likely to take risks. You just need to remain flexible in finding solutions to obstacles as they arise.

Passive jobs are ones where both demands and control are low. Under such circumstances, you are less likely to find purpose or satisfaction in your work. This is usually the case in big bureaucracies that have workers follow an antiquated procedure. You do not feel strained by your work necessarily, but the lack of autonomy coupled with the lack of purpose may make work feel like just a way of getting your bills paid. The lack of challenge can, once again, lead to disengagement and boredom.

MANAGING DEMANDS WITH RESOURCES

How many hours per week do you work on average?

- ❑ Less than 40
- ❑ 40-49
- ❑ 50+

2. How do you manage the demands on your time and energy?

_____

_____

_____

3. What are you sacrificing in the process?

_____

_____

_____

---

4. In the table below, categorize the level of resources (autonomy, instrumental/emotional support, opportunities for growth) you have as low, medium or high.

Resources	Autonomy	Instrumental Support	Emotional Support	Opportunities for Growth
Low				
Medium				
High				

5. If your resources are low, what can you do to increase them?

_____

_____

_____

Personal Stressors

The demands of a job itself are often what lead workers to the point of burnout.[11] While there is much truth to the fact that job sites are placing overwhelming demands on their workers while providing them with inadequate support, there is likely much more to the equation. Could the overwhelm stem from within?

Usually, workers have little or no control over their environment, so they attempt to gain control of their situation by placing high demands on themselves. In this next section, we explore the effects of such internal demands on stress at work and where these self-imposed demands stem from.

HIGH ACHIEVERS AND UNRELENTING STANDARDS

What is a high achiever? According to the Merriam-Webster dictionary, it is "a person who is hardworking and successful."[12] This definition implies that your input creates your output. You first have to have motivation, which will translate into investing tremendous effort, and this will lead to your success.

29

However, there are lots of people who work hard but are not successful, and there are those who are successful but perhaps do not work so hard. By its name, the term "high achiever" implies that the hard worker *is* successful, but we will focus more on the person as the "high aimer," because it is their mindset and efforts that get translated into action and which lead to their ultimate success.

THE MINDSET OF THE HIGH AIMER

Ambitious people often work very hard to attain their goals. They have an inner drive to prove themselves, to succeed, and to be recognized for their accomplishments. Many of them set the bar very high and will not settle for mediocrity. Even when everyone around them believes their work is exceptional, the high aimers may still not feel satisfied. That is indicative of a perfectionistic mindset.

If you are a perfectionist, you are not perfect. You just want everything you do to be perfect. You may have unrelenting standards where you feel like nothing you do is good enough. This keeps you striving to do better, do more, and can create the opposite effect of what you want.

Some of the biggest problems perfectionists face include a critical inner voice that tells them they are not good enough, a fear of failure, and a tendency toward procrastination. This trifecta, shown in Figure 2.3, is crucial to understanding what drives high aimers who are perfectionists and what can lead them to burn out.

If you do not believe in yourself enough or if you worry so much about what other people think, you will be less likely to take risks. This can lead to procrastination, where you put off your efforts until the last minute so that if you do fail, you can save face by saying that you only worked on the project for a short time, and it is not indicative of your actual ability.

Perfectionism is not attainable. It is an unrealistic standard we set for ourselves, intended to push us to achieve greater and greater results. Precisely because the standards are impossible to reach, we are setting ourselves up for failure. Ironically, this is what perfectionists fear the most, and that is why this is a cycle of self-sabotage.

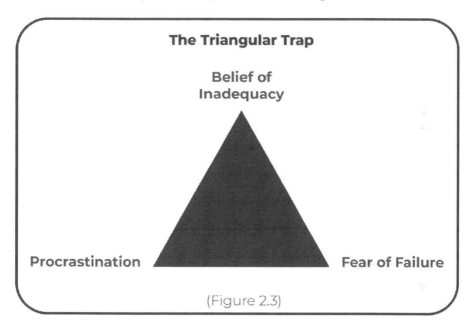

(Figure 2.3)

Perfectionism takes up tremendous time and energy. While, in some instances, it can lead to increased performance, the satisfaction is transient. Perfectionists are not typically satisfied because they always expect more from themselves. Even when they attain the desired result, they dwell on ways to improve or run ahead to the next challenge rather than take time to celebrate their win.

It is not surprising that perfectionists exhibit such extreme behaviors: they think about life in black and white terms. It is all or nothing. It is either perfect or it is garbage.

I will explore antidotes to perfectionism later in this book.

IDENTIFY WHETHER YOU ARE TRAPPED

1. Does your inner critique make you feel like nothing you do is good enough?

   ❏ YES

   ❏ NO

2. Does your fear of failure lead to procrastination?

   ❏ YES

   ❏ NO

3. Do you hold yourself to perfectionistic standards?

   ❏ YES

   ❏ NO

If you answered yes to any of these questions, you are likely stuck in the Triangular Trap. Don't despair. You will find the answers in this book to get you unstuck.

Mismatched to Your Work Environment

The Transactional Model of Stress theorizes that stress is not found in either the person or the environment, but in the interaction between them.[13] In other words, there is the environment, the person's perception of the environment, and the attempts to cope with the stressors that arise.

In their book, The *Truth About Burnout*, Maslach and Leiter address problematic interactions between the employee and the job environment by looking at six contributors, that if not adequately addressed can lead to a job-person mismatch. These contributors include excessive workload, low autonomy, lack of acknowledgment, lack of support, poor ethics, and unfair treatment.[14]

When the workload is excessive, and you feel like there is too much to do in the allotted time with the resources available to you, this will initially lead to anxiety and irritability as you struggle to get the job done. Because you are not able to accomplish it during office hours, you are more likely to stay late or take work home to complete. This over-commitment to your job robs you of personal time, and you end up feeling guilty about not spending enough time with your family or having the necessary personal time. As I will show you later in this book, without proper time for recovery, you will inevitably burn out.

You might feel mismatched with your job if you have too little autonomy. This is usually the case when you feel micromanaged by your boss, resulting in a lack of influence and accountability which can leave you feeling powerless and can also lead to burn out over time.

When your efforts are left unacknowledged, you feel devalued. If you are not proud of your work or if you are not gaining a sense of purpose from it, you will place more emphasis on external rewards, including money, prestige, and career advancement. If you feel dissatisfied with these rewards, you are more likely to burn out.

The community aspect of work is often overlooked, but it is a crucial component that can make or break your experience on the job. Humans are wired for connection, so if you feel alienated, if you lack support, or if you are surrounded by constant conflict, you will feel frustrated and on edge. Over time, these feelings can build and push you over the edge to unbearable levels of stress.

If your boss is so focused on results and efficiency that you end up acting unethically, you will lose any sense of meaning you might have other-wise gained from your work which will also lead to burn out.

As with any relationship, you want to be treated fairly. If, however, you get blamed for aspects of the job outside of your responsibility, get unequal pay, or see others in your company getting ahead by cheating, you will feel disrespected. This negativity will gnaw at you and can eventually lead to burnout.

Julie was one such client who experienced unfair treatment at work. The CEO of the company put her in charge of several accounts. Julie's manager was someone who had been her peer and who had moved up in the company. When Julie went on vacation, her manager went behind her back and contacted one of Julie's accounts attempting to change the contract with the account holder.

When Julie returned to work and found out what happened, she contacted her company's CFO to discuss the financial ramifications of changing her account's contract. In finding out, her manager demanded that she come into his office for a face-to-face meeting. He felt that Julie made him look bad in front of the company's upper management and was in a rage. Julie, on the other hand, felt that her manager was threatening and condescending to her, and not only neglected to take the time to understand her job responsibilities, but had tried to undermine her work. This made Julie feel a mixture of outrage and loss of confidence.

In addition to the six contributors to a job-person mismatch, you must understand the responsibilities tied to your role.[15] Without such clarity, you are unable to perform adequately. It is not surprising, then, that role ambiguity has also been linked to job burnout.[16]

MATCHING YOURSELF TO YOUR JOB

1. Check off any of the following that contribute to a poor job match for you:

   ☐ Excessive workload

   ☐ Poor autonomy

   ☐ Lack of acknowledgment

   ☐ Lack of support

   ☐ Poor ethics

   ☐ Unfair treatment

   ☐ Role ambiguity

2. In the lines below, write down everything that you focus on about your job that isn't working for you. Be sure to include items you've checked off.

   _____

   _____

   _____

   _____

   _____

3. Now re-write your story by focusing on what is going well and what went well in the past. Include information about challenges you've overcome, good role models you have come across, and about what you learned along the way.

   _____

   _____

   _____

   _____

   _____

Perception and Coping

In addition to identifying any mismatches between you and your work environment, you need to explore two additional factors that may contribute to burnout: (1) the perception you hold of your work environment, and (2) your coping style.

Returning to the Transactional Model of Stress, your appraisal of any given situation plays a big role in your stress response and works in two stages.[17] The primary appraisal is when you see potential stressors as threatening. You might reflect on past losses, consider future potential harm, or engage in a current situation that feels challenging.

The secondary appraisal is a consideration of your coping resources. In other words, if you see the situation as challenging as opposed to threatening, it is easier to deem it something you can handle, and you will be less likely to experience stress. It is when you feel you cannot cope, whether because there is too much on your plate, too little time, or because you lack the necessary skill to undertake the task, that you feel stressed.

When you appraise a situation as threatening or challenging, there are different ways in which you can cope. To better understand how this works, let us examine work through the lens of a relationship. When you feel frustrated in your love relationship, you can easily find fault with your partner. And some of the time, you would be justified in doing so. But even in the cases of apparent grievances like an affair, it is typically not so one-sided. When romance falls apart, you might seek out stimulation elsewhere. You might get bored with the relationship when it starts to feel status quo and lacks any sort of excitement.

In these situations, as always, you are faced with several choices. You can bury your head in the sand, convinced that this is "as good as it gets" and keep trudging along. You can look for a quick fix, perhaps finding excitement outside of the relationship to enliven you. Or, you can dig deep into the problem and seek out solutions.

The first choice is often the easiest for it requires no change. The problem with doing nothing is if you are unhappy with your situation, the prospects for improvement are meager.

The second choice, as noted, provides a quick or substitute solution. Rather than focusing on the root cause, you can look for a distraction, a shiny new object in which to invest time and interest. This often takes the form of drugs, alcohol, or emotional eating and can lead to addiction and health problems. What you often find is this approach does not have the effect you want because now you are in a bind. You are living a conflicting double life.

The third option, one that requires quite a bit of courage and determination, is where you can change things around for the long-term. Does this option guarantee you will get the results you want? Not entirely. You only have control over yourself. You cannot be sure how your counterpart will behave. But by shifting your mental and emotional framework, you can experience the situation on an entirely different level, regardless of any external changes.

The same principles apply at work. To be effective, you need to have insight into what led you to burn out. Then, consider what other ways you can look at your situation. When you can see it through a different lens, you can change your feelings about it as well as you coping strategy. In many cases, by examining the problem and seeking solutions, you will reduce your stress level without changing the job environment.

MANAGING PERCEPTIONS

1. Now that you changed your perception of the situation from "threatening" to "challenging," how well do you think you can cope?

   a. It feels beyond my scope

   b. I have some ideas, but I'm not super confident

   c. I trust myself to figure this out

   d. I know exactly how to handle this

2. If you picked option A, the uncertainty of the situation is likely contributing to your stress. Who can you approach for support and guidance?

    _____

    _____

    _____

3. If you picked option B, you might still want to seek out consultation, but you might want to take a leap of faith and try your ideas out first. If you have any fears about that, write about them below.

    _____

    _____

    _____

4. If you picked options C or D, write below what your plan is and then tackle it!

    _____

    _____

    _____

Conclusion

Your work environment, your personality, as well as the interaction between the two can all lead to burnout. When it comes to your environment, the ideal scenario that leads to engagement is where demands and resources are both high, where demands are challenging rather than hindering, and where you have adequate autonomy.

Personal stressors can be minimized by overcoming beliefs of inadequacy, overcoming fears and a tendency to procrastinate, and by not holding yourself to perfectionistic standards. If you find a mismatch between yourself and your work environment, focus on changing your perception and increasing your coping strategies. Of course, if all else fails, find a more fitting setting for your skills and talents.

Symptoms of Burnout

WE NOW KNOW that stress results from perception. When you perceive the demands as far exceeding your resources or ability to cope, you feel stressed. If this stress continues to build over time, not only does performance go down, but you become depleted of energy and experience burnout.

Burnout can affect you in many ways. Emotionally, you feel discontented when you put in the effort and cannot produce your desired outcome. Maybe you are used to giving so much of yourself, but are so worn out that you feel frustrated when you physically cannot do what you want or perform what is expected of you. The excessive stress can lead to impatience. Even when you achieve your goal, you might find that you get less satisfaction from it.

When you are under duress, you might be more prone to emotional reactivity, but once you burn out, you are at risk for extreme anxiety, depression, and anger. Because you lack energy, it becomes nearly impossible to manage your feelings. Over time, the emotional rollercoaster can leave you even more drained or bring you to a state of numbness that blunts even positive emotions. Physicians, for example, who are commonly burned out, are often so hopeless about their situation that they were found to be twice as likely to commit suicide as the normal population and more than any other profession.[1]

Physical symptoms of burnout include dizziness, rapid heartbeat, shortness of breath, insomnia, nausea, and chronic fatigue. Because your immune system is compromised, you are more prone to illness. If you are feeling down and exhausted, chances are you are not taking care of your health. You might find that you do not have the energy to exercise or prepare healthy meals. When you are burned out, you are already in a state of depletion. But without taking time to recover, your situation cannot improve.

Cognitive impairments include forgetfulness and poor concentration, making it even harder to get the job done. This can cause you to lose motivation. Negative thoughts continually surface, especially when you lack a sense of accomplishment from your work. If productivity is crucial to your self-worth, you will feel inadequate. Eventually, you will become apathetic to the situation, isolate from others, and even find excuses for why you should skip work.

Because all these effects can feel overwhelming, you will attempt to stay afloat, but simply coping may be a struggle. You might look for a quick fix, something to distract your mind and numb your feelings. If you find yourself reaching for alcohol the first chance you get when you come home, be forewarned. Addiction commonly develops from burnout. You will need to find real solutions to burnout, not merely an escape.

As I highlighted, burnout can impact your emotional, physical, and mental functioning, but there are three main burnout symptoms to be aware of. These include emotional exhaustion, cynicism, and reduced personal accomplishment.

To provide you with a visual depicting the symptoms of burnout, I've created an infographic that you can access on www.BurnoutToResilience.com.

Emotional Exhaustion

Emotional exhaustion is a state of mental fatigue due to an accumulation of stress. People experiencing emotional exhaustion often feel like they have no power or control over what happens in their lives. They may feel "stuck" or "trapped" in a situation. The lack of energy, poor sleep, and decreased motivation they experience can make it even more difficult to overcome the problem. Over time, this chronic, stressed-out state can cause permanent damage to their health.

Karasek's Demands-Control model of job stress, described in the section What Leads to Burnout, helps us understand what bring about exhaustion. In no uncertain terms, a major cause of emotional exhaustion is a high workload coupled with low autonomy on the job.

High Demands + Low Autonomy = Emotional Exhaustion

If you are tired all the time, it is likely you are burning out. You put in a long workday, commute home, and then work from home some more. Your work responsibilities are never done and you feel like you are living to work instead of working to live. There is no time for anything else. When the weekend finally arrives, if you actually find time not to work, you might notice that you do not have the energy to do anything fun. You just want to catch up on sleep or veg out in front of the television.

Once you are over "the hump" of emotional exhaustion, subtle signs of stress become more pronounced. Healthy engagement, which enables stress hardiness, becomes over-engagement with high stress levels. There is a heightened sense of urgency and hyperactivity in this frantic state. You intend to invest more of yourself to conquer your task list, but when expectations are too high and time and resources are depleted, you lack the energy required.

While no one wants to burn out, researcher and author Brené Brown points out that exhaustion has become a status symbol.[2] We live in a culture that emphasizes the importance of work and accomplishment. Too often, you can get caught up in over-working and feel proud of your self-sacrifice, like skipping lunch or never taking a vacation. When you are adequately tired, this is a sign you are a hard worker, which is culturally admirable.

In reality, if what you care about is accomplishment, you have to think about how to maintain your energy, not drain it, so that you can keep going.

While exhaustion may seem like an easily identifiable symptom to observe, it is often misunderstood and under-appreciated. To find out whether you are indeed exhausted, tune into your energy level. If when you started your job you felt energized and now you are feeling drained to the point that you are dragging yourself around, you are burning out.

Emotional exhaustion is an indication that you need to recover from work-related stress. Some indicators that you are energy-depleted include the inability to relax at the end of the day when you are home. You continue to ruminate in your mind about your work and find it hard to focus on personal tasks. Physically, you feel tired and it may take you a couple of days to recover your energy. When you are overly fatigued, you may find that upon arriving at home you need to be alone for a while before interacting with others, lack the energy to engage in any leisure activity or even engage with your work.

When you are worn out, this can bring a sense of dread about going to work. Not only do you struggle while at the office, but also during recovery attempts. It may be hard to fall asleep despite your fatigue. When the energy you need is not restored, it undermines your ability to do your job well by making it difficult to concentrate and remember critical details.

EXHAUSTION INVENTORY

Before you move forward to delve into solutions, find out how exhaustion or other burnout symptoms may be impacting you.

To measure early signs of fatigue at work, consider these items that were adapted from the **Need for Recovery Scale**[3]. Give yourself 10 points for each "yes" response. Scores fall in a range of 0 to 100. Higher scores indicate a greater need for energy recovery after work.

#	QUESTIONS	YES	NO
1	Toward the end of the workday, does fatigue keep you from being productive?		
2	Do you feel worn out by the time you leave work?		
3	Do you have trouble relaxing after work?		
4	Do you find it hard to show interest in other people when you arrive home?		
5	When you get home after work, do you need to be left alone for some time?		
6	After work, does it take over an hour to feel entirely recovered?		
7	Do you find that after dinner, you are still in bad shape?		
8	Do you feel so tired after work that you lack the energy to engage in leisure activities?		
9	Is it hard to focus outside of work?		
10	Does it take two consecutive non-working days before you can start to relax?		
TOTAL:			

Passionate people may destroy their relationships or physically pass out from emotional exhaustion but not burn out the way a frazzled worker might. When you are not clicking with your role, when you feel over-loaded, and when your duties are not aligned with your expectations or values, it is not merely the stress that gets to you, but you will experience a perspective shift. You will feel like you cannot make progress, and consequently disengage and become cynical and pessimistic over time.

Cynicism

When you are exhausted, you are extremely low on energy. You might feel like things are not working out. Maybe you are trying to do all the things that you typically do, but you do not get the same results. In essence, you go from being effective to being ineffective at your job. It can feel frustrating because it is not that you lack the skills or the knowhow; something is getting in the way. This frustration might fuel you to invest even more energy to get the results that you are used to getting, but if that doesn't work, over time, your attitude changes. You go from a place of feeling enthusiastic and excited about your job to feeling cynical. This is when you feel like your work is "just a job."

Cynicism is mentally distancing from work, minimizing engagement, and giving up on ideals. This is an attempt to protect your energy and prevent further disappointment.

If you are working with customers, you might stop seeing them as people with needs and start thinking of them as "just another part of my day I have to get through." This leads to decreased customer service, increased errors, and can negatively affect how you feel about yourself, especially if you typically take pride in your work. You might feel angry at your company for putting you in this situation or you might feel like you are stuck in a job that brings you no joy or sense of purpose.

In fact, upon reaching burnout, you have less capacity for empathy. Coupled with impatience and irritability, this renders you unable to have working relationships with your customers or coworkers.

According to the Job Demands-Control Model (Figure 2.2), while high demands lead to exhaustion, low autonomy is what brings about cynicism.[4] This is especially true for workers who struggle with time management and who have few resources with which to work.

When a job is very demanding of your time, energy, and focus, and when you feel like you do not have enough resources to stay afloat, you are likely to push yourself harder and harder. At first, you might be successful at getting some projects completed. But soon, you will recognize how unsustainable this pattern is and start to feel anxious about how you are going to manage. This anxiety is especially pronounced when you feel as though you are running out of steam.

If you find yourself in this position, turn your anger into a fight for increased support, more resources, and for getting tasks taken off your plate. Over time, however, when you are met with resistance, your anger can turn into a sense of detachment and cause you to feel deflated. You may feel like a lone soldier on the battlefield trying to fight a war that is way over your head. You know it's *mission impossible*, but you stick it out and think, "I have to keep going."

If high demands are the equivalent of you drowning, then cynicism is you making it to shore. The shore, however, is that of an island. While on this island, isolation leads you to feel disconnected from others.

You lose your sense of enjoyment at work as you indulge in negative self-talk. Consequently, you look for ways to avoid work by calling in sick more, coming in late, or not answering calls and emails.

PROBLEM-SOLVING AROUND CYNICISM

When you give up on yourself, it's only a matter of time until you fail. Whether you think you can or can't do your job, you are right.

In the lines below, write about a work situation where you currently feel cynical about your ability to accomplish a task and why.

_____

_____

_____

_____

_____

45

Now problem-solve about how you can turn this situation around.

_____

_____

_____

_____

_____

Reduced Personal Accomplishment

Given that burnout leads to reduced capacity for concentrating, decision-making, and overall coping, what might have been easy to do in the past becomes increasingly more difficult. Because operating in a hectic manner is unsustainable, overtime you will become disengaged, noticing that despite all efforts, you are not accomplishing as much as before.

A sense of helplessness and hopelessness can set in and can negatively affects not only performance and motivation, but the appraisal of performance at work. You may no longer see your work as an opportunity for accomplishment; you may stop believing in your ability to be productive, or you might blame yourself for not being able to keep up. When your mind is filled with negative self-talk, you stop taking risks, thereby accomplishing less, which only reinforces your belief that you "CAN'T do this job."

Journalist Ulrich Kraft discusses a burnout model proposed by psychologists Freudenberger and North which is comprised of 12 stages (Figure 3.1)[5]:

Stage 1: The cycle begins with a compulsion to prove yourself and is predominantly found in perfectionists.

Stage 2: You are led to work harder because you want to be irreplaceable.

Stage 3: The excessive drive eventually leads you to neglect your needs.

Stage 4: Sleep, meals, and social interactions all become erratic. You become aware that something is wrong, but you don't notice the physical symptoms of stress that are upon you.

Stage 5: In an attempt to adjust to the environment and make it work, you revise your values. Everything that is not work-related you deem unimportant, and notions of work-life balance, friends and family, as well as hobbies are dismissed, all in an attempt to get the job done.

Stage 6: When problems emerge, you deny them, become cynical, or place blame on the demands of the job and the timeframe rather than the changes that have occurred in your life.

Stage 7: To release the stress, you withdraw by using substances.

Stage 8: You become fearful, apathetic, and experience feelings of worthlessness. You exhibit odd behavioral changes that concern your friends and family.

Stage 9: Your sense of self and ability to tune in to your own needs is lost.

Stage 10: A sense of emptiness sets in and you become reactive and impulsive. This may lead to an overreaction to situations that feel stressful and to looking for ways to compensate and fill the void through the consumption of excessive food, alcohol, or drugs.

Stage 11: You become depressed and life loses its meaning.

Stage 12: Finally, you are burned out and mentally and physically collapse.

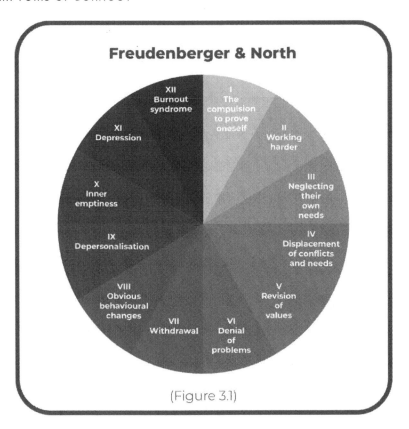

(Figure 3.1)

Conclusion

Burnout can affect you emotionally, physically, and cognitively. When demands are high, you are more likely to experience emotional exhaustion. When autonomy is low, your attitude about work might turn cynical. When you run out of steam, your performance and, hence, your accomplishments decline.

Life doesn't have to be so grim. Burnout is something that can happen for various reasons and can express itself in various ways, but there are proven systems to overcome burnout as well as prevent it. You're about to uncover seven different strategies to deal with burnout before it's too late.

PART II: DOING

E#1 EMOTIONAL INTELLIGENCE

"Knowing others is intelligence; knowing yourself is true wisdom."

– Lao Tzu

In this section, we will examine the two essential competencies of EQ, personal and social. You will gain wisdom and power as you improve your personal competency, and you will increase intelligence and strength as you develop your social competency.

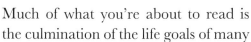

Much of what you're about to read is the culmination of the life goals of many of my client—being productive, self-motivated, and influential. In a word: effective. This section will highlight the skills you will need to develop in order to withstand external obstacles with grace.

PERSONAL COMPETENCY

Often, our biggest obstacles include distrust in ourselves or others, being overcome with fear, feeling overwhelmed by stress or anxiety, lacking motivation, and believing we are inadequate. Each of these can be addressed by increasing your EQ.

Personal Competency begins with an understanding of yourself through which you can better manage your reactions. To help you fully grasp the concepts and the associated skills, I have divided this competency into four chapters.

In the first chapter, we will examine how to increase self-awareness. This is followed by a chapter discussing emotional literacy and examining six of the most common emotions. The third chapter looks at how you can use your awareness, self-control, and self-expression to master your emotions. The final chapter helps you put your skills to use to achieve optimal performance. The idea is that when you know yourself, you can manage yourself better which leads to better performance results.

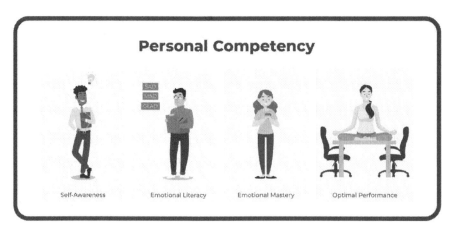

Self-Awareness

BEING SELF-AWARE is the cornerstone of Emotional Intelligence. It is vital to decision-making, to satisfy your needs and desires, to feel safe and in control, and to live with purpose.

Think about the last time you were at a job interview or on a first date. A question that we often struggle with is, "What can you tell me about yourself?" Sure, this question is vague, very general, and you may not know where to start. Likewise, due to your blind spots, it is a tough question to answer adequately.

There are a variety of ways to increase your self-awareness. We will focus on seven areas to master:

1. Know Your Strengths and Weaknesses

I recently worked with a client who was feeling burned out at work. She was not even aware she was burned out, but upon reflection on her work history, she noticed a pattern. She would push herself to work hard, but there was a misalignment between what she wanted to focus on and the work she was assigned. After a while, she would quit her job and look for a new one.

I had her take the Myers-Briggs personality assessment so we could gain insight into her strengths and weaknesses. Armored with this new information and discussing how her strengths and weaknesses applied to her job, it was easy to see where she could thrive at work and what she needed to leave behind. This conversation inspired her to talk to her manager and feel enthusiastic about changing the course of her job responsibilities.

If you want to be effective, you need to play to your strengths. You also need to know your weaknesses so that you minimize the amount of time and energy you spend on those areas and focus on improving them over time. By understanding and accepting your limitations, you avoid overestimating your abilities and can strategically delegate certain tasks to others whose strengths are more aligned with those areas.

We often have a hard time acknowledging our talents because they are just part of what makes us who we are. But consider this: let's say that from the age of eight, you spent 30 minutes a day practicing piano. What do you think motivated you to sit down and play every day when you could have been watching television or playing outside? Perhaps it was determination because you believed in your abilities. Are you the kind of person that once you make up your mind about something, you persevere? If so, how can you use that in the work setting?

Maybe playing the piano was an activity that allowed you to get into a meditative state. When working, what types of activities enable you to get into a state of flow? What are the circumstances that allow you to relax and allow your talents to shine?

When you play cards or board games, do you strategize and think two or three steps ahead of your opponent? If so, how can you apply this ability at work to anticipate what other people want, think, and might do? This is your superpower. Use it wisely.

2. Know Your Personality

According to researchers and authors of the Myers-Briggs Type Indicator (MBTI)[1], Isabel Briggs Myers and her mother Katherine Briggs, one dimension of personality is extroversion-introversion.

Your coping strategy for dealing with stress should be modified based on where you are on this dimension's spectrum. As an example, you need to set realistic expectations for yourself. If you are an introvert, this means allowing for recovery time from social exchanges because being around others takes its toll. If you are an extrovert, this means seeking out social opportunities when your energy is low because being with others gives you the boost you need.

One of the traps you can fall into is comparing yourself to others. If you are an introvert and see a colleague accepting more social invitations after work, going to one networking event after another, or discussing weekend plans at lunch with the entire team, recognize that they are likely extroverted. Rather than consider yourself inadequate in comparison, focus on your personal strengths that make you unique as an introvert.

If you are an extrovert, you might notice how easily a colleague creates intimate interactions with coworkers or works alone, focusing well without the need for socializing, or that their ideas seem introspective. Instead of feeling inferior, note that your extroverted tendencies just mean that you have different areas of strength.

INCREASE YOUR SELF-KNOWLEDGE

To know your strengths, weaknesses, and other dimensions of your personality, take the MBTI (available at https://www.myersbriggs.org) or a free version of a similar such instrument (available at https://www.16personalities.com).

Based on the feedback you get, answer the following questions below:

1. What are you good at? When you think about the work you've done in the past, what was easy for you? Perhaps you found yourself able to do something that was a struggle for others around you. If so, what was that? Think back to your past jobs, volunteer positions, and life experiences. What do people compliment you on? Is it your ability to make decisions, your time-management skills, your ability to lead a team, or your creative solutions to problems?

    _____
    _____
    _____
    _____
    _____

2. What are your personality type's stated weaknesses and how do you see these affecting your work?

    _____
    _____
    _____
    _____
    _____

3. How can you maximize your strengths and minimize your weaknesses in your job?

    _____
    _____
    _____
    _____

3. Be Aware of Your Emotions

It is easy to know when your car needs gas because the gas gauge serves as a visual reminder. Unfortunately, you do not have a visible indicator for your emotions, but you can become more attuned to your feelings.

Emotions are energy which manifests differently in the body depending on the emotion you feel. Close your eyes and scan your body. Where do you feel tension or discomfort? Ask yourself to associate a feeling with that bodily sensation and see what comes up.

Emotions are contagious. Just because you feel something does not mean it belongs to you. Ask yourself, "Who does this stress belong to?" You might realize you have absorbed your partner's or your colleague's stress just by being around them. In that case, focus on letting it go. It is not your stress and you do not have to hold onto it.

You can also go back in your mind to past experiences. If, for instance, it is hard for you to associate physiological symptoms with angry feelings, bring to mind an experience that made you angry in the past. With your eyes closed and your mind focused, notice what sensations arise. This is how anger manifests for you physically. Consider making a note of that sensation, and next time you feel this way in your body, let it be an indication that you are angry. You can do this for each of the emotions.

The more you are aware of what you are feeling, the more authentically you will come across in conversations. Your body language gives away your true feelings, so being aware of your emotions allows you to be mentally in sync, express your thoughts and feelings accurately, and get your needs met, thereby addressing the issue at hand.

As mentioned earlier, we all have blind spots. Getting feedback from a boss, coach, or through leadership assessments, helps you understand perceptions others have of you and will shine a light on your behavioral patterns.

Journaling provides you with an opportunity for self-expression and is something on which you can look back to identify patterns. Meditation is another useful tool. It helps to increase mindfulness which is an opportunity to delve into yourself to notice and release thoughts, emotions, and bodily sensations. By raising awareness of yourself, you will make more intuitive and fitting decisions.

REFLECTING ON YOUR EMOTIONS

Think back to a time when you felt each of the emotions below and write down how the feeling manifested in your body (e.g., heat, tension, pain).

1. Fear

_____

_____

2. Anger

_____

_____

3. Sadness

_____

_____

4. Guilt

_____

_____

5. Shame

_____

_____

6. Joy

_____

_____

---

4. Know What You Need and Want

Imagine you are driving a vehicle. You need to have a destination in mind. Your goal will determine the destination. If you need to buy milk, you will drive to the grocery store. If you want to visit a friend, you will drive to their house. If you want to combine them, you will figure what route to take so you can buy milk on your way home. By focusing on your needs and desires, you will direct your actions to be purposeful rather than being reactive and wasting your resources.

When you are clear on your needs, you can communicate them to others and increase the likelihood of getting them met. But you may ask, "What is the best way to identify my needs?"

Abraham Maslow talked about needs in terms of a hierarchy or pyramid (Figure 4.1).[2]

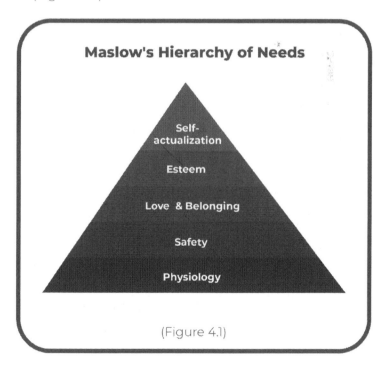

(Figure 4.1)

It makes sense that before you can focus on anything else, you have to meet all of your physiological needs, including food, water, clothing, and shelter. Once you take care of the basics, you can focus on safety and security issues such as employment, money, and health.

Next, you can focus on the need we are all wired for: connection. As human beings, we require "love and belonging" and this includes friendship, family, and sexual intimacy.

The next level of the pyramid focuses on esteem. This is where we seek ways to feel confident, get the respect of others, and gain a sense of achievement.

Lastly, we reach the highest level: the need for self-actualization. According to Maslow, we are self-actualized when we behave morally, use our creativity, can be spontaneous, problem-solve, and accept the facts. When it comes right down to it, this need is when the right and left sides of our brain are working together to bring logic in touch with our feelings so we can flourish. You will read more about the hierarchy of needs in the section bearing its name.

You can tune into your emotions to better understand your needs. If, for instance, you are feeling angry, this is an indication one or more of your needs are not being met. Ask yourself, "What do I need to turn down the dial on my anger?" But to be accurately attuned, you need to differentiate between primary and secondary emotions.

Anger is a secondary emotion, which means that there is another feeling underneath it. Anger is the feeling you have about your primary feeling, and it can intensify long past the triggering event. The patterns you experience may go back to childhood, so if it feels familiar, it may be a long-stemming way of interacting in the world.

To understand how you truly feel rather than be reactive, first find out what might be beneath the anger. Are you lonely, sad, or afraid? Once you identify the primary emotion, you need to deal with it rather than mask or avoid it. This reduces the emotion's intensity and allows you to powerfully cope with situations as they present themselves.

Each emotion connects to a thought. While you have tens of thousands of thoughts per day, you will need to do some detective work to find the notion that relates most closely to your emotion. Then notice whether the thought is about something or someone else. If it is, you will need to dig deeper to identify what your belief is about yourself.

Let's say, for example, that someone at work confronts you about the way you handled a procedure. When you think back on the incident now, you recognize that you were upset about the confrontation and were defensive in your response. In hindsight, you might be aware that you tend to one-up others in situations like these.

This is where you will need to get curious to figure out the unmet need. When you reflect on your life, what is the motivation that leads you to try to prove yourself right during conflicts? Maybe it's because you worry that others will not take you seriously. If that is your perception, what would it mean about you if this were true? You might believe that you are not important. Your need might, therefore, be to feel significant and heard. Once you recognize your need, you might consider more effective ways of meeting it.

GET FAMILIARIZED WITH YOUR NEEDS

Take a look at Maslow's Hierarchy of Needs and note below on which level of the pyramid your main needs lie at the moment:

_____

_____

Identify the emotion that best represents how you currently feel about your situation at work:

_____

_____

What is the unmet need beneath this emotion?

_____

_____

5. Know Your Triggers

Triggers are emotional overreactions you have to circumstances happening now that have roots in one or more events from your past.

You might notice that every time you drive by a place where you used to work, you feel nauseous. Perhaps when your friend arrives late to your dinner date, you find yourself panicking about her safety. If you are hyper-vigilant even when walking down a very safe street, this fear is an overreaction.

Saying that you are overreacting is not a judgment, but an observation. If you consider the situation and your reaction to it objectively and realize the two are not congruent, chances are you feel triggered.

You may have a perfectly good reason to react the way you do. The old workplace may have left an emotional scar, making it challenging to be around without reliving old memories. If at one time someone you waited for no-showed because something terrible happened to them, you will likely remember that story each time you are waiting on someone. And if you have ever been accosted while walking outside or heard of a physical attack happening to someone else, it might trigger you to be extra vigilant whenever you walk alone.

Neurobiologist R. Douglas Fields identified that our triggers usually fall into one of nine categories. He came up with the acronym LIFEMORTS to capture these trigger types:

- **L**ife or death: These are survival-based triggers, like the example of being hyper-vigilant while walking alone outside. You are trying to protect yourself from harm.

- **I**nsults: When someone hurls a hurtful phrase at you and degrades your integrity, you might feel triggered. When this happens, you might become angry and try to defend yourself. It may lead to rumination and to internalizing the insult, which can result in having other feelings like depression.

- **F**amily: This refers to protecting family members from danger.

- **E**nvironment: Protecting your home is an example of an environmental trigger. It is also imperative to your survival.

- **M**ate: You might be triggered when there is a threat against your mate because you want to keep them safe.

- **O**rder in society: You may feel triggered when you perceive a social injustice happening to yourself or others.

- **R**esources: This refers to obtaining and protecting resources such as money. When something threatens your resources, you might become triggered.

- **T**ribe: When the group you identify with (e.g., your country or religion) is negatively affected, you might also feel adversely affected.

- **S**topped: You may feel triggered as a result of being prevented from pursuing what you want. Examples include imprisonment or being physically cornered.[3]

The more you know your triggers, the more you will be able to avoid triggering situations that put you at risk for an extreme emotional reaction or at least prepare yourself in advance. Conversely, by identifying what you are avoiding, you will be able to familiarize yourself with your triggers and use that information to prepare for facing challenges.

FIND YOUR TRIGGERS

Identify your triggers in each of the LIFEMORTS areas, where applicable:

❑ **Life or death:**

_____

_____

❑ **Insults:**

_____

_____

❑ **Family:**

_____

_____

❑ **Environment:**

_____

_____

❑ **Mate:**

_____

_____

❑ **Order in society:**

_____

_____

❑ **Resources:**

_____

_____

❑ **Tribe:**

_____

_____

❑ **Stopped:**

_____

_____

What can you learn from your triggers to protect your energy?

_____

_____

6. Get In Touch With Your Values

We all seek meaning in our lives. When we are clear about what we value, we can direct our decisions and behaviors to be more purposeful. Do not let ego get in the way of your decisions. Instead, be true to yourself and others.

When you know your values, you can optimize your environment. This is key to avoiding burnout. If you are a doctor, for instance, you might consider whether you prefer a fast-paced work environment where you expend energy throughout the day (e.g., an emergency room setting) or a slower-paced environment that focuses on relationship building (e.g., a health clinic). Your values can shape your preferences and inform your decisions.

One value that determines how I live my life is balance. I love my work, I love my family, and I love my time alone. To feel complete, I have designed my life so that there is time for each of these aspects.

When you are not intentional about creating your experiences based on your values, you can easily fall out of balance, primarily if you are focused on only one aspect of your life, like your career. You will learn more about values in Why Enlightenment is Important.

7. Know Your Beliefs

We all identify with our story. It is our personal history, our collection of memories, and early experiences that have shaped the way we see ourselves and others around us. What is your story? What beliefs do you hold as a result of your early life experiences? The more in touch you are with your beliefs, the more you will see how they affect your interpretation of events, your feelings, and your decisions.

For example, my client Tammy showed up to our session upset the week after Mother's Day. Her father, with whom she had a problematic relationship, had sent her a package of hats as a Mother's Day gift. These were hats he had received as free giveaways. Tammy was upset because she interpreted the gesture as an indication that she was not important to him to actually buy a gift. Meanwhile, her husband asked her why she had not thanked her father and threw out the hats.

Tammy and her husband had different reactions to the same event because they had different upbringings and associated beliefs. The reason Tammy had the reaction she did was that she has been carrying around a belief since childhood that her father does not think she is important. Our brains try to find evidence to justify our ideas. In this case, Tammy was able to associate the "thoughtless" gift with her importance.

Throughout our work, Tammy was able to widen her lens—which is an essential aspect of changing personal stories. The more she thought about it, the more she realized that, in fact, her father was the only person who had given her a Mother's Day gift at all. While the hats were not what she wanted, she was able to recognize that the contents were not a reflection of her. Instead, they were a reflection of her father, who liked to collect free samples and wanted to share them as a thoughtful token.

Through the process of changing your story, you can change your state of mind. Therapy is one of the best avenues to help you identify and overcome limiting beliefs. I cannot overstate the importance of this work. It allows you to get beyond your stuck points, which start in your mind. Noticing triggers and working through them is an opportunity to break old patterns, whether in behaviors or relationships with others.

IDENTIFY YOUR LIMITING BELIEFS

Identify if any of the limiting beliefs[4] from the list below apply to you and check the corresponding boxes:

- ❏ My needs won't be met.

- ❏ I can't be successful.

- ❏ I can't control myself.

- ❏ Other people's needs are more important than my own.

- ❏ I have to stay vigilant/perfect, or something terrible will happen.

- ❏ There is something wrong with me.

- ❏ I am not enough.

- ❏ Other people cannot be trusted.

- ❏ I don't belong with other people.

- ❏ I can't do my work without other people's help.

- ❏ I am a failure.

- ❏ I am better/smarter than anyone else around me.

- ❏ I care more about people's perception of me than about being authentic.

- ❏ If others knew how I feel, they wouldn't like me or they would judge me.

- ❏ When people make mistakes, they should pay the price.

- ❏ Other:
  _____
  _____

- ❏ Other:
  _____
  _____

Conclusion

Being aware of yourself is very important. It serves as the basis on which one builds self-mastery. When you do not know yourself or what is driving your emotions and needs, you will not be your best self and can easily take on the identity other people want you to have. This leaves you feeling empty inside.

Self-awareness is a work in progress. It requires you to continually check in with yourself and notice what is happening within you. Assessing your strengths and weaknesses, personality, needs, triggers, values, and beliefs is a start, as these are typically stable over time. From there, you can focus on your emotions, which will be affected daily and change throughout each day. Once you are equipped with self-knowledge, you can begin to manage your reactions and be more in control.

Emotional Literacy

WE LEARN ABOUT ourselves through self-reflection and mindfulness. Through this knowledge, we can direct our energies to gain control over our reactions and thereby accomplish more and feel better about ourselves. In honing our self-competence skills, we gain true wisdom and power.

Awareness is always the first step to creating change. We have to be aware of what aspects of our lives make us unhappy, draw motivation to change them, and then exert effort consistently over time to see results.

But simply being aware is not sufficient. As the Buddhist proverb says, "To know and not to do is not to know." We must take the knowledge we have gained and use it for self-mastery.

There is a Buddhist tale about two monks bound to cross a rushing stream. They are approached by a beautiful young woman who asks if they would carry her across, so she will not get wet and have to endure the cold temperature of the water. The young monk was disgusted by her request. He ignored her and crossed the stream alone. The old monk picked her up, carried her across and set her down on the other side. The woman thanked the monk and went on her way. The two monks continued down the road.

The young monk remained furious. At first, he was silent, but after a while, when he could not hold back any longer, he finally exploded. He yelled at his companion for carrying the woman stating, "You know it is forbidden for monks to touch women!"

In response to the young monk's anger, the older monk said, "Oh, no! Are you still carrying that woman? I put her down an hour ago."

We have all had instances where we got swept away by a strong emotion. Life can feel stressful and overwhelming at times, and it is easy to succumb to such experiences by crumbling or letting the feelings build inside us until we explode. We have to manage our emotions the way a tightrope walker maintains their balance. These artists must perfect their craft, focusing solely on biomechanics. They must be present in mind and emotionally calm.

To truly master your feelings, you must first understand them. Here are six of the most common emotions we experience regularly:

Fear

Our survival instinct kicks into gear when we believe we are threatened. Our body produces adrenaline and goes into what is known as a *fight or flight* response. We become energized in the face of danger to either fight off the threat or remove ourselves from the perceived danger.

While this response is appropriate and vital when we are indeed in harm's way, the majority of our fear lives in our mind, not in any physical reality. Our brain has not adapted from the time we were cave dwellers to know the difference.

Fear is associated with stress and anxiety. When we are afraid, we experience a stress response and have anxious thoughts about the future. Stress is an experience we have based on our interpretation of events. A testament to this is when an event takes place, each person's reaction to that same event is different. This is because we view the event through a lens shaped by our life experiences.

So the next time you notice your heart fluttering, your head swimming with anxious thoughts, and your breathing as shallow, remind yourself that you are safe. Gaining perspective on the situation can help calm you down so you can focus on problem-solving.

What you need most to act in the face of fear is courage. Without it, you feel dis*couraged*. Having the support of others will give you the confidence you need to feel en*couraged* to take action.

Anger

We often feel angry when faced with an injustice, like when someone falsely accuses us of an act we did not commit or when we feel disrespected by others. When anger sets in, you might notice your temperature rising. Anger creates heat inside of us, and if we do not manage our anger properly, it will reach its boiling point, and we will likely explode.

Rather than think of yourself as a pressure cooker, someone who lets resentment build and build over time, it is best to notice when you begin to feel upset and take immediate charge of the situation.

One way to do this is by paying attention to your language. Have you ever dismissed someone's complement of you? If it is possible to keep positive influences out due to our determination to deflect praise, we can say the same about negativity. Make up your mind that others' criticisms and judgments have no influence on your mood.

Daniel J. Siegel, an American neuropsychiatrist, coined the phrase "Name it to tame it," explaining that by naming your emotion, you can begin to gain mastery over it.[1] The other piece to consider is what to call your emotional experience. The richer your vocabulary of emotional terms, the easier it will be to intervene.

Let's say your manager promised to meet with you each Friday at noon to go over your weekly progress and discuss upcoming projects.

Somehow, as you get to the end of the week, you notice that your manager has a completely booked schedule. He bumps your meeting off until next week. The following week, he is 20 minutes late. The week after that, he tells you he has to leave early. You value these meetings as they are part of your plan for getting a promotion. You tell yourself that if you are not able to have face-to-face time with your manager, you will likely stay stuck in your current position.

After the first occurrence of neglect, you feel frustrated but try to stay optimistic and maybe even understanding of your manager's busy schedule. The next time he brushes you off, you feel annoyed. By the third time he cancels your meeting, you are furious.

By naming your emotions, you can see where on the spectrum you are. By using different labels such as "frustrated," "annoyed," and "furious," you stay aware of the intensity of your emotions.

The more an injustice takes place over time, the more we go from irritated to enraged. The danger is that when we escalate emotionally, our rational brain goes offline. It becomes harder and harder to control our behaviors, and we are more prone to overreacting by saying or doing something we will likely regret. Instead, we need to intervene sooner by asserting ourselves. In the above scenario, you might firmly remind your manager how significant you find these weekly meetings and check-in to see what is getting in the way of him making it a priority.

Anger, as previously stated, is a secondary emotion. While it is true that we are angered when someone crosses our personal boundary, underneath that anger is typically another feeling. In some instances, anger is an externalization of our sadness. By getting angry, we become energized to make a change rather than become deflated and immobilized. Alternatively, anger can also be a mask for fear.

As in the example above, not meeting with your manager may be infuriating if you are afraid of staying stuck in your position when what you desire is an upward career move. By understanding what you are feeling and how deeply you are feeling it, you can take proactive steps to recover.

Sadness

We experience grief whenever there is a loss in our lives. Examples may include losing a loved one or a job, a geographical move, or experiencing a disappointment when reality does not match our expectations. Sadness forces us to slow down physically and mentally. We tend to become sluggish and have a hard time focusing our mind. It is essential to take time to grieve as a way of releasing these feelings. One way we do that is through our tears. They shed the pent up anguish we feel and cleanse us from the inside out.

Children have a much easier time releasing their sadness than do adults. Stigmas do not inhibit children. When they experience a loss, they easily cry about it. Although, as we age, we learn that crying is not socially accepted. In a work setting, it is often considered unprofessional. Many cultures deem crying a sign of weakness. This belief contributes to the stigma of emotional expression.

There is a fine line between expressing our feelings in a healthy way and being out of control. When we push our feelings down, we become numb. The tricky thing about this phenomenon is that when we numb our feelings in one realm, we become numb in other realms as well. So, when you don't allow yourself to feel sadness, for example, you will also become numb to joy.

The key is to find healthy outlets for your feelings and to express yourself assertively, so you meet your needs. That way, you can stay emotionally balanced.

Guilt

Our moral code is something we develop through family and cultural norms. We are taught right from wrong and then add our interpretations of what we should and should not do.

It is when we believe we have crossed our moral line in the sand that we feel guilty. The purpose of this emotion is to remind us of our rule to keep us in line.

There are two optimal ways to handle guilt. One is to learn from your mistakes, so you do not step out of line again. It might include repenting for your actions as in asking for forgiveness. It is righting your wrong.

Other times, you might feel guilty for having an antiquated rule in place that no longer fits. Now that you have changed your way of thinking, you feel guilty for not sticking to your original method of doing things. In that case, ask yourself a simple question, "Does this rule still make sense for me?" Rather than being loyal to an outdated rule, this is an opportunity for revision.

Once you take action by either learning from your immoral act or changing your moral code, you can release the guilt. It has served its purpose.

Shame

Of all the emotions we experience, shame is the only one that does not help us in any way. Unlike guilt, where you believe you have done something wrong, shame is your belief that there is something wrong with you.

It is easy to see why you may feel shame. Growing up, you may have heard adults say, "You should be ashamed of yourself." Shame is other people's way of controlling you, and when you hear it enough from others, you internalize it. You start to believe that there is something wrong with you, that you are not enough.

From all my years of professional experience, I have found that many of the problems we face internally boil down to a feeling of inadequacy. We often lack confidence, suffer from chronic self-doubt, and fear failure because of internalized shame.

When you recognize shame in yourself, ask yourself whether it is related to an immoral behavior—in which case you can substitute guilt—or to a belief that there is something fundamentally wrong with you. If the latter rings true, investigate the origin of this belief and any evidence for it. Then consider the aspects of your character that are positive. If you were to ask your loved ones why they care so much about you, what would they say? We are often so harsh with ourselves that we omit evidence contrary to our beliefs even though it is staring us straight in the face. To achieve a balanced perspective, we must consider both sides.

Joy

The underlying goal we all have in common is the desire to experience joy. I often ask my clients what they want most in life. While for some people, it is evident that they want to be happy, many others focus on achievement or material possessions. The quest is to dig deeper and ask why you want what you want. When you dig deep enough, what typically will surface is the desire to feel joy. There is nothing beyond it in the line of questioning. It is our biggest wish.

One of the emotions that gets in the way of joy is guilt. When you believe that you do not deserve to experience joy, you block yourself from pleasure. Some people tend to put others' needs ahead of their own and will sacrifice their happiness as a way to feel important. Having a sense of purpose is vital, but it does not have to be at the expense of joy. Ideally, you can find a way to experience joy and attain a sense of purpose. It is not impossible. It is a state of mind.

EMOTIONAL UNDERSTANDING

In the exercises below, consider your relationship to the six major emotions mentioned in this chapter.

FEAR

What things scare you, and what can you do to lean into your fear?

_____

_____

ANGER

What resentments or grudges do you carry, and how does holding onto them affect you?

_____

_____

SADNESS

What losses have you experienced about which you feel continually depressed or numbed out?

_____

_____

GUILT

What do you feel most guilty about? What are the lessons you can glean from this?

_____

_____

SHAME

Identify areas of your life where you feel shame. Would it be appropriate to substitute guilt here instead? Whose voice is shaming you? Is it your inner critic? If so, who does that remind you of in your life?

_____

_____

JOY

Do you believe you deserve to feel joy? If so, do you behave accordingly, or do you put other people's needs ahead of your own? If not, identify the belief that is blocking you.

_____

_____

Conclusion

To engage in the world in an emotionally intelligent way, you must begin the journey with yourself. Pay close attention so you can know yourself, and then make use of that knowledge to manage your own emotions.

Self-management is a skill that requires you to examine your beliefs and challenge your perspectives. By understanding the purpose of each emotion, and by expanding your emotional vocabulary, you can more accurately name what you are feeling. This practice helps decrease the emotional intensity you feel. With the knowledge of what you are feeling and how deeply you are feeling it, you can take proactive steps to recover.

You must look for healthy outlets for your feelings, examine your moral code when guilt gets triggered, focus on what you can control, and remember that ultimately you want to have purpose and to feel joy.

Emotional Mastery

MALCOLM GLADWELL MADE popular the notion that with ten thousand hours of practice, usually over a period of ten years, we attain mastery.[1] Emotional mastery, thankfully, does not have to take that long. It is more about creating daily habits and repetition over time than it is about years of experience.

Despite all your training and good intentions, it is still likely you will have a strong reaction every once and again. You are engaging in an emotionally intelligent way as long as you stay mindful of what triggers you, how you react to certain events, and what you can take away from an experience to minimize your reaction the next time around.

In this section, we will explore three aspects of emotional mastery, namely: Awareness, Self-Control, and Self-Expression. Within each of these areas, I have highlighted specific practices you can adopt to strengthen your sense of mastery. You do not, by any means, need to engage in all of these behaviors to reap the benefits. Instead, review the list and find the methods that work best for you.

We will focus on anxiety as it is the emotion most closely related to burnout. Before we delve in, you need to truly understand anxiety.

Anxiety is an experience you have when you must do something that scares you or when you worry about something bad happening. But contrary to popular belief, anxiety is not necessarily bad for you.

Think of anxiety on a scale of 1 to 10, with 1 being a state of no anxiety which you might experience when you are completely Zen or in peaceful sleep, and 10 being in the midst of a panic attack. If 5 is the midpoint, anything below that number can be considered a motivating factor. If you have minimal anxiety, you will likely be lazy as opposed to taking responsibility. Thus, having some anxiety helps motivate you to do the things you need to do. When your anxiety goes above the midpoint, you start to feel distressed and will see a decline in functioning and handling of responsibilities. Too much anxiety impedes your ability to do what it is you need to do (Figure 6.1).

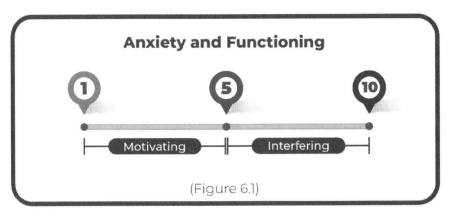

(Figure 6.1)

Anxiety shows up when you interpret your circumstances as threats, especially when you do not believe you can adequately cope. This usually incorporates a lot of "what if" thinking. What if I miss my flight? What if I lose my job? What if I get lost? What if I show up and don't know anyone? Your brain and body prepare you for facing a life-threatening situation when, in fact, you will make your flight, keep your job, find your way, or are just going to a social event. Overkill, right?

"Worrying is carrying tomorrow's load with today's strength—carrying two days at once. It is moving into tomorrow ahead of time. Worrying doesn't empty tomorrow of its sorrow, it empties today of its strength."

– Corrie Ten Boom

When you create these tragic scenarios in your mind, actually seeing yourself missing your flight and being late to your meeting, you may neglect to notice the physiological manifestations of your anxiety in the body. Anxiety is physiological arousal, so when you feel anxious, the physiology in your body changes. As you will see, there is usually an external circumstance that triggers an innate response.

Physiological symptoms of anxiety can bring up a state of alarm. When you notice something happening in your body that you do not understand or know how to control, this can create even more anxiety.

In the section below, you will find approaches to identify your anxiety and deal with it effectively.

Awareness

The first thing you want to be aware of is how anxiety manifests for you in your body. For each person, it will be a little different. There are a wide variety of symptoms, so just notice what happens for you. When you are feeling anxious, is your mind racing? Do you feel dizzy and faint? Is your heart beating fast? Do you have butterflies in your stomach? Are you sweating? What is happening for you when you are feeling highly anxious at work? Take note. That way, you can become familiar with your pattern and you can prepare yourself, or at least know that when you feel it, you have a name for it.

You need to identify your work-related triggers. Is it the way that somebody looks at you? Is it a tone of voice? Is it a dynamic between you and other coworkers? What triggers you the most? You can prepare for future scenarios by looking at past triggering episodes.

You are more likely to experience anxiety when you either lack the skills to deal with the situation or lack the confidence to utilize your skills. If, for instance, you are feeling overwhelmed or have too much on your plate, your anxiety might be related to poor time management. Alternatively, if work is placing unrealistic demands on you, there might be a need for asserting yourself. This includes letting your boss or whoever is delegating you the excessive work know that it is not realistic. You may need to revisit what your responsibilities are for that job.

Lastly, consider how your environment affects you. Moods, we said, are contagious. If the people around you are anxious and you start to feel similarly anxious, recognize that this anxiety may not be your own. In such a case, it would be best to surround yourself with individuals who are more mindful and in control of their emotions.

COPING WITH ANXIETY

How does anxiety manifest in your body?

_____

_____

What triggers an anxiety response in you?

_____

_____

Which coping skills might you benefit from working on (e.g., time management, assertive communication) to reduce your anxiety?

_____

_____

What can help you feel more confident to use the coping skills you have?

_____

_____

Do the people you surround yourself with struggle with anxiety? If so, how does that affect you?

_____

_____

Self-Control

Having control over your emotions and, thus, your behavioral response requires you to build up the skills of tolerance and discipline. Once you become aware of your emotional state, you need to be able to ride the wave of your emotions. Knowing that feelings come and go, and mindfully noticing what is happening within you rather than becoming fearful or overwhelmed will help you stay calm. The alternative is suppressing the emotion, which is a form of avoidance. While avoidance, as a coping strategy, may distract you from an unpleasant experience at the moment, it is not a long-term solution. Suppressed emotions tend to get stored in the body and can result in physical pain, autoimmune diseases, and eventually rupture in emotional outbursts.

To gain mastery over any area of knowledge or skill, you need an investment of time and energy. What can get in the way of mastery is either boredom or a preference to engage in pleasurable activities.

Imagine that you want to write a book. This requires thought, research in some cases, and many hours of writing and editing. While you have good intentions to sit down and write, you may become distracted by a television show, or feel tempted to go out with friends for fear of missing out on the fun. All this temptation causes distraction and procrastination and prevents you from making strides toward your goal. Mastery requires discipline and a delay of instant gratification.

What this has to do with Emotional Intelligence is that your behaviors are a result of your emotional state. If the reason you are procrastinating or giving up on your goal is that you are bored with the repetition of your work, you need to manage your boredom to stick with the task long enough to master it. Similarly, if you are blowing off your commitments to engage in fun, you need to manage your mindset, remember the benefits you will reap in the long-run, and set up rewards for milestones along the way. This keeps you moving ahead and will lead to a sense of purpose in your life, which will outlive any short-term gratification you could attain in this moment.

It is not only when you are bored that you seek stimulation and forego possible long-term goals. If you experience low frustration tolerance, this may drive you to impulsivity in many situations. A standard illustration of this is on the road when a person becomes impatient with other drivers, red lights, or pedestrians that cause traffic to slow down. When they act out impulsively, they increase their own risk of being in an accident and hurting themselves and others.

Being aware of how impatient you feel and then taking some deep breaths can help to get your rational brain back online, just when your emotional brain is taking over. Infusing your frustrating moments with relaxation can improve your mindset and sometimes mean the difference between life and death.

Set your intention on building up your tolerance of negative feelings and on having the discipline to delay gratification so you can reach your ultimate goals. There is a time and place for everything.

Although you don't have direct access to your emotions, you can manipulate your feelings through your thoughts and behaviors. I have included several cognitive and behavioral strategies below to help you attain a greater sense of control over your emotions.

REPLACING AVOIDANCE/SUPPRESION WITH TOLERANCE AND DISCIPLINE

Identify which tasks bore you and how you handle them (e.g., distraction, procrastination).

_____

_____

In the table below, list your goals in column 1. Then identify milestones toward those goals in columns 2 and 4 and rewards associated with those milestones in columns 3 and 5.

Reflect on situations in which you acted impulsively because you felt frustrated. Identify ways to relax next time you feel this way so you can be more in control of your actions.

Goals	Milestone 1	Reward 1	Milestone 2	Reward 2

COGNITIVE

We experience anxiety when we think about a future event in a worrying way. Therefore, we should consider various methods to change our thinking to lower our anxiety. We also feel anxious when we experience a failure of sorts and catastrophize what this will mean moving forward. To this end, we will explore cognitive solutions focused on what to do before, during, and after an event.

Before

If you are finding it difficult to make progress, it is likely because you are overthinking things. When you indulge in "what if" thinking, you anticipate everything that might go wrong. By focusing on potential problems, you remain stuck in anxiety. Instead, you need to focus on a solution. You also need to visualize what the worst-case scenario might look like and what you would do if you were in such a dire situation. Quickly allow yourself to figure out what you would do if this were to happen. With your preparation for the worst, you can handle anything less.

As you prepare to move ahead, you need to manage your expectations. When you build up expectations in your mind about the outcomes you want, you can become highly disappointed. These situations can lead to sadness, fear, or anger. Accept that you will face failures as well as successes. Keep in mind the goal you want to attain and stay focused on making headway, even if it means having to change your approach along the way.

During

When an intense emotion such as anxiety absorbs you, it might be hard to step out of it enough to apply any intervention. This is where mindfulness is helpful. Once you are mindful of your experience of anxiety or another challenging emotion, you can ask yourself, "On a scale of 0-10, how strongly do I feel this negative emotion?"

Negative emotions are an indication that something is out of alignment. If you are experiencing negativity, you want to do something to change your state. If the intensity is a 7 or above, you want to focus on de-escalation. The goal is to bring the intensity down to a 6 or below. A quick way of doing this is through breathwork. For a visual guide on breathwork, go to my website: www.BurnoutToResilience.com.

Recognize that your feelings result from your thinking. Negative emotions, therefore, result from skewed and unhelpful thoughts. Once you are in control enough, start applying some state-altering interventions. Consider doing a mental inventory of evidence for and against your thoughts and this will widen your lens of the situation and assess for accuracy.

What you experience is not necessarily the truth; it is just your version of the truth, which will likely be different from other people's versions. When the negative emotion you feel is associated with your thoughts of another person, you need to do some reality testing.

In her Netflix documentary, Brené Brown demonstrates a useful technique to check in with others.[2] It asks you to put your interpretation of an event in the context of something your brain made up, which gives you the opportunity to reality test with the other person. If Tammy, who received what she considered to be a thoughtless gift from her father, were to apply this method, she would call her father and say something like, "The story that my brain is making up when I look at the contents of what you sent me is that I am not important." This would allow her father to explain his intention and how he cares very much about her.

Events happen around you continually. Your interpretation of these events leads you to feel the way you do. If your emotions emerge from a thought in your mind, by changing your unhelpful thought to a more helpful one, you can alter your emotional state.

To change your unhelpful thought, use the 3Cs method, which comes from Cognitive Behavioral Therapy (CBT).[3] This is a three-step process to help deal with worries, catastrophes, or negative interpretations of events that are causing anxiety.

Step 1: Catch it. What are you thinking about? This is where you identify the thought that is leading to anxiety.

Step 2: Check it. Is this thought accurate? Even if it is valid, is it helpful for you to think this way? Consider how you want to feel. If this thought is causing anxiety and you want to feel calm, it is not helpful. When an idea is either inaccurate or unhelpful, go on to Step 3.

Step 3: Change it. Change your thought to a more accurate (rather than one based on false information your mind makes up) or helpful idea (one that makes you feel how you would prefer to feel).

After

Only certain aspects of the road ahead are in your control. The things you cannot control you need to accept. Learn from and continually adapt to your environment. This is especially important when things do not go your way. Keep things in perspective, and do not allow one disappointment to ruin your mood and spoil the entire day.

COGNITIVE STRATEGIES TO INCREASE SELF-CONTROL

Next time you catch yourself worrying about what might go wrong, stop yourself and substitute the following exercise.

On a scale of 0-10, how anxious do you feel?

If you scored 7 or above, focus on taking cleansing breaths until your anxiety goes down to 6 or below. Then proceed with any of the following:

Visualize the worst-case scenario and write it below.

_____

_____

Now visualize what you would do to solve the problem should this worst-case scenario really happen and write it below.

_____

_____

Identify the belief(s) that is (are) creating your anxiety. In the table below, list evidence for the belief being true in column 2 and evidence that goes against your belief in column 3.

Belief	Evidence for	Evidence against

Catch the thought: _____

Check the thought (helpful or unhelpful)?

Change the thought to a more helpful one: _____

Is this a situation over which you have control (y/n)?

If not, focus on letting go of control and accepting the situation.

BEHAVIORAL

You may recall a time when you became very emotional and impulsively reacted to a situation. This is often the case when you are driving a vehicle. Someone cuts you off or does something that either triggers a thought of being disrespected or a fear of being unsafe, and you become angry and lash out.

Regulating your emotions is about creating a space between the external event and your response to it. In the road rage example, it might be as simple as taking a deep breath or reminding yourself that the other driver's behavior is not a personal attack against you. When you take steps in the moment to slow your reaction time down or to challenge your automatic negative thoughts, you are gaining control of yourself.

You may experience strong negative emotions when something goes wrong and other people are involved. It is vital that you take responsibility for your part rather than focus on shaming or blaming the other person. Instead, you can request that they behave in a way that is preferable to you, but remember that ultimately it is not their behavior that is causing your distress. Rather, it is your thinking about their behavior that is distressing you.

It is always wisest to focus on what you want and how to make it happen, rather than focus on what you don't want. If, for example, your partner seems disengaged at a party, rather than judging, shaming, or feeling frustrated, focus on re-engaging her. By taking action, you are moving toward your goal rather than staying stuck in thought.

Because anxiety is associated with several physiological responses, it is necessary to have a strategy for managing anxiety in the body. Panic is the epitome of anxiety and it can include a pounding heartbeat, sweating, shaking, dizziness, feeling out of your body, or nausea. If anxiety is an emotion you struggle with often, build up your immunity in advance. Practice relaxation every day to prepare your mind and body for dealing with stressful situations as they arise.

Grounding practices are a great way to immediately shift the energy in your body when you are feeling anxious. There are many ways to ground, including walking in nature, lying on the floor, and standing with two feet firmly on the ground while imagining you are a tree sending roots into the earth.

BEHAVIORAL STRATEGIES CHECKLIST TO INCREASE SELF-CONTROL

- ❑ Create a space between the event and your response by taking five deep breaths or counting to 10

- ❑ Take responsibility for your part of the situation

- ❑ Assert yourself if you experience negative feelings due to someone's behavior toward you

- ❑ Practice relaxation daily to build up your immunity to stress

- ❑ Ground your energy when you feel anxious

Self-Expression

Emotional mastery is not just about self-control. It is also about self-expression. What you are aiming for here is to get your needs met. You must first understand yourself and use this knowledge to be proactive in communicating to others about your experience.

In an online study, researchers examined responses to an Emotional Intelligence test taken by 1324 people.[4] The data distinguished between responders who were able to apply both self-control and self-expression, and those who managed to control their emotions, but were unable to talk about their experiences with others.

The group that expressed their feelings experienced advantages to the other group in every category including self-awareness, comfort around others, and contentment. The group who refrained from sharing their feelings was not only less assertive, but tended to feel less confident, more awkward around others, and be less successful in accomplishing goals. The group's greater need for social approval might explain this finding.

Consider why self-expression is such a crucial component of Emotional Intelligence. If you genuinely want others to like you and do not share your authentic self with them or refrain from empathizing with their situation in a compassionate way, your relationships will suffer. Your health will also suffer because you are not getting your needs met when you favor compliance over self-care.

Self-expression is one of the ingredients through which you can communicate and attain your goals. We will explore effective communication later in this book.

The way that you talk to yourself is another form of self-expression. It is how you silently express your inner-most thoughts. Because thoughts, feelings, and behaviors are interconnected, your self-talk can determine how you feel and affect your performance. If you want to manage your emotions, you need to pay attention to your inner dialogue.

Are you harder on yourself than you are on others? Perhaps you tell yourself that you should "just get over it" after a challenging experience or that you are "a failure" because the task you worked on did not turn out as well as you had hoped. This approach lacks compassion. There is a better and more effective way to relate to yourself if you want to increase resilience and performance.

Think about somebody else who is struggling. Say your friend Sally had the same struggle that you are currently facing and she was sitting right next to you. What would you say to her? Put yourself in her shoes. Imagine how you might try to comfort her, or how you would advise her to move forward with her situation. Then, apply some of that compassionate talk to yourself. While it might seem like being hard on yourself is the key to improvement, the opposite is true. Compassion builds you up to face challenges and stressors and is what leads to greater resilience.

If you can have compassion for others but not for yourself, tune into your inner voice. Determine whose voice is speaking to you. Does it sound like someone in your life, perhaps a family member or your boss?

To counter this harsh and judgmental voice, identify someone kind. It can be someone you know or even a fictional character. Imagine inserting this voice of compassion into your head to counteract this otherwise very critical voice. This can help you distill the negativity, instill more compassion, and become more resilient to perform in a demanding environment.

CHECKLIST TO INCREASE SELF-EXPRESSION

❑ Pay attention to your inner dialogue

❑ Name your inner critic

❑ Recognize that your inner critic is trying to help

❑ Practice self-acceptance and forgiveness

❑ From a place of self-awareness and compassion, assert yourself with others

Conclusion

To respond to pressures in the workplace, you must have clarity of thought, think objectively, and remain calm. Mastering your emotions is part of your arsenal for becoming effective. To begin this journey, you must first be aware of what you are feeling, allow yourself to face these emotions, and extract lessons from them.

Negative emotions stem from worried, judgmental, or other unhelpful thoughts. By applying mindfulness, you can alter your interpretations of events and gain more control over your feelings. Focusing on responding mindfully rather than reactively demonstrates a form of self-control.

Emotional mastery results from mindful habits of self-care, self-examination, and self-expression. When you know yourself, you can communicate to others what you feel in order to get your needs met.

By tackling your anxiety from various angles, you will be better prepared to manage it when it arises. This will give you the proper balance and motivation to stay focused on what matters so you can get through your day with ease and peace of mind.

Zone of Optimal Performance

IF YOU CARE about achievement, you care about your performance. The quality of your performance is affected by your arousal level. Both high and low arousal levels lead to compromised work, so it is important to understand what determines these states of arousal and how to manage them. By doing so, you will enter the Zone Of Optimal Performance (ZOOP).

When you become overly aroused, you experience high levels of anxiety. For instance, when work demands are high, you go into overdrive, trying to get tasks done in a frenetic pace. Overtime, this leads you to feel drained and burned out (see Figure 7.1).

While it is commendable that you dive into action when faced with a challenge, paradoxically, you need to lower your arousal. By reducing activation, you can release tension and prevent exhaustion. You can accomplish this by improving your time management skills through minimizing distractions, prioritizing essential tasks, undertaking a realistic amount of work, and delegating everything else. Additionally, avoid taking on too many responsibilities. Remember, if your job requires that you do more than is feasible in the time you have, you need to put some boundaries in place.

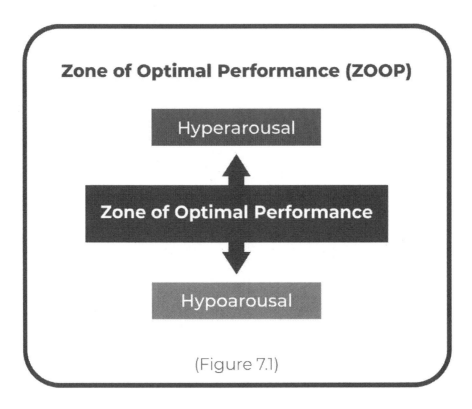

(Figure 7.1)

It might be difficult to catch yourself in the moment of an elevated arousal state to implement change. If that is the case, sit down and think about past instances where you became frenetic or shut down. List out what events led to this behavior, how they made you feel, and what you would do differently if you were to do them over again. Look for patterns of thinking, feeling, and behaving, and you will be on your way to a more mindful understanding of yourself.

The more you can see your tendencies, the more you can plan accordingly. Create a "When-Then" contingency plan for how to handle commonly triggering situations. Decide in advance what you will do by stating, "When this happens, then I will..." For example, if you notice a pattern that when you are up against a time crunch, you turn into the Energizer Bunny, rushing about and feeling overwhelmed, consider doing the opposite. Your plan can read, "When a deadline is stressing me out, I will sit in a quiet place, meditate on what is the most essential task that I need to get done to push the project forward, and then I will focus only on that essential item." This can help you stay grounded and centered while avoiding unnecessary stress.

On the other end of the spectrum, you might experience hypo-arousal. This is where you underperform and typically results from sticking to your comfort zone. Instead of operating frantically, trying to accomplish those to-do items, you are more likely to disengage from the work. If you find yourself procrastinating, avoiding, or feeling bored on the job, you are disconnected. Start paying attention to body signals to get out of your head. Incorporate exercise into your routine so you can handle and thereby release the physical stress that you carry around. This will help you restore your energy, improve your focus so you can become more integrated, and free you to do your best work.

One evidence-based technique that can help you overcome procrastination is temptation bundling. Research by Dr. Katherine Milkman (as discussed by author Eric Barker), a professor at the Wharton School at the University of Pennsylvania, focused on how to improve self-control through limiting access to temptation.[1]

While we all know how vital it is for us to exercise, getting to the gym might be difficult. In her study, Dr. Milkman set out to discover what level of motivation would be most successful in getting 226 students and faculty members to engage in physical activity.

Milkman placed participants in three distinct groups. The first group received an iPod and was able to access audiobooks only at the gym. Members in the second group had audiobooks loaded onto their personal iPods and were encouraged to only listen to them at the gym. The third group received a gift card and an encouragement to work out more.

The results showed that the first group worked out 29 percent more than the second group and 51 percent more than the third group. The relative success of the first group resulted from bundling the temptation of the audiobooks with the challenging activity of working out, which increased the group's motivation and follow-through in facing the challenge.

Consider how you might physically restrict access to temptation to boost your performance in challenging tasks. Notice that the temptation used in the study did not sabotage the results of the challenge. If you are interested in optimal performance, don't load yourself up with sugary foods as a reward. This may give you immediate energy but will only lead to your energy dropping in a short while. Instead, consider a more inspiring, motivating, or relaxing reward such as a ten-minute meditation, stretching, or a music break.

When in a hypo-arousal state, in order to release negative emotions, you are more likely to do things without being aware. For some people, emotional eating becomes their retreat from stress. You might recall stuffing food into your mouth, unaware of how much you are eating until you have reached the bottom of the ice cream container. If this is happening with you, there is a solution that has nothing to do with dieting. Instead, you need to become more mindful of your emotional state and deal with it effectively.

IDENTIFYING YOUR COPING STRATEGIES

When you feel stressed, what is your go-to comfort?

- ❑ Web surfing
- ❑ Playing video games
- ❑ Watching endless YouTube videos
- ❑ Engaging with pornography
- ❑ Daydreaming
- ❑ Browsing social media
- ❑ Shopping on Amazon
- ❑ Smoking
- ❑ Using drugs or alcohol
- ❑ Eating

Which of these healthy alternatives can you substitute instead?

- ❑ Meditation
- ❑ Taking deep breaths
- ❑ Listening to music
- ❑ Walking in nature
- ❑ Chatting with a friend
- ❑ Drinking water
- ❑ Taking a bath
- ❑ Other

If you find that when you feel pressed to perform, you tend to run away to social media, invade the refrigerator, or distract yourself with mindless television, take some time out to regroup. Go for a walk to clear your head. Engaging in physical movement can release pent up energy and help you get into your body. This is also a form of self-care that will restore your energy and improve your focus on the task at hand.

The goal is to function in the ZOOP. When you are in the "Zone," your performance is optimal because you are practicing self-awareness and self-management. This mindfulness will also let you know when you need to incorporate self-care. When you are in the ZOOP, you are more engaged with your work because you have the appropriate energy and are prioritizing the most crucial tasks. You are stretching yourself to achieve goals outside of your comfort level, but not ones so audacious that they create panic.

To enter the ZOOP, start each day with the intention to accomplish what is in the best interest of you and your family. Each time you engage in an action, ask yourself if it aligns with your intention.

What helps keep you in the ZOOP is continued self-care, social support, and a positive mindset while continuing to push the boundary over time. Doing difficult things and coping adaptively increases self-esteem. It changes your perception of yourself, especially when you are determined to achieve your goals and don't allow initial failure to stop you short.

Resilience starts in the mind and includes a sense of realistic optimism for what lies ahead, gratitude for the goodness around you, and acceptance of anything that is not in your control or that has not gone as well as you would have liked.

True control is trusting that you can handle anything that comes your way because you know it is temporary. By managing your emotions, you gain control of your behaviors. By being curious about your thoughts, you remove the assumption that they are factual. You must not allow negative thoughts to create anxiety about the future. Instead, question whether these thoughts are based in reality or not, and let your intuition guide you.

GETTING IN THE ZOOP CHECKLIST

- ❑ Release tension before jumping into action and instead of procrastinating

- ❑ Manage your time well

- ❑ Avoid taking on too many responsibilities

- ❑ Pay attention to body signals

- ❑ Try temptation bundling to build healthy habits

- ❑ Look for patterns of thinking, feeling, and behavior from past instances of hypo- and hyper-arousal

- ❑ Create a when-then contingency plan

- ❑ Start each day with an intention that is in your best interest

- ❑ Before engaging in an activity, ask yourself whether it aligns with your intention

- ❑ Trust yourself to problem-solve

Conclusion

Your arousal level is a good indication of your performance. By paying attention to your behaviors, you can gain insight into whether or not you are performing in the optimal zone. Put your self-competency skills into practice to increase mindfulness and bring yourself into the Zone Of Optimal Performance (ZOOP).

When you boil it down, the heart of the matter turns out to be trust. You have to be able to trust yourself to problem-solve and to know that even though you are imperfect, you can improve over time with the right intention, mindset, and actions.

By focusing on what you can control, you can regulate your emotions and behaviors and make good decisions. Know that you are capable, and with the right effort and hard work, you will build resilience and succeed.

SOCIAL COMPETENCY

Being in control of yourself is highly valuable, though it is your relationships that are the most critical aspects of your existence, as you will learn further in this book. This is why developing your Social Competency is vital to cultivating the best possible relationships with others and feeling connected to them.

I have divided Social Competency into three sections. Section 1 focuses on empathy, a skill that helps you better understand another person's situation. Building on this understanding, you will be more adept at managing your relationships with others, which will be the focus of Section 2. In Section 3, you will learn skills for effective communication. This is where you bring together your self-management and empathy skills to effectively navigate your relationships.

EQ is a highly valuable skill in the workplace and few people are actually trained in this. It has been shown to lead to greater success than your intelligence and it makes sense. People who are relatable and who are not overly emotional or irrational make better leaders. And, even if you are not in a leadership role, when you are likable and relatable, you get further in your career.

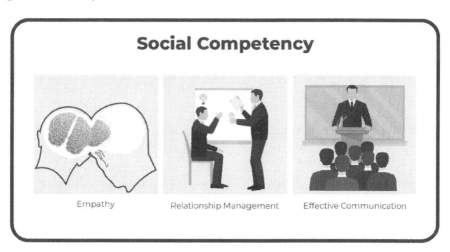

Empathy

IN THE STORY "Peter and the Wolf," the bird and the duck have an exchange. The bird says to the duck, "What kind of bird are you if you can't fly?" To this, the duck retorts, "What kind of bird are you if you can't swim?"[1] Each is seeing the world from his point of view, which makes it harder to relate to each other. For the two birds to truly connect, they need to look at the situation from the other's perspective. This is what we call empathy.

When an event stirs you, you can apply your self-awareness skills to recognize what you are feeling and why you are feeling it. With empathy, you are applying this process to another person's experiences. If, for instance, your manager is doing something that is upsetting you, try to put yourself in his shoes and consider: Why is he acting like this? What do I know about him and his situation that can shed light on this for me? What might be going on behind the scenes? The better you can understand what makes other people tick, the more easily you will be able to relate to them.

When someone tells you about a personal struggle, listen carefully. Resist the urge to judge the person or the situation. Resist the urge to interrupt and share your experience. Resist the urge to propose a solution. You do not have to fix it. Instead, focus on understanding the how and the why: how the person feels, and why they feel that way. Once you have a better understanding of how the other is feeling, try to relate to their emotions. Ask yourself, "When have I felt similarly to what this person is describing?"

As human beings, we are wired for connection. That is why relationships and our management of them are crucial to our success. We want to feel connected. We need to feel connected. It is when there are interfering factors that conflict can arise or lead us to disengage.

Psychologist Richard Ryan (as quoted by Daniel H. Pink) said, "One of the reasons for anxiety and depression in the high attainers is that they're not having good relationships. They're busy making money and attending to themselves and that means there's less room in their lives for love and attention and caring and empathy and the things that truly count."[2]

In a 2016 survey conducted by the National Opinion Research Center at the University of Chicago, researcher Emma Seppaia and professor Marissa King found a significant correlation between work exhaustion and loneliness. When you are more focused on production than connection, your work can quickly drain you and leave you feeling lonely. Conversely, when you have social support at work, burnout rates decline as work satisfaction and productivity rates rise.[3]

While social support comes in several forms, the type of support most helpful to diminish burnout is emotional support. This includes empathy, love, and understanding. Instead, when people burn out, they tend to want more instrumental support, someone to help them get things done. Instrumental support is most helpful when it also provides the worker with emotional support. A work culture that allows you to adjust your hours so that you can better attend to family demands is indirectly providing emotional support.

Emotional support is so vital to workers' job commitment that even the perception of such support can increase engagement. It turns out that when your boss is understanding of your family demands, you are more willing to put in long hours on the job, and, despite working longer hours, you are less likely to reach burnout when you receive this workplace emotional support.[4]

In this section, we are going to focus on how to harness empathy to understand others better and then couple that understanding with our competency skills of self-awareness and self-management to maneuver around conflict and build healthy relationships.

Are You Overly Empathetic?

Empathy is an essential skill for relationships. If you are in the helping field, chances are that instead of struggling to understand others, you may have the opposite issue. You might be so empathetic that you experience compassion fatigue.

Compassion fatigue is when you feel so much for another person that you end up feeling emotionally exhausted. This happens especially when you put in a tremendous effort to help someone else but are not seeing the desired results. Nurses are notorious for experiencing this phenomenon. The nature of their job is to meet the needs of their patients. They are drawn to their field because they are caring, but the long hours and heavy demands can lead them to a state of emotional saturation, especially when they sacrifice their own needs in the process.

The online blog for nurses, *Nurse Buff*, provides insight into how this unfolds by sharing statements from nurses who have experienced compassion fatigue. For example, a nurse from Maryland shared: "I've been working hard to take care of my critically ill patient. Sometimes, I don't even mind skipping my meals and ignoring my urge to drink or pee just to keep up with his nursing care demands. He thankfully recovered but one day he got off from his bed and fell. When I saw him sick again, I was crushed."[5]

I have discussed the importance of self-care to maintain a balanced lifestyle and recover the energy expended throughout the workday.

Compassion fatigue is a version of over-engagement that leaves you in a deficient state and more vulnerable to disappointment when your self-sacrifices do not give you the desired results.

To avoid this emotional drain, you need to shift your perspective. Consider how you can be there for somebody without taking on their distress or total responsibility for their wellness. Keep in mind the big picture idea of how your work brings a sense of purpose to your life rather than honing in on each person you are helping, by putting all your "purpose eggs" in that basket. Know that you do the best you can without overgiving to any one individual so that you can sustain your energy in the long run.

When you reach compassion fatigue and burnout, you have less capacity for empathy. As mentioned previously, one of the main signs of burnout is cynicism, which is when you lose your ability to relate to others, and when you max out. This is why you should simultaneously channel your empathy for others alongside empathy for yourself.

When Empathy is a Struggle

It might seem challenging to apply empathy during a conflict. If you feel blamed for something that is not your fault or over which you have no control, you are likely to focus your efforts on defending yourself rather than tuning in to the other person's point of view. While this is understandable, it is a reactive response, and it will only fuel the conflict more.

To de-escalate a conflict, you need first to apply your self-competency skills. Notice what feelings are coming up for you. Take a deep breath and keep those feelings under control in whatever way works best. Only then will you be able to apply this more advanced skill of empathy, which requires that you understand the other person. It does not mean that you have to agree with them.

Always keep in mind when you are interacting with others that your goal is to connect with them. When you are defensive or accusatory, you are saying, "I am separate from you," which works against your goal. Connection is an art that requires mastery over time, but if you keep this premise at the forefront, it will help you be mindful of your responses.

You might find it hard to offer apologies when appropriate because you worry about losing face. This is an indication of all-or-nothing thinking. Saying "I'm sorry" takes humility, but it makes others appreciate you more. In essence, you are acknowledging your mistakes and the other person. Try to see the situation from their perspective and consider whether you would want an apology if you were the one wronged. By offering an olive branch, you are making a statement that you value the relationship more than your ego.

You might find it challenging to apply empathy if you internalize other people's actions as an indication of how they think or feel about you. This is true whether you know the other person or not.

Imagine the following situations:

You are taking a family walk in the morning to drop your kids off at school. You want to hold your partner's hand during the stroll, but so do both of your kids. When your partner opts to keep your children's hands rather than yours, you decide to break off from the group because you feel shunned.

You are a safe driver. You stop, look, and follow the rules. You get to a four-way intersection and it is your turn to go through, but a car crosses in front of you. You have to wait a few more seconds for that car to pass so you can finally go. You feel disrespected and annoyed.

You are on vacation. Your boss contacts one of your accounts to let them know that he is changing their terms. You find out about the change when you return to the office, and you are fuming about the sabotage your boss is enacting without discussing it with you first.

In each of these situations, you can read into the other person's intentions. You can make it about you, which will make you feel angry at the other person and possibly badly about yourself.

When you tell yourself that what is happening is an indication that the other person does not care for or respect you, you will become upset. These interpretations result in a spiral of negative emotions which can sometimes lead to reactivity.

News flash: It is not always about you.

Think about it. People are focused on themselves more often than not. They want the fastest, biggest, and best rewards, and this blinds them to how their actions may cause harm to others.

When your partner chooses to hold your kids' hands on the walk to school, it is not because he does not want to keep your hand. It is because his focus is on holding your children's hands.

When that driver takes your turn at the intersection, it is because she is focused on getting to her destination quickly. You just happen to be another car on the road.

When your boss goes behind your back, it is because he wants to look good and feel in control. He likely does not have an agenda against you.

The more you can zoom out and look at the big picture and try to think about what makes other people tick, the less you will personalize what is happening and be able to let things go. So stop inserting yourself into other people's brains, assuming you know why they do what they do. Stop inserting poison into your mind and filling it with ideas of mal-intent. Adjust your expectations, take a deep breath, and focus on your intentions rather than those of others so you can lighten your load.

TIPS FOR APPLYING A HEALTHY AMOUNT OF EMPATHY

- ❑ Try to understand the other person's point of view

- ❑ Resist the urge to judge, interrupt, or propose a solution

- ❑ Focus on understanding how the person feels and why they feel that way

- ❑ Try to relate to their emotions. When have you felt that way?

- ❑ Focus on creating social relationships to buffer you from stress

- ❑ Elicit emotional support more so than instrumental support

- ❑ Remember to be supportive of others without taking on their distress or responsibility for them

- ❑ Practice having empathy for yourself and others

- ❑ To de-escalate a conflict, apply self-competency skills before empathy

- ❑ Avoid being defensive

- ❑ Offer an apology and acknowledge your mistakes and the other person

- ❑ Avoid assuming you know other people's intentions

Conclusion

Empathy is a skill that helps you create human connections. It requires that you take into consideration the other person's experience so you can better understand them. Ultimately, this understanding leads to important protection against burnout: social support. That said, it is important to keep your support of others in check, too much or too little can bring you out of balance.

Relationship Management

WHILE EMPATHY BUILDS a bridge between yourself and others, what can help direct your interactions is an understanding of communication styles.

There are four styles of communication: passive, aggressive, passive-aggressive, and assertive. What drives us to communicate is our underlying belief about the importance of our own needs and the needs of others.

Consider the following situation: Your boss asks you to stay late to finish a project, but you already have evening plans. If you tend to be passive, you will put your boss' needs ahead of your own because you believe your needs are less important. You will forego your evening plans and stay late at the office. The problem with this model, as you might imagine, is that you build up resentment over time, which might lead to your acting out aggressively.

What happens if you are passive but then become momentarily aggressive? You will feel guilty about your outburst and then go right back to being passive to compensate for your behavior. This keeps you in a never-ending loop of problematic communication and misses the mark on addressing your needs.

If your communication style is aggressive, it is usually an indication that you view your needs as more important than those of others. When your boss asks you to stay late, by saying "no" without any consideration for the situation, you are acting aggressively. While this strategy might help preserve your needs, it can be damaging to your relationships. You may be perceived as selfish and uncaring and might unintentionally intimidate others.

A common communication pattern is a combination type called passive-aggressive. The belief underlying this style of communication states that "my needs are more important than yours," but the person wants to avoid potential conflict. Instead of denying the boss' request, a passive-aggressive person might say "yes" but then leave anyway without finishing the project. This style of communication is problematic because even though you might be able to avoid conflict in the moment, when your boss realizes that you did not follow through on your promise, you will likely be faced with the consequences down the road.

Finally, if you use an assertive communication style, you believe that both your needs and those of the other party are important. This more desirable belief will help you incorporate self-awareness with empathy and be open to negotiating.

Managing Others' Emotions

Paying attention to how others communicate tells you about their beliefs and can help guide your interactions with them. For passive people, it is best to appreciate them and then elicit from them what they need. Encourage them to advocate for themselves and show them that they are safe to do so with you.

For aggressive people, use reflective statements such as, "I can see how important this is to you. I wonder if we can find a solution that meets both of our needs." This helps them feel seen by you and will make them more likely to take your needs into account.

If someone is passive-aggressive, you might let them know that you don't judge them for wanting to get their needs met and that they can feel free to share them with you instead of just telling you what you want to hear. Let them know you prefer their authenticity over their compliance.

Because assertive people are already considering both sides, they are easiest to negotiate with in an effective way. Chances are you will not need to manage their communication too much.

Assertive Communication

Dr. Marsha Linehan, the founder of Dialectical Behavioral Therapy (DBT), came up with an acronym that can serve as a guide for asserting yourself. It is a 7-step solution called DEAR MAN.[1]

The first four steps describe *what* to say and the order in which to say it:

Describe the Facts. When you conflict with someone, you want to get them on the same page as you by stating the facts. For example, you might state to your boss, "Over the past month, I have stayed late at work six different times to meet deadlines." By objectively describing the situation, you are more likely to get them to agree, an indication that you are seeing eye to eye.

Express Your Feelings. Now that you have described the scenario factually, you have an opportunity to talk about how you feel about it. Relating to our former example, what you might say to your boss is: "I understand that we are in a crunch period and I want to be a team player, but this cuts into my time with my family and does not allow me as much of an opportunity to recover from the stress of the day." By using "I" statements, you reduce any possible friction.

Assert Your Needs. This is where you make a direct request for things to change. Sticking to our example, you might add, "I would like to minimize these late nights to no more than once a week."

Reinforce Your Request. Keep in mind that people often find change difficult. Whenever you are asking to change the status quo, expect to be met with resistance. In this step, you are motivating the change. This can take two different forms. The first is positive reinforcement, where you explain the benefits. For example, you might say, "Having proper rest would allow me to come in fully restored the next morning so I can bring my best self to work."

In his book *Influence* by Robert Cialdini, he explains that when you give someone a reason for what you are doing, you are more likely to get compliance out of them.[2] So, when you explain why you need to cut out at five o'clock, it will be better received than if you just state your wish with no explanation.

Alternatively, some situations may call for negative reinforcement in which you explain the consequences of not changing a behavior. If, for instance, your boss had an aggressive communication style and showed a lack of empathy for your needs, you might say, "If I continue to stay late night after night, I will surely burn out, and I won't be as capable of doing my work well."

Hopefully, whatever conflict you are facing does not require such dire measures as threatening to leave your job if things don't change, but it might. If the situation goes against every grain of your being, you must listen to your intuition. Otherwise, you will become disempowered.

Now that you know what to say, we will examine the second half of the process which reveals *how* to practice assertiveness:

Mindfulness. You need to stick to your agenda regardless of what fears or thoughts might come up that attempt to cloud your mind, or what tactics the other person tries to throw out to distract you. If your boss talks over you, attempts to change the subject, or becomes defensive, you can either ignore him and continue on or become a broken record. You might start from the top until he gets the message that you mean business. You might even shift gears and use the DEAR part to address what is happening between the two of you in that moment. It might sound something like:

- "I noticed that as I'm explaining something which I deem important, you keep interrupting [Describe].

- This is upsetting because it seems like you don't want to listen to what I have to say [Express].

- I would appreciate it if you could give me two minutes to explain myself through [Assert].

- That would mean a lot to our relationship [Reinforce]."

Appear Confident. This is imperative if you want to be taken seriously. Be aware of your body language, tone of voice, and filler words. If you have an in-person conversation, make sure that your posture is erect, that you make eye contact, and that you speak up so the other person can hear you. Keep an open stance. Closed stances (e.g., crossing your arms) may signal defensiveness. If you are really in tune with the other person, you might find that you mirror their position. Remember, you have an effect on others and by staying aware of your body, you can come across as more inviting. Paying attention to the other person's body language can also reveal unspoken truths and can help you with complex reflections (see The Essentials for Effective Communication). Lastly, pay attention to what you are saying. You want to sound like you are serious about your request. Avoid using phrases such as "I think" or "I don't know." These indicate that you are feeling intimidated or unsure of yourself. When you take yourself seriously, others are more likely to take you seriously, as well.

Negotiate a win-win situation. By now, you have asserted your request but remember: if you believe that the other person's needs are also important, it is time to bring the conversation back around to them. This is where you check back in with the other person and see how your request fits in with their needs.

117

When conflict arises, if you can look at the situation from different angles and focus on the solution rather than assigning blame, you will have an easier time reaching a resolution and keeping your professional relationships intact.

LEARNING TO ASSERT YOURSELF

In the table below, identify the (non-assertive) communication style of the person with whom you are interacting and how to approach them assertively:

Communication Style	Assertive Approach
Passive	• Appreciate them • Elicit their needs • Encourage them to advocate for themselves • Help them feel safe with you
Aggressive	• Use reflective "I" statements that express how you understand them • Be curious about finding a solution that fits both your needs
Passive-aggressive	• Let them know you don't judge them for getting their needs met • Encourage them to be transparent rather than telling you what they think you want to hear

---

Conclusion

By looking at communication through a lens of needs, you can gain great insight into what people believe and why they behave as they do. You can then customize your approach to their style. Through assertive communication, you can minimize conflict and get both your needs and those of the other person met.

The Essentials
for Effective
Communication

*"When you talk, you are only repeating what you know. But if you
listen, you may learn something new."*

– Dalai Lama

THINK ABOUT A TIME when you had a strong urge to share an
experience with someone else. Perhaps during times of trouble, you
wanted the other person's support or understanding. If you experienced
a conflict with someone in your life, you might have felt tempted to
communicate to them why what they are doing is problematic. This is
your opportunity to assert yourself.

When you are in conversation with someone, you want to feel heard,
understood, and validated. The other person may not necessarily agree
with your position, but if they are respectful, listen carefully, and you
think they "get you," that alone will meet some of your needs.

Now that you are able to tune into what you would like when you are
sharing something difficult with another person, let us flip the script. It
is time for you to be on the receiving end and to do so effectively.

Step 1. Reflective Listening

Very few of us have ever had training in how to listen. Many of us are born with the ability to hear, but listening is an art.

Imagine you are arguing with your coworker, roommate, or romantic partner. You may be so worked up that all you want to do is jump in and tell your side of the story. There might be a part of you determined to convince the other person why they are wrong and you are right. This impulse is natural. But being "natural" and "effective" are two different things.

To have quality relationships, you need to contain yourself even in the heat of the moment. You will have a chance to give your version of the story, but it's critical you first listen intently to the other person. When you listen without an agenda because you want to truly understand what the other person is feeling, thinking, and wanting, you have information you can later leverage in problem-solving.

Let's take a deep dive into what quality listening means:

- You agree to understand the other person before you tell them what you have to say.

- You reflect to them what they said.

- You see whether they agree with your summary statement. This is an invitation for them to add anything you may have missed. You can then re-summarize to ensure you got everything right this time.

- Only after they feel understood do you share what is on your mind.

This process provides role modeling. If the other person is not trained in listening the way you are, you can remind them of how you took the time to understand them and that you would like them to do the same for you. Ask them to check in with you without jumping in to make their point.

Step 2. Empathic Understanding

To be truly effective, you are not just listening for content. You want to read between the lines, carefully examine body language, and find out what the person is feeling. By understanding the other person's emotional position, you can put yourself in their shoes and try to sense what it must be like for them. This does not mean that you have to feel their pain and over-exert yourself emotionally. You can just relate to their experience as an emotional being.

Reflections are used in Motivational Interviewing (MI), a form of therapy that focuses on helping people resolve their ambivalence and overcome their resistance by mirroring their experience back to them.[1] According to MI, there are two kinds of reflections: (1) Simple Reflections which focus on the content of what the person is saying, as in paraphrasing; and (2) Complex Reflections which focus on the emotions and meanings behind what is said. To be able to reflect in such a way requires deep listening. It may require you to jump ahead and fill in the blank when the other person has not yet said what they mean. According to William Miller, the co-creator of MI, "two-thirds of the change in therapy clients is attributed to accurate empathy."[2] The same outcomes are expected outside of a therapeutic setting. Empathy can help you effectively understand the other person in order to find a fitting solution to the problem.

Empathy is not the only helpful tool in understanding others. There is also the use of compassion, where you show caring and a willingness to help. According to the Dalai Lama, compassion is an uncompromising attitude that remains constant regardless of the other person's actions. It is a commitment to stay kind and focus on removing the other person's suffering no matter what they do. While the Dalai Lama acknowledges that this is a challenging practice, he advises that you start by removing anger and hatred from your heart.[3]

Empathy is about being a sponge, absorbing the other person's experience, and fusing it with your own knowledge. When both sides have done this, the outcomes are superior to any result one of you could have made alone.

Step 3. Sharing Your Point of View

Now it is your turn to talk. You have been patient enough, holding back with the goal of first understanding the other person. To continue going down the road of effective communication, you will need to express yourself in a way the other person can hear you. What that requires is for you to avoid blaming or criticizing the other person, which only raises defensiveness in them. Instead, stick to the facts. Share with them what has transpired. Tell the story by first pointing out elements they are likely to agree with.

Only after you have been successful in getting them to agree to what you expressed, do you continue on. This is your opportunity to share your point of view. It may be that they said or did something that hurt your feelings. Explain how that made you feel but be careful not to say that they made you feel this way through their behavior. Instead, use "I" statements and focus on your emotions as a result of the facts stated above. Once you are satisfied that they understand you, move on to the next step.

Step 4. Emotionally Intelligent Problem-Solving

If you have followed steps 1 and 2, you should have a good understanding of how the other person feels. By the end of step 3, they should have a sense of how you feel. Step 4 is about putting the two sides together and coming up with a solution that is satisfactory to both parties. This is not about compromising. It's about an attempt to get both people's needs met. It requires creativity, patience, and goodwill.

When the person you are speaking with feels understood, they will be open to moving the focus from the problem to the solution.

It's best to take the "teach a man to fish" approach to empowering them to solve their problem rather than try to fix it for them. Elicit this problem-solving mindset through questions such as, "What do you think will help in this situation?" When they come up with their answers, they are more likely to follow through. If, however, they become stumped, you can ask permission to provide a suggestion. By preempting your solution with this request, you will help the person be more receptive to hearing what you suggest.

Step 5. Finding The Essence

In every situation, some elements repeat themselves. You may recognize a part of the current conflict because it reminds you of the arguments you used to have with a family member. To grow as an effective communicator, boil down the problem-turned-solution and see what you can learn from this experience. This can help you circumvent future interpersonal issues. Use the knowledge you gained about how you affect others emotionally and consider what lessons might be in store for you. You can also reflect on any triggers you experienced and think what you can do the next time you are in a similar situation. By extracting the essence of the case, you are setting yourself up for more effective communication moving forward.

TIPS FOR EFFECTIVE COMMUNICATION

❏ Reflective listening: listen without interruption, reflect what you've heard, and get to an agreement before sharing your side.

❏ Empathic understanding: examine body language and cultivate compassion.

❏ Sharing your point of view: use "I" statements.

❏ Emotionally-Intelligent problem solving: find a solution that fits both sides. Elicit the answer from the other person and ask permission before making a suggestion.

❏ Finding the essence: boil down the problem-turned solution to see what the takeaways are.

Conclusion

Social Competency is the key to successful relationships. It provides you with the framework for effective communication, which includes the right balance of empathy for yourself and the other person, deep listening, and problem-solving. These are vital skills that allow you to not only talk in a way in which you can be heard, but also to understand what the other person is experiencing, and to come up with a solution that incorporates both sides.

E#1: Empowering Exercise

There are many ways you can increase your EQ, but for our purposes, let's start by focusing on the most fundamental of the necessary skills to help you manage your stress at work: self-awareness. More specifically, the goal of this exercise is for you to gain clarity about your needs, even if you aren't sure what your needs are.

In the interactive table below, you will have three different ways to elicit your unattended needs. The first is by honing in to your emotional state. How do you feel when you are at work, given the demands and resources available to you? If, for example, you feel overwhelmed, write "overwhelmed" in column one. Then ask yourself, "What is the story I am telling myself that leads me to feel overwhelmed?" You might be telling yourself, "This is too much for me." Whatever the thought, put it in column two of the table.

If you do not have access to your emotions or thoughts, it is best to notice your behavior. What are you doing that relates to burnout? For example, if you are disengaging from your work, put down "disengaging" under the third column of the table.

Finally, ask yourself, "What do I need in order to reengage in my work?" Reflect on any needs that are not being addressed. These may include feedback on how to improve, learning to prioritize, social support, minimizing distractions, connecting to purpose, taking breaks, and incorporating self-care or other needs. Write down the most essential need that, if met, could change your experience at work.

If you need more space, draw a table in a notebook and label it like the table shown here:

Emotion	Thought	Behavior	Need
Overwhelmed	*This is too much for me*	*Disengaging*	*Prioritize*

E#2:
EMPOWERMENT

"Energy, not time, is the fundamental currency of high performance."

– Tony Schwartz

To change your reality, you first needed to be in touch with yourself and have the skills to negotiate relationships with others. Now that you have these EQ skills under your belt, it's time to make use of them to *empower* yourself.

Burnout is about feeling disempowered, like you lack control over your situation. You feel inadequate to manage the demands on you and start to question your competency. As we've shown, these experiences are simply symptoms of the problem, but there is a solution.

In this section, we will focus on ways to increase personal power so that you get your needs met. As you read about the various areas related to this process, beware—it may lead to quite a transformation!

Personal Power

OFTEN, THE WORLD presents us with challenges. Work can be demanding and feel stressful. Even with the best of intentions, you might come across obstacles such as a shortage of time, a lack of energy, or a gap in your knowledge or skill set, all of which can make moving forward seem overwhelming. Precisely when you come to this point, you need to tune into your power.

Empowerment is the process of permitting yourself to act responsibly, to take control of your life, and to use your resources to get tasks done. Even when your job feels draining, when you are empowered, you wouldn't automatically opt for the easy way out and quit. Instead, you would buckle down and face your challenges.

In a recent study, researchers found that a better indicator of cardiovascular health than running on a treadmill was whether you could do forty pushups during a timed test.[1] If you do not regularly exercise your arm muscles, doing forty pushups might seem nearly impossible. Instead of giving up on ever being able to accomplish this feat, if you are determined to succeed, you could break up the task. Start with five pushups and add one more each day. Over time, you will build strength and also, your daily practice will help keep the momentum going.

Like an athlete who trains intensely before a marathon, you have to strengthen yourself to deal with hardships. In the process of increasing your inner strength, you will experience challenges, embarrassments, and repeated failures, but these are milestones along your path to make you into a warrior. A successful person does not wake up one day to realize their strength. Being successful is something you have to develop with intention and focus. When you develop personal power, you can apply it to any situation that requires you to take action or be fierce.

People often confuse confidence with motivation. They believe they will try something when they are certain they can do it, but waiting for confidence to show up is futile. Instead, we must drive ourselves by tapping into our inner strength to tackle challenges. From this perspective, confidence will result. We feel stronger knowing that we have climbed a steep mountain, that we have successfully faced a confrontation with a coworker even when we are uncomfortable with conflict, and that we persisted when giving up was an option.

You may have experienced some adverse events in your life. We all have, but sometimes when this happens, we can adopt a victim mentality. There is a sense of helplessness, and we can feel sorry for ourselves, eliciting empathy from others to counteract any negativity we might be experiencing. Along with this mentality, we often adopt negative thinking patterns. For instance, we may overgeneralize and state that everyone is out to get us just because one person harmed us. We may start to see the world as either "good" or "bad." We might not recognize the knowledge we already have, doubt our ability to do something we actually can do, or feel like we have no available choices, all of which will leave us feeling trapped.

Although a victim mentality may help us suppress our anger, get attention and compassion from others, and bring about some momentary relief, it promotes a feeling of helplessness. It can trigger fears and anxieties and can bring about feelings of shame, guilt, and despair.

In contrast to a feeling of powerlessness or a perception of deficits, empowerment is focused on personal strengths. When you feel empowered, you can create the changes you want in your life rather than succumb to a victim mentality. This concept emphasizes self-sufficiency, which may require you to learn new skills along the way. It requires that you take responsibility for yourself, take proactive action toward achieving your goals, and forgive yourself for any past doings.

In the song "Solsbury Hill," Peter Gabriel wrote about a spiritual experience he had when he left the band Genesis that prompted him to start a solo career. According to Gabriel (as quoted in Billboard), "It's about being prepared to lose what you have for what you might get...It's about letting go."[2]

Imagine you have a beat-up car in your one-car garage. You want a brand new car, but so long as you hold onto the old one, you will not have room for the vehicle you desire. You can attain personal power when you let go of your story, the narrative that limits you. By letting go of the old, you make room for new opportunities to show up. Let go of your limiting ways of thinking about things, of your attachments, and your habitual patterns so you can see the possibilities that await and make good choices through your newly adopted lens.

A paradoxical effect can happen when we are not paying attention to our energy. When we are exhausted, we often engage in activities that demand the least amount of effort, like watching television. This can become a procrastination habit. Even if you intend to increase your leadership skills by watching a YouTube video on the subject, if you do not intentionally turn off your computer and focus on putting your newfound knowledge into action, you can end up wasting hours watching additional videos on subjects that have nothing to do with your intended project.

Whether you are losing power from activities that cause laziness or from people around you who are critical or create conflict, replace them with more positive influences that allow you to gain power.

You might find that you feel drained, that your attention is weak, or that you lack enthusiasm about most things in life. By understanding what drains your energy and closing the door to those influences, you can reclaim your personal power and find that you have the energy you need to be productive.

We will keep coming back to the topic of energy, as it is relevant to burnout's primary symptom of exhaustion and its solution, self-care. Energy is also applicable to self-awareness, our emotions, engagement in tasks, and mental resilience.

TIPS FOR EMPOWERING YOURSELF

❑ With intention and focus, work to build up your inner strength

❑ Persist during hardships rather than wait to feel confident before tackling difficult situations

❑ Forgive yourself for anything you may have done wrong

❑ Increase self-sufficiency

❑ Take proactive action

❑ Be prepared to lose what you have for what you might get

❑ Mindfully reduce activities and affiliations with anything that makes you lose power

---

Conclusion

Empowerment is your personal power that develops with intention and focus, strengthens as you overcome mounting difficulties, and helps you stay determined in the face of challenges. Empowerment is associated with a strength-based mindset that requires you to be self-sufficient and take responsibility. Let go of the old to make space for something new, surround yourself with positive influences, and eliminate energy drains.

Ways to Increase Power

THERE ARE TWO primary methods to augment your power. The first is identifying what depletes your energy and then doing the opposite. The second is being intentional about times and seasons, noticing how they affect your power, and making decisions accordingly.

Energy Drains

One of the most significant contributors to your lack of power is your mind. When you have negative thoughts or fears, you are less likely to take action and more likely to be avoidant.

An easy way to understand the importance of self-talk is to examine the influences of criticisms from others. Recall a time when you had your heart set on doing something you deemed meaningful and you told someone else about it. The other person did not share in your enthusiasm and, instead, criticized your idea or said you lack what it takes to be successful. Ouch! What this sort of narrative does is discourage you from persevering. So now imagine that this negative voice is your own. If you are telling yourself everything that could go wrong, how you will embarrass yourself if you fail, how it will be too difficult or take too long, chances are you will disengage. This negative headspace short-circuits your opportunity to stretch yourself and test your limits.

When a task feels difficult or when the demands of the job seem excessive, you might find your mind overthinking, predicting catastrophes, and fearing failure. This self-deprecation leads to anxiety, which is energy depleting and, therefore, counterproductive. If you make excuses, you are just getting in your own way.

Perfectionism is another energy drain. It is an attitude of servitude because you are a slave to external circumstances. No matter how much you accomplish and how hard you try, it is never enough. It always feels like something is missing, like your outcomes are insufficient, and like there is a lot left to be desired.

If you are a perfectionist, you might believe that your needs come last, so you spend all your energy taking care of other people's requests. When you are overloaded, you will not ask for help. You will not delegate tasks to others because you hold firm to the idea that you "should" do it all yourself. You also lose power when you focus externally on the need for control or seek the approval of others.

Perhaps you are not quite a perfectionist, but you are a high achiever who has a go-go-go mentality. This need to continually produce can be incredibly draining. In this case, you may not be focused on quality, but simply the quantity of what you do. Not only does this approach use up a lot of your energy, but if you are working through lunch or think sleep is overrated and stay up late to get more done, your productivity will end up suffering in the end.

When it is time to recharge, you might inadvertently choose activities that zap your energy. When you are tired, if you are habitually choosing to watch television, play video games, or surf the internet because they are sedentary activities, you are not getting adequate rest. There is nothing wrong with kicking your feet up and engaging in entertainment, but these activities cannot be a substitute for proper relaxation.

If you are exposed to brainwashing commercials or get caught up in comparing yourself to friends on social media, these activities will further drain you.

When your energy is low, you are inclined to relax and you might be tempted to reach for something that will give you an immediate boost. While this may increase your energy in the moment, it can be problematic in the long-term. If you find yourself eating junk food, consuming caffeine or sugary snacks, smoking, or drinking alcohol, it is a sign that you are energy-deprived.

Being around certain people may also be an energy drain. People who take the victim role, for instance, are likely to be full of self-pity and avoid taking responsibility for themselves. Those who have narcissistic tendencies can be manipulative and solely focused on their own needs. People who try to dominate others can be intimidating and off-putting. Those who are always in a crisis mode seem to create drama wherever they go. Judgmental folks may try to make you feel insignificant so they can feel more important in comparison. Also, the person who is always acting helpless might elicit your sympathy and convince you to help, but you will likely find yourself caught in a futile cycle. If the person you are around is more of a taker than a giver, if by being around them you feel more negative than positive, or if you feel exhausted merely by spending time together, you need to minimize contact with this person.[1]

To increase your personal power, you need to identify your energy drains and reverse engineer them. If you have a critical mind, move beyond thought so you can see the ultimate truth. Our thoughts cloud our vision of reality. We experience feelings associated with our interpretation of events. Our perceptions are often flawed and can mislead us.

You need to have a positive outlook. Identify thoughts that stop you from having what you want and declare that you will do whatever it takes to make your goal come to fruition. Pay close attention to the language you use. It can make a big difference in how you feel and in your productivity. By quieting the mind, you can attain greater clarity, which will allow you to make decisions with greater ease and avoid potential obstacles.

Engaging in selfless acts demonstrates that you are acting out of your best interests. If, for instance, you feel stressed and frustrated about all you have to do, such as taking care of your children, keeping your home organized, providing financially for your family, you might notice how depleting this feels. But once you redefine your actions as selfless, you stop anticipating reciprocity and drop expectations. This simple mind shift can give you more energy and help you feel empowered, knowing that you are responsible, caring, and strong.

Rather than focus on controlling your circumstances, turn inward to gain ultimate control of your mind, the intensity of your emotions, and your reactions. If you live with integrity, you can validate yourself rather than feel a need for someone else to recognize you. This can boost your confidence and help you show up charismatically.

Have compassion for yourself and slow down. Instead of focusing on getting an exponential amount of work done, focus on quality. Pace yourself and stay attuned to your energy levels throughout.

Consider what will truly replenish your energy. Sitting still and breathing can energize your body, release internal stress, and free the mind from negative chatter. Nourish your body with high energy foods. Hydrate with lots of water. Declutter your environment and then your mind will also feel less cluttered and you will regain your focus and vitality. Surround yourself with people who are enthusiastic, supportive, and loving.

Showing up powerfully requires you to be aware of your energy. Like a light switch, you have to know which direction turns you on and which shuts you down. When inspecting your circumstances, consider what gives you personal power and what takes your power away. This awareness can help you make better decisions that are aligned with your integrity, your goals, and your values.

REVERSING ENERGY DRAINS

Identify your energy drains and write next to each one what you will focus on instead:

- ❑ Negative thinking:
- ❑ Fear of failure:
- ❑ Making excuses:
- ❑ Perfectionism:
- ❑ Not asking for help:
- ❑ Not delegation tasks:
- ❑ Needing to always be in control:
- ❑ Having a relentless go-go-go mentality
- ❑ Not getting adequate sleep:
- ❑ Not taking breaks:
- ❑ Consuming negative media:
- ❑ Eating poorly:
- ❑ Drinking alcohol:
- ❑ Smoking:
- ❑ A cluttered environment:
- ❑ Negative people:
- ❑ Other:

Times of Power

Energy is all around you and is continuously shifting. It changes from situation to situation, from morning to night, and from season to season. Notice how differently you feel when you wake up than when you go to sleep. If you are a morning person, you likely feel energized early in the day and sleepy in the evening. Alternatively, if you are a night owl, it might be hard to find the energy to leave your bed when the alarm goes off in the morning. It's harder still to go to bed because this is when you feel most alive and energized, have your clearest thoughts and most productive hours late into the night.

Each season brings different energy with it as well. In the wintertime, we feel more sluggish. There is less sunlight and we are more likely to hunker down in the cold weather and feel a need to be still. The spring is a new beginning, and we feel revitalized to clean and organize our home. The summer can be a time of robust activity as we have the most energy this time of year. Like the leaves of a tree, during the fall season, we are ready to let go of anything that may be limiting us or draining our energy. As the seasons change, our energy can speed up, slow down, or bring us into balance.

Do you have a time of year when you typically feel burned out? One lawyer I spoke with stated that he finds himself getting burned out around the end of the year. November, December, and January are the months when he starts to feel the accumulation of stress from the year's entirety. What about you?

It is essential to understand how your energy changes with the seasons and not take a one-season approach all year. If, for example, you push yourself all year, as you might do in summer when your energy is highest, you will feel exhausted. To set yourself up for longevity, you need to tailor your approach based on the time of year.

In-between each season, there is a two week period of transition. In the middle of each seasonal change is either a solstice or an equinox. During each solstice (usually June and December), the sun is furthest away from the equator and, thus, we have the longest and shortest amount of sunlight, respectively. This is a time to think about what in your life you want to change. What do you want more of and what do you want less of? During each equinox (usually March and September), the sun is closest to the equator, so we have equally long days and nights. The equinox is when there is balance in the universe, which is why it is an excellent opportunity for you to focus on cultivating more inner stability.

Listen to your body, pay attention to your energy gauge, and work in harmony with your circadian rhythm as well as with the seasons.

Be aware of what gives you power and what takes your power away. These are critical aspects of empowerment, which can alter stressful situations and provide you with the energy, the confidence, and the motivation to act. However, merely having power is not enough.

You need to have a developed sense of self to know what to go after and investigate the internal challenges that show up. By having clarity and removing obstacles in your path, you can mobilize your energy to continue expressing and gaining personal power.

TIMES OF POWER INTENTION CHECKLIST

Create an intention related to each of the following:

Times of the day

☐ Early bird: focus on getting the most important and challenging tasks done early in the day

☐ Night owl: carve out undisturbed time at night to get your work done

Season of the Year

☐ Winter: focus on recharging through meditation, journaling, grounding, and resting

☐ Spring: clean and organize your environment while planting seeds for new projects

☐ Summer: combine diligent work with taking breaks, limiting distractions, and reaping what you've sewed

☐ Fall: review where you are and let go of anything that stands in your way of growth

---

Times of Transition

- ❑ Solstice: release the old, reflect and journal on your findings

- ❑ Equinox: cultivate inner balance through meditation and apply balance in your life through your actions (i.e., achieve financial balance)

Conclusion

To increase your personal power, you need to eliminate energy drains (e.g., negative thinking, perfectionism, putting your needs last, controlling others, seeking outside approval, doing too much and recovering too little, seeking immediate gratification) and do the opposite. To this end, you need to have an awareness of your energy level and employ a positive outlook, be selfless, engage in healthy and energy replenishing activities, and surround yourself with positive influences. Also, pay attention to times of the day and the season so you can be aware of when you feel most energized and in harmony with the forces around you.

Becoming More Yourself

WHEN YOU FACE an event, such as exceedingly high demands from your job, it is not uncommon to experience a range of reactions to it. While some people complain because they are upset, others become anxious and easily overwhelmed, while still others take charge and become more focused. We can link the differences in these reactions to different beliefs within each person, beliefs that define how you see yourself. But what leads to these different beliefs in the first place?

Psychiatrist Dr. Murray Bowen came up with a theory about the influence family systems have on how individuated a person becomes.[1] The less your sense of self is developed, the more others will be able to influence you. If you depend heavily on external approval and acceptance, you will be more likely to adjust your way of thinking and your behaviors to please others. Alternatively, you may try to control others by telling them what they should be like and pressure them to change.

When your sense of self is well developed, you do a dance between your sense of autonomy and your reliance on others. This means that when those you are closest to become critical or rejecting, you do not allow their actions to cloud your judgment. You stay focused on your goals while acknowledging that your progress may not be accepted or understood by some people in your inner circle.

Based on this theory, it is probable that you would want to be in the latter scenario, where you feel confident and can stand your ground regardless of what feedback you receive from others. This would enable you to feel connected and avoid becoming overly dependent or easily manipulated by others.

Bowen stresses that people do not usually shift their level of self-differentiation unless they consciously make an effort to do so. If you are searching for ways to function more optimally, focus on ways to more authentically be yourself.

To become self-differentiated, you first need to understand the layout of this concept and figure out where you fall within it. To begin, think of a time when you had to make a major decision that did not sit well with your family. Perhaps you wanted to marry someone your parents did not approve of or enter a field of study that was different from the family business. Whatever the situation, reflect on your consequent behaviors. Did you listen to your inner voice, or did you capitulate under pressure? If you rebelled against your parents, did you feel guilty, or were you able to balance your decision and emotional reaction to it?

Self-differentiation consists of two elements (see Figure 13.1). The first is being able to tell the difference between your thoughts and your feelings. You may feel guilty about not listening to your parents, but if you have a strong sense of self, you will understand where those feelings are coming from and choose your own decision. Part two of this process is choosing whether you let your intellect or your emotions guide your decision-making. The more differentiated you are, the more you let your mind be your guide.

This is a simplified understanding of differentiation. As mentioned above, there is an intricate dance you have to do between autonomy and intimacy. Being extreme in either direction can lead to problems. When you are too autonomous, you become isolated. This can lead to loneliness and depression. On the flip side, when you are too fused with others, you are not living your life the way you want to, which can create a sense of meaninglessness and propel constant anxiety about what others think of you. The latter is also a way of giving up your personal power.

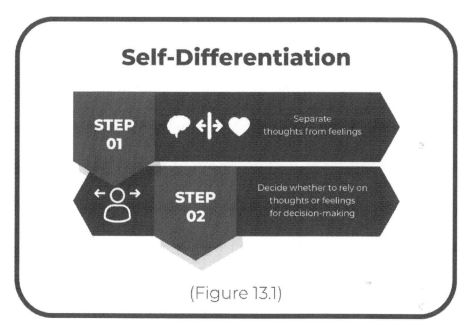

(Figure 13.1)

To help you increase your sense of self, let us focus on seven concrete areas: responsibility, authenticity, resilience, vulnerability, self-governance, courage, and mindfulness. Wherever you may find yourself at the moment, remember that self-awareness is the first step. By recognizing where you lie on the spectrum between autonomy and connection, you can start to make the necessary changes to bring yourself into balance.

Responsibility

Do you take responsibility for yourself, including for how you think, feel, and act? Or do you expect others to make you feel good? When people make comments similar to, "I will be happy when...," they are externalizing the responsibility for themselves. Such comments set an expectation that circumstances will change your life and create a passive stance. Focus instead on what you can do to change your life for the better so you can find the happiness you desire. This may sound something like, "I am actively working on ways to improve my level of satisfaction," or, "I take responsibility for my state of mind."

It is all too common to hear people say phrases like, "You made me so mad!" Other people cannot make you feel anything. Similar to how situations affect people differently, your reaction to your environment is your own. It is not what your environment or other people are doing that is causing your feelings. It is your interpretation and your ability to control your thoughts that lead you to feel a certain way.

The other aspect of responsibility to consider affects your beliefs about being of service to others. Do you take responsibility for "fixing" those around you who are suffering, or do you recognize that it is their responsibility to fix themselves? Remember that just like you, others need to be responsible for meeting their own needs. When you take their responsibility onto yourself, you enable the person to stay stuck, which ironically is the opposite of what you want for them.

Differentiation is a balancing act, so while you are focused on becoming responsible for yourself, you are also focusing on cultivating closeness to those you care about. Be accountable to others, not responsible for them.

Authenticity

As mentioned earlier, those around you may disapprove of your plans. Being differentiated means that you stay true to yourself and continually work toward achieving your goals while letting others around you know who you are. This requires you to be clear on your identity, a process of self-awareness that results from exploring your values, needs, and desires. You are born to be unique and it is your gift to yourself and the world when you express your authentic self.

Let's assume that you are determined to travel the world for a year. You have saved up your money, purchased your airline tickets, and are finally sharing your idea with your coworkers as you give your notice. Not everyone will be enthusiastic about your plans. When you are in a situation where the people around you are not supportive, you have a choice. You can either try to fit in and give up on your dreams, or you can stick to your plans and look to build a community of like-minded individuals. So if your coworkers criticize your plan, tap into your personal power to not let them dissuade you or bring up self-doubt. Likely, when you are traveling around the globe, you will meet others who have a similar sense of adventure to your own.

Resilience

When there is interpersonal tension, your instinct might be to flee. But avoiding conflict does not solve anything and can keep you stuck in a perpetual pattern. You can focus on reducing friction by removing blame and acknowledging the other person's point of view. Even if you do not agree with them, this simple act of listening to their perspective can lower resistance. Remember that being differentiated means being internally strong and able to withstand disagreements without being easily manipulated or elusive. Being resilient means recovering from such interpersonal clashes quickly.

Recently, I had an incident with a woman with whom I was splitting a lane in the swimming pool. Because it was just the two of us in the lane, I stuck to the right side for my laps while she was on the left. At one point, though, she began swimming on a diagonal, and I accidentally made contact with her. I was surprised at her reaction. She stood up and started screaming, "You should stick to your own lane!" My immediate inclination was to explain what had happened from my point of view. However, she did not receive my perspective well. When I said that perhaps she was sticking out into my lane, she yelled out, "Oh! So now it's my fault!" I instantly understood that my defensive response only increased the conflict. I self-corrected, reassuring her that it was no one's fault, that I'm not blaming her, and that I am not complaining.

What followed further surprised me. Instead of continuing to yell, my pool partner immediately pivoted 180 degrees and said, "You are so kind!" The next thing I knew, she was introducing herself to me with her first name. She then apologized and informed me that she has a physical condition that makes it difficult for her to swim in a straight line. Indeed, she went from blaming me to admitting fault, but only when she felt it was safe to do so. This instance solidified for me the importance of non-defensiveness regardless of whether you are at fault or wrongly accused.

You can also be resilient when the conflict does not involve you directly. Judd came to see me because his girlfriend did not get along with his parents. He felt like he was in-between the two parties and that he had to choose a side. This brought up feelings of helplessness that were familiar to him from childhood when, as an only child, he watched his parents constantly argue and yell at each other. Rather than stay passive and watch an argument unfold between his girlfriend and dad, I encouraged him to acknowledge both sides and move the conversation along. By taking charge rather than sitting at the sidelines, Judd became more empowered.

Vulnerability

While focusing on your goals, you may recognize areas of weakness that keep you from forging ahead. This is an opportunity for increased connection where you can elicit the help of those around you and simultaneously remain responsible for your own needs. Use effective communication to let others know what you can use help with, but stay mindful not to be demanding or let your expectations get the better of you. If the person you approached is unable or unwilling to help at this time, don't ruminate or give up. Focus on people you can reach out to for assistance. Keep in mind that there will be needs that may not be met, so stay realistic to avoid disappointment.

Being vulnerable does not mean that you are weak. It takes courage to admit you have a deficit or that you are not perfect. It's hard to be vulnerable if you worry too much about what others will think of you. Remember, being self-differentiated and powerful means thinking for yourself. Don't let your imagination about what other people might say turn you around. The truth is, many of these projections are unfounded and usually don't happen the way you may anticipate. When someone is not on your side, you can harness your resilience to sustain your vulnerability.

Self-governance

When your emotions get the better of you, they are in control and can lead you to be reactive and make poor decisions. Reflect on past instances where you were either unaware of your feelings or were overwhelmed by them. Recognize that it is perfectly normal for you to have emotional responses to events around you and that the feelings that emerge are there for a reason. Slow down enough to consider what you are feeling and why you are feeling this way. This will give you a better understanding of yourself, which you can use to make decisions that align with your goals for connection and that will not detract from your sense of self.

So often, I hear from my clients that they are not even aware of their feelings; they push their feelings down so they can keep forging ahead. It is true that just because you are sad, scared, or upset, the world does not stop. You still have the same level of responsibility at your job and often at home, and having all of these feelings inside will get the better of you if you do not deal with them. Over time, their intensity increases until you feel overwhelmed by your emotions or until they manifest into disease in your body, keeping you from being able to function.

One of my clients compared her tendency to push her feelings down to pushing a balloon under water. The balloon does not stay down for long, and eventually, it pops up with a vengeance. When she is going through difficult times that lead to strong negative emotions, she tends to busy herself as a distraction. She worries that facing her negative emotions will incapacitate her, and then she will be unable to do what she needs to get done.

Through our work together, she recognized that just because she was not focusing on her emotions did not mean they were not negatively affecting her. Instead of continuing to evade her feelings, she came up with a system to manage her feelings and where she will be able to make decisions under less than ideal conditions. She asked herself, "What would a CEO do?" This mindset allowed her step into a position of leadership and confidence. As we practiced embracing and honoring her feelings, her distress went down. She found it helpful to acknowledge what was inside of her and put into practice what she imagined a CEO would do. This provided her with the inner guidance she needed when she was under duress.

Courage

We all have fears that can keep us from making progress. Even with the best intentions in mind, we can become stuck in a rut. Work to overcome your fears by focusing on your life's purpose. Steer clear of extreme thinking that leads to extreme behavior. Life is not black or white. Let the many colors of the rainbow expand your thinking. The more you understand that your brain is trying to keep you alive, the more you will be able to remind yourself that you are not in a life-or-death situation that warrants such fear. Take it one step at a time in the direction of whatever scares you. When you get to the other side, you will feel a sense of pride and increased confidence in your ability to take on other fears and challenges. This will also remove any notion that you need others to save you from your struggle or any need to use others to attain your goals.

Many of my clients have felt stuck because they lacked clarity about what they wanted. When no other options seemed viable, they just stayed stuck in their current situation and felt hopeless that it will change. It takes courage to admit that you want to change, as change can be scary. It takes further courage to act in a way that brings about change. Get clear on what you want and ask yourself what you need to do about it. Sometimes change means altering your circumstances while other times, change is simply a shift in perspective that can make all the difference.

Mindfulness

Your early life circumstances, especially those events that left a wound, can be triggers for future events. You might find that you are having strong reactions to situations that are seemingly mild. This is an invitation to work on neutralizing your triggers, a process you can engage in with a trauma-trained therapist. Regardless of whether or not you get this kind of help, remember that you need to remain present. What is happening right now has nothing to do with your past. By differentiating between the past and the present, you will be able to stay focused on the moment and enjoy it for all that it is worth. Similarly, you want to stay in the here-and-now rather than focus on the future. When you feel anxious or preoccupied, it is a sign that you are future-focused. One method to bring yourself back to the present moment is to ground your body by exhaling all your air out several times.

Much of the process of differentiation is understanding that you have a right to be unique while focusing on creating strong relationships with others. This balancing act requires boundaries, which start in your mind. By getting clear on how you define yourself, you can draw lines in the sand about what is appropriate and what is not. You can start to differentiate between what feelings you have that are your own and which you may have absorbed that belong to someone else. Once you identify that you are holding onto unnecessary angst, let it go.

In this sense, what is true and right for you may not be true and right for others. Release any judgments or criticisms you have about others who are pursuing their path. Replace such negative opinions with compassion and give them the same opportunities for personal growth, even when they are struggling, without either trying to deter them or save them. We all have to experience failure to learn how to improve. Accepting others for their differences and celebrating those differences will enrich your relationships.

Having a greater sense of self allows you to have the best of both worlds. You can live your life more fully, finding a sense of fulfillment from being authentic to yourself while cultivating connections with others around you. The more self-differentiated you are, the more capable you are of functioning well under stressful conditions and, therefore, problem-solving with increased effectiveness.

You benefit in many ways as you become self-aware and can manage your feelings. You gain more control of important life decisions, your health, and reactivity to stress or others' emotions. You establish more definitive boundaries and are less likely to engage in behaviors that do not suit you. By validating yourself rather than focusing externally on approval from others, you gain more confidence.

The more differentiated you are, the better you will be able to manage work stresses such as excessive demands on your time and energy.

This is due, in part, to being able to transform your beliefs, which affect your emotional outcome and your coping. Your beliefs about meeting your needs while effectively addressing conflict help you cope even in the most intense situations because you can focus on both the circumstances outside of yourself as well as your inner experience.

Stress is not the enemy. Other people's agendas are not your roadmap.

You need to take responsibility for getting your own needs met. Stay true to yourself by focusing on what you desire for your life. Remain mindful of your emotions so you can manage them and make good decisions. Lastly, have the courage to be vulnerable and learn to cultivate intimacy rather than dependency on others so you can remain resilient, powerful, and increase your confidence.

Once you are empowered and self-differentiated, you need to know how best to utilize your power, and for this, you need to have clarity about your needs.

CHECKLIST TO INCREASE YOUR SENSE OF SELF

- ❏ Take responsibility for how you think, feel, and act.

- ❏ Be accountable to others, not responsible for them.

- ❏ Surround yourself with like-minded individuals.

- ❏ Reduce conflict by eliminating blame and acknowledging the other person's point of view.

- ❏ Recognize personal areas of weakness and ask for help.

- ❏ Keep expectations realistic to avoid disappointment.

- ❏ Consider what you are feeling and why you are feeling it.

- ❏ Ask yourself, "What would a CEO do?" and act accordingly.

- ❏ Focus on your life's purpose and take it one step at a time.

- ❏ Stay focused on the present moment.

- ❏ Ground your anxiety.

- ❏ Release judgments about others.

- ❏ Accept and celebrate others' differences.

- ❏ Have compassion for other people's struggles.

Conclusion

According to the theory of self-differentiation, external events affect people differently based on their sense of self. A poorly differentiated person focuses on external approval. Someone with a well-developed sense of self incorporates both autonomy and reliance on others. By separating your thoughts from your feelings and knowing which of these forces leads you to make decisions, you can become empowered and strengthen your sense of self.

Hierarchy of Needs

AS MENTIONED UNDER Self-Awareness, Abraham Maslow claimed that our needs are hierarchical, and we must meet those needs based on a sequence.[1] Maslow identified five human needs and in this section, we will discuss the first four. The final need is discussed in Why Enlightenment is Important.

Human Needs

PHYSIOLOGY

Starting with our most basic physiological needs that sustain us, we focus on getting shelter, food, water, and sleep. Without these vital life-sustaining elements, it is fruitless to focus on anything else.

Since you are reading this book, chances are you have secured the first level of the pyramid (refer back to Figure 4.1). You have met the most basic needs that keep you alive. Even though this is true, when you become highly stressed in your life, your sleep suffers, you start to eat poorly, and you substitute caffeine and sugary drinks for water. So rather than take this first level of needs for granted, you must continually monitor your behaviors and make the best choices for your well-being. By doing so, you are establishing a strong foundation that will lead you to your ultimate desires.

SAFETY

Once we establish our foundation, we climb up to the second tier of the pyramid. We focus on issues surrounding safety. Beyond physical safety, we want to create stability in our lives. We attain financial security through employment, entrepreneurship, and investments. While there are good reasons why we focus so intensely on this aspect, we need to be careful, as we often get stuck here.

I have worked with many smart and talented individuals who were making far more money than I ever made at their young age. And yet, it seemed that despite their economic success, they were struggling. You might be able to relate to this, especially if you have a job filled with high demands that requires you to sacrifice much of yourself.

You might find that you pour all of your energy into your work, yet it never feels done. You have no choice but to stay late and, even then, sometimes you take it home with you. If this is sounding like your story, your job is taking up two of your most valuable resources in exchange for one: time and energy in exchange for money.

Many of the people I have worked with struggle with feeling like what they make is never enough. When they get a raise, they upgrade their lifestyle. They buy fancier cars and eat at more expensive restaurants, so they need more money to continue to match their expenses. Some of them think about retirement and the need to create passive income. Planning for the future is crucial, especially because so many of them are miserable at their jobs and want an exit strategy. I am certainly a proponent of planning and creating multiple streams of income, but what I see with a lot of my clients is that they get stuck around issues of safety, so much so that they never attain the next level of the pyramid. As a result, no matter how much money they make and how great their lives may seem on the outside, they are unhappy.

Often, people have difficulty attracting a hefty paycheck because they believe they do not deserve it. If they are making a lot of money, they may feel like they have to stretch out their work hours to justify their pay. Others have a hard time holding onto money due to beliefs that they are not good money managers. Whether you are not making what you are worth, are working so hard that your life is out of balance, or have a hard time saving your money to create financial security, you can benefit from working on your mindset.

Our money beliefs are usually tied to our personal history and tend to go back to childhood. Consider the relationship your parents had to money. Were they struggling financially? Did they fight a lot about money? You may have picked up a notion that money is scarce. Alternatively, you may associate negative ideas with cash (e.g., greed or materialism).

Lenny came to me because he was unhappy in his relationship. His partner had a change of status after selling his stock and wanted to use his money windfall to travel. Lenny could not afford to travel based on what he was making at his job. And the fact that his income was low was no accident. Money was a trigger for Lenny. We uncovered that the limiting belief that had kept him making too little was that he did not believe it was possible to make more. Lenny also considered himself a spiritual person and said he did not feel good focusing on money.

Through further exploration of these historical beliefs, Lenny realized that he indeed wanted more money so he could have the financial freedom that his partner now had. That said, he still did not believe he could do it or that he deserved an increase in pay. Because he was not making as much as he wanted, he saw himself as worthless, which made it challenging to ask for more money.

To rewire his limiting belief into one more aligned with his new goal, Lenny started reciting an affirmation daily about his worth. Within three weeks, his belief in himself had tripled. He quickly set a new financial goal, updated his resume, and began job searching. Seven weeks later, he was offered a new position with a twenty thousand dollar raise.

If you have anxiety about money or anything else, chances are you do not feel secure. Work on grounding your anxiety so you can feel calm enough to take action and progress up Maslow's Human Needs Pyramid.

LOVE AND BELONGING

Level three of the hierarchy of needs is about love and belonging and your relationships with other people, including friends, family, and your romantic partner. We are social beings, and we cannot derive real meaning from life without connections with other people. In fact, in the book, *The Top Five Regrets of the Dying*, a palliative nurse collected the regrets of her dying patients.[2] Here are some things we can learn about life not fully lived:

"I wish I'd had the courage to live a life true to myself, not the life others expected of me." Sometimes, as an attempt to be loved and to belong, we take on other people's wishes and make them our own. We forget to listen to ourselves. We get lost. We live inauthentically to please others. So while we need connections, we need to be true to our desires and, rather than fit in, strive to belong. Consider your behaviors and the choices you make. Are they what you truly want? Is someone living vicariously through you even though you would rather be doing something else? Be honest with yourself.

"I wish I hadn't worked so hard." It is standard in 21st Century America to work a minimum of 40 hours a week with only two weeks of vacation. But if you are reading this book, you are not average. You likely fall into the high-achievers camp, which means you work upwards of 50 hours per week, if not more. High achievers are often those who fail to take their vacation days. It is no wonder high achievers burn out. They have so much to prove to themselves and others, and the work feels like it is never done.

When you are on your death bed, and you look back at your life, will you think you focused on the wrong things? Did you pass up on opportunities because you were too busy? Did you avoid taking the easy road, even part of the time, because you had something to prove? Did you want to feel accomplished, but never felt like what you do is enough? It is time to rethink this paradigm, so you do not end up with regrets. How can you work less, relax more, and enjoy the lifestyle you are working so hard to build?

Ana came to see me because her husband was working long hours, which left her feeling lonely and confused. She was often anxious about making advanced plans, especially for long weekends, because she knew that without something in hand, her husband would run off to the office. Sure, he had a justification. He knew he could get more work done when no one was around. He had a lot of work to do being that he was part of a start-up and wanted it to succeed. From this perspective, his work ethic made perfect sense. However, after two decades of this pattern, Ana started to wonder, "How much do I really matter to him if he's never around?"

Deep down, Ana knew that she did matter to her husband and that he was a high achiever with a deep desire to feel accomplished. He wanted his family to have financial security and he took it upon himself to be the provider for them. This made it easier to choose his work over his family because it was, in a sense, a form of self-sacrifice.

Ana's husband is not alone in this paradigm. How many times do we hear of people who work around the clock, whose entire identity is wrapped up in their work, and who, as a result, do not have much time to enjoy a personal life? It is often when the time has run out and only in retrospect that the high achiever realizes they have missed out.

"I wish I'd had the courage to express my feelings." Relationships are about the communication of our innermost worlds, including our needs, desires, thoughts, and feelings. We all want to be seen and understood, but if we do not express ourselves, how will others know our authentic self? In many cultures, talking about feelings or simply showing feelings to others is considered a sign of weakness. We learn to zip up our emotions

and keep tight-lipped. Like any limiting belief, we need to challenge this one. It is outdated. Research confirms that holding our emotions inside can cause our foundation to crumble.[3] When you refrain from expressing yourself, your emotions can turn into physical pain and even auto-immune diseases. You suffer inside, and your relationships to others will suffer on the outside.

When someone shares a story of personal hardship, how do you think of that person? Often, we consider this an act of courage. Still, we forget that showing vulnerability brings us closer to others. When it comes time for us to be vulnerable, we often shut down. We are afraid of people's judgment. It is time to end the double standard. If you want to maintain your health and cultivate relationships, you must open yourself up as well.

"I wish I had stayed in touch with my friends." Are you so caught up in your stressful life that you have no time for your friends? The older we get and the more entrenched we are in our work, the more isolated we become.

Why are friendships important? According to Aristotle, the Greek philosopher and scientist, friendships serve several purposes. He said (as quoted by Volney Streamer), "In poverty and other misfortunes of life, true friends are a sure refuge. The young they keep out of mischief; to the old they are a comfort and aid in their weakness; and those in the prime of life they incite to noble deeds."[4]

Tom Rath, director of Gallup, researched friendships and came up with these three notable findings:

1. We are five times more likely to lead healthy lives if our best friend does so.

2. Married people conveyed that the friendship they have with their partner is five times more important to their relationship than their intimacy.

3. We have only a 1 in 12 chance of feeling engaged at work when we have no friends there, but when we have strong relationships with even one coworker, we are seven times more likely to feel engaged at our job.[5]

Relationships can be both stressful and stress-fighting, depending on the nature of the interaction. We are affected by our proximity to others and the level of intimacy we have with them. When you surround yourself by people who are very negative, critical, or unsupportive, you tend to shut down. When despite your innate desire for closeness, you are unable to convert this individual into being your personal fan, you may want to run the other way. Conversely, when you surround yourself with others who are loving and supportive, you flourish. Thus, it is a prominent reminder for you to actively pursue people who are positive and encouraging, as well as environments that attract like-minded individuals.

"I wish that I had let myself be happier." As you get caught up in the rat race, you often forget to slow down and enjoy the journey. You might seek happiness in the form of accumulating material possessions, but find this unsatisfying. So, why not pursue more happiness? For many, it boils down to the belief, "I don't deserve it." Maybe you believe that you are not worthy, that you are "bad," or are unaware of your true value by not realizing when you aren't doing well. Author Mel Robbins wrote a book about the latter in the hopes of getting us to wake up to the truth and push the boundaries to reach our true potential. In Stop Saying You're Fine, Robbins outlines how we are often our own worst enemy.[6] We get comfortable in our old ways, even when they keep us miserable. We fear change, so we convince ourselves that everything is "fine."

How can you push the envelope and fill your life with greater joy?

If you could have the kind of life you only dream of, what would be different? Surely, you would not be working as hard as you are, you would not be as lonely as you feel, and you would enjoy the comforts of your life more. So why not turn that dream into a reality? With the right mindset you can.

ESTEEM

Assuming that you have created heart connections with others and have cultivated the friendships and love relationship you desire, what is your next need? According to Maslow, level four is about esteem. This corresponds with your personal power, your sense of self, or how you project yourself into the world. It starts with how you see yourself.

Do you feel confident in taking on new challenges? When someone acknowledges your efforts or pursues your friendship, do you feel worthy? Often, although you have earned the comforts and warranted the relationships you have, if you believe you are inadequate, you will resist opportunities to advance your life.

This belief pattern that gets in the way of confidence is evident in the story of Jillian, my 25-year-old client who struggled in the first year at her job. After getting a low-performance review, she decided to buckle down and work harder. This translated into putting in more time and energy than anyone else at the company. By the end of her second year, she received recognition at the company party as the *Most Improved* worker. Even though she earned this award through her hard work, she felt she didn't deserve it. Her belief about her inadequacy held firm.

The same belief pattern was also evident in her romantic relationship. She had been dating the same man for five years. When I inquired about the plan for the next stage of their relationship, she said her boyfriend wanted to wait until he had enough money to buy a home for them. She saw this as a personal rejection, which drove her to prove herself to him even more. Despite all his praise and acknowledgments of her, she kept blaming herself for his stalling. Only after I pointed out that he seemed to have a similar belief to her own of feeling inadequate, did Jillian consider this alternative possibility.

To compensate for a lack of confidence, perhaps you have taken the "fake-it-'til-you-make-it" approach, and are shaking in your boots each time you think someone will discover the truth about you. If you struggle with a sense of inadequacy or imposter syndrome, chances are you see others as being more capable.

Remember that while you are keenly aware of your anxieties and limitations, what you know of others is only skin deep. While you do not know the inner workings of those around you, you can be sure that everyone has some regrets, makes mistakes at times, and has insecurities with which to contend.

When you have stage fright, the standard recommendation has been to imagine the audience members as naked. Why is this supposed to help calm your nerves? Because by picturing everyone else as vulnerable, you feel more in control.

PRIORITIZING YOUR NEEDS BASED ON THE FIRST FOUR LEVELS OF MASLOW'S HIERARCHY

Physiological:

❑ Make good choices for your well-being, especially when under stress.

Safety:

❑ Work to eliminate any limiting beliefs about financial security.

❑ Live within your means.

Love and belonging:

❑ Be authentic rather than focus on pleasing others.

❑ Express your feelings to increase connections to others.

❑ Work to overcome your fear of change.

Esteem

❑ Stop comparing yourself to others.

❑ Replace unrealistic ideals with realistic expectations.

Conclusion

According to Maslow, your needs are hierarchical, and you should pursue them in order starting with the basic needs.

Meeting the four human needs of Physiology, Safety, Love, and Esteem can bring a sense of contentment. Depending on where you are in the hierarchy, this will inform what you need to prioritize.

You must first have your needs met in order to do your best work. This will allow you to focus and engage in what you are doing and feel more fulfilled by it.

E#2: Empowering Exercise

If you find yourself drowning in a sea of never-ending to-dos and more tasks seem to pour in continuously, it is time to strategize. Get out a pen and paper and follow these three steps:

Step 1: In the table below, list all the tasks currently on your plate under the "Task List" column. Determine which of these items are tasks that only you can do given your skills, expertise, and know-how. Put a checkmark next to those items in the column labeled "Tasks Only I Can Do." Delegate the items that you did not check to someone else. Mark these by putting a checkmark next to those items under the "Tasks to Delegate" column.

Priority	Task List	Task Only I Can Do	Tasks to Delegate

Step 2: Of the items on your list that you choose to keep, which of them would have the most significant impact? Put a "1" next to the first of these items in the "Priority" column and start on that one first. Then put a "2" next to the item that would have the next most significant impact. Continue to sort through your list by asking this question for the remaining items and marking them accordingly in column 1.

Step 3: Do you have control over your schedule at work, or are other people interrupting your flow and pulling you into constant meetings?

If you deem certain meetings to be essential for you to attend, focus on those. However, any meeting that you can skip and have someone else attend in your stead who can report back with what you missed, would give you more time to focus on your essential tasks. Determine which meetings are not the best use of your time and communicate that to your higher-ups.

By engaging in these three steps, you will prioritize your tasks, take control of your schedule, and minimize the demands of others, freeing up your time to be maximally effective.

E#3: ENGAGEMENT

Now that you are emotionally in control of yourself and in your power, you can optimize engagement in your work.

Engagement is the antithesis to burnout. It is what happens when you have resources (versus burnout when you lack them).

You can then meet those high demands and still thrive.

As part of this burnout solution, I discuss what poor and optimal engagement look like, how to get into a state of flow, what resources you can hunt down that will increase your engagement and then teach you how to best manage your time and tasks to get the most done.

Engagement is how you express yourself through your work on a cognitive, emotional, and physical level. When you are optimally engaged in your work, you are most productive.

Think about a time when you were in a state of flow, when you were so immersed in what you were doing, that the time seemed to pass by much more quickly. This is what optimal engagement is like. It is when you are simultaneously inspired and challenged. When you are engaged in such a way, you are less distracted and will get more done.

Poor Engagement

AS ARE MANY concepts in this book, engagement, too, is found on a spectrum (see Figure 15.1). On one end of the engagement range is a frenetic or overly-engaged state. We often see this when demands are high, control is low, and you put everything you have into doing your best work and trying to get it all done. This lofty effort strategy may work well for a short period, but over time, it will take a toll, not only on your work, but on your mental and physical health.

While work demands will undoubtedly contribute to your frantic behavior, there are internal demands attributed to your personality that will also be a driving force. If you are unable or unwilling to acknowledge failure, if you neglect your personal needs, or if you are prone to anxiety or irritability while also being highly ambitious with lofty goals, then you are a contender for over-engagement.

According to Christina Maslach, a primary researcher on the subject of burnout, when employees are overly-engaged, it may be a sign that they are stressed out.[1] Consider Julio, who works intensely all day. He stares at his computer screen and tries as hard as he can to get the work done before nightfall. But the demands of his job are so high that he feels buried by his responsibilities. In an attempt to lessen his load for the following day, he stays at work late and even when he goes home, he continues working into the night.

Poor Engagement

Over-Engaged   Engaged-Exhausted   Disengaged

Figure 15.1

On the surface, we can say that Julio is highly engaged in his work. Is he a workaholic? Not necessarily, at least if what is meant by being a workaholic is that you don't want to get away from your work. Julio might just feel so overwhelmed with the amount of work he has to get done that he is not able to step away. To an outsider, it may seem that Julio is obsessive. Despite his intense focus, energy, and time invested in work, Julio would love to have more personal time and feels stressed that he doesn't but instead has to work so much.

So, what will happen to Julio if his situation at work does not change? Over time, his energy will wane. Now imagine yourself in Julio's position. The demands of your job have not changed, but you no longer have the energy to dive in. You notice how exhausted you feel and now experience difficulties in performing tasks. You consequently start neglecting your responsibilities and feel bad about yourself or hopeless about your work. This is what Maslach (1976) refers to as engaged-exhausted, and it is associated with feeling worn out, having a low sense of control, and low self-efficacy. In other words, you start questioning your ability to do the work.

What we know about burnout is that it is a result of chronic stress over time. On any given day, Julio can go from being overly-engaged to disengaged. Disengagement is a sign of burnout. It is when demands are so low that you feel under-challenged. In Julio's case, if his exhaustion leads him to drift too far away from the demands of his job, he will ultimately become detached.

When we are disengaged, even work that at first seemed meaningful will now feel unfulfilling. The stress of the work leads us to feel irritable and impatient. In contrast, the sense of monotony and boredom from work results in a lack of personal development, which may very well lead us to contemplate changing jobs. When we burn out, we become depleted of energy, we feel exhausted, our engagement turns into cynicism, and we become ineffective.

A 2018 Gallup poll found that nearly 70 percent of U.S. workers were not engaged or were actively disengaged.[2] Clearly, the workplace is getting it wrong with such a profoundly negative impact on employees. Now that you know what makes the difference between engaged and disengaged, and the difference between optimally engaged and engaged-exhausted, you are ready to learn how to harness more optimal engagement, which I will cover in the next section.

Identifying Poor Engagement

Next to each item in the table below, mark "yes" for items that correspond with your current situation:

	Poor Engagement	YES	NO
1	Demands are high		
2	Control is low		
3	I am highly ambitious		
4	I am unable or unwilling to acknowledge failure		
5	I neglect my needs		
6	Demands are high		
	Overly-Engaged/Frenetic Total =		
7	I have low energy		
8	I find it difficult to perform my regular job duties		
9	I have been neglecting my responsibilities		
10	I feel bad about myself		
11	I feel hopeless about work		
12	I have low self-efficacy		
	Engaged-Exhausted Total =		
13	Demands are too low		
14	I feel detached from work		
15	Work feels unfulfilling		
16	I am impatient		
17	I feel bored at work		
18	My work lacks opportunities for personal development		
	Disengaged/Underchallenged Total =		

Scoring: Count how many items from questions 1-6 (overly-engaged/frenetic), 7-12 (engaged-exhausted), and 13-18 (disengaged/underchallenged) you answered "yes" to and tally your totals under each heading. The area where you have the highest total score reveals how your engagement is poorly affected.

Conclusion

When work becomes more than you can handle, you may go from being overly-engaged to disengaged as you run out of steam. Despite your best efforts, as your energy depletes, your work may no longer feel meaningful, and you may lose your effectiveness. Once you recognize the spectrum of engagement and your place within it, you can aim for an optimal state of engagement.

Three Dimensions of Optimal Engagement

OPTIMAL ENGAGEMENT IS work-related well-being. When you are productive without overexerting your energy resources or becoming detached, you thrive. There are three dimensions associated with engagement (Figure 16.1)[1]. The first is *activation*, which ranges from exhaustion to vigor. This is similar to the engagement continuum and it also includes the physical and mental energy needed to persevere.

Research by Hakanen and colleagues[2] looked at the intersection of activation at work and the degree to which the person experienced their work to be pleasant. According to this model, when workers exhibit high activation in unpleasant tasks, they experience negative emotions that correspond with workaholism such as agitation, irritability, and tension. When, instead, they engage in unpleasant tasks with lower levels of activation, workers might feel depressed and lethargic, which correspond with burnout.

When you focus on pleasant tasks, the outcomes you experience are positive regardless of your level of activation, but there are subtle differences. High activation on pleasant tasks leads to engagement, enthusiasm, and feelings of happiness. Low activation on these same tasks leads to feelings of contentment, relaxation, and calm.

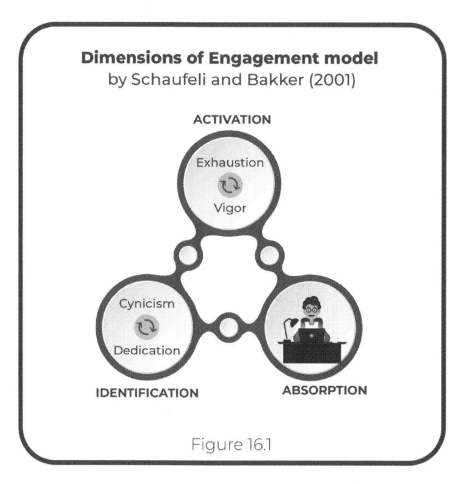

Figure 16.1

As such, we can conclude that it is best to focus on pleasant tasks. Your level of activation will then determine whether you have higher or lower intensity feelings associated with the task.

The second dimension is *identification* ranging from cynicism to dedication. This is about how inspired and challenged you feel by your work, your particular tasks, and how proud you are of your efforts.

When activation and identification are both low, you can expect to feel exhausted and cynical. The antithesis to this, of course, is vigor and dedication, two factors which exemplify optimal engagement.

The third dimension for optimal engagement, which is not found on a spectrum, is *absorption*. This is about being so intensely and happily immersed in your work that time passes quickly, and ultimately you have difficulty detaching yourself from the task. Absorption is the opposite of the detachment (experienced by the under-challenged) and is similar to what author Mihaly Csikszentmihalyi calls "flow."[3]

Think back to a task where, although it demanded your full attention, your mind was clear, and focusing on it felt effortless. Because you were so immersed in the task and were enjoying yourself, you were surprised to find how time flew by. That is flow.

In the next section, I will teach how you can establish a sense of flow and enjoyment through everyday activities, even with your chores.

SHIFTING POOR ENGAGEMENT TO OPTIMAL ENGAGEMENT

In the last chapter, you identified signs of poor engagement. Now is your opportunity to turn it around.

Overly-Engaged/Frenetic:

❑ Focus on changing your activation. Negative emotions such as anxiety and irritability are signs you have high activation in an unpleasant task. Exhaustion is a sign your activation level is low and the task is unpleasant.

❑ Focus on tasks that you find more pleasant or find ways to change your perception of the current task until it feels pleasurable.

❑ When you have high activation in pleasant tasks, you increase engagement. When you have low activation in enjoyable tasks, you increase satisfaction.

Engaged-Exhausted:

❑ Find tasks in which you can easily become absorbed. Clear your mind so you focus effortlessly on your work.

❑ Create the conditions in your environment to get into a state of flow without disruption.

175

Disengaged/Underchallenged:

❑ Focus on changing your cynicism to dedication. Look for ways to become inspired.

❑ Find tasks that are challenging, even if they seem outside the scope of your job description.

❑ Consider what new aspects you want to learn to grow in your career. When you've achieved something, be proud of the effort you put in.

Conclusion

Optimal engagement is about activation, identification, and absorption. For the best personal experience, you need to find pleasure in your work. Engagement will then follow, and regardless of how activated you feel, if you derive pleasure, inspiration, and a sense of challenge from the task, you will experience a positive outcome. Vigor and dedication can help prevent burnout. Lastly, immersion in your work can help make it feel effortless and the time will fly by.

Being On Fire

"The best moments usually occur when a person's body or mind is stretched to its limits in a voluntary effort to accomplish something difficult and worthwhile."

– Mihaly Csikszentmihalyi

As a teenager, I took note of one activity I would engage in regularly that stood out from the rest: playing the piano. What was different about this activity was that I was able to lose myself in it, even though this was not always the case.

I spent the beginning portion of every practice doing warm-up exercises to strengthen my fingers. When I was learning to play a new piece, I would have to concentrate on small segments of the music until muscle memory took over and I was able to play it correctly from memory. It was not until I had the piece memorized that I could play it without much effort. My mind would drift away, making piano playing an enjoyable activity.

My friend Pamela has a similar experience when she puts together puzzles. She can spend hours and days working on a jigsaw puzzle. When I asked her what in particular she likes about it, Pamela said she appreciates that there is one given solution to the problem and that when she has completed the puzzle she feels accomplished. Over time, she increases the challenge by assembling more difficult and larger puzzles and has created works of art by gluing the pieces together and hanging them on her wall. She has something to show for her efforts and continues to admire her accomplishments.

People typically complain about housework, yet my husband insists on folding our laundry. On any given week, I can find him listening to music while organizing newly washed clothes. He dumps heaps of our clean laundry onto the bed and begins separating them into piles. He places pants separately from shirts, socks separately from underwear, and adult clothing separately from the children's clothes. What he likes about the act of folding is the order he gets to create. It gives him a sense of control. He finds the physical action therapeutic, which puts him in a meditative state. The bigger the pile, the more easily he says he can get in the zone. Like Pamela, he knows there is a positive outcome to creating order from chaos.

When do you get the most enjoyment? Could playing piano, putting together puzzles, and folding laundry top the list? Can tasks that are not normally considered "fun" or tasks that you find difficult also be enjoyable? According to Csikszentmihalyi, enjoyment has nothing to do with our leisure activities. Instead, enjoyment is about how immersed and challenged we feel by the task on which we are working.[1]

The Goldilocks Rule

Whether you are maniacally focused on productivity or just want to get more enjoyment from your work, flow enters you into an efficient state of mind. Being in the flow requires that you set clear goals that are suitable for your skill level.

The other day, I played cage bingo with my two children. The experience for each of us was quite different. For my nine-year-old, calling out the numbers and keeping track of the numbers she called by placing chips on her bingo card, all made for an engaging and enjoyable experience. For my six-year-old, the simple act of matching the number called with the numbers on his bingo card was plenty challenging. For me, it was quite different still. I found it so elementary just waiting to hear the next number being called (so that I could place a chip on my card), that I felt bored playing this game.

The takeaway is that the same game or task can and likely will be experienced in profoundly different ways.

To get into flow, you need to differentiate between different levels of challenge (see Figure 17.1) and find the tasks that are challenging yet completable. In other words, you have to be well-matched to the task. To do this, you have to consider both task difficulty and your skill level. When task difficulty outweighs your skill level, anxiety ensues. When the opposite is true, and the task lacks challenge given your skill level, you will likely feel bored.

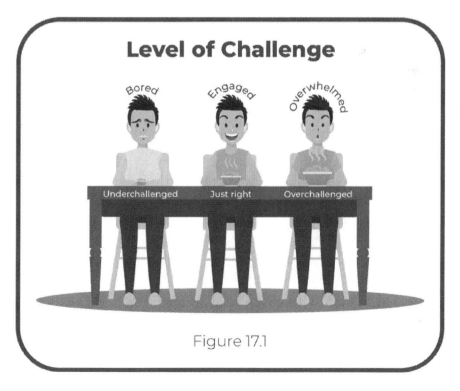

Figure 17.1

The Importance of Feedback

Once you have a job with the right level of difficulty that keeps you challenged enough so you can stay focused without anxiety or boredom, it is time to consider how you will go about completing the required tasks. Csikszentmihalyi notes the importance of setting clear goals rather than just plugging away.[2] Often, we show up at work and try to pick up where we left off, working until it is time to go home and always feeling like there is so much more to do. Instead, we need to focus ahead of time on what we are working on specifically so that we can eliminate unnecessary distractions and activities that pull us away from our goal.

However, a clear goal is insufficient on its own. The tasks need to offer immediate feedback. When I was practicing my piano pieces, I knew when my efforts amounted to the desired outcome because I could hear the finished piece. When Pamela worked on her puzzle and a piece did not fit, that was immediate feedback that she needed to find a different piece. When she completed the puzzle, it was another source of feedback that she had followed the steps correctly. And for my husband, when all the clothes are folded and sorted into piles, he has immediate feedback that his chore is complete.

Having immediate feedback lets you know whether you will get your intended results or if you need to change course. It also informs you when you are finished with that particular task. What follows a completed task is feeling a sense of accomplishment.

The Optimal Experience

Work can sometimes feel tedious. There may be demands on your time over which you have little control and which feel unenjoyable. It may seem at times that you are keeping busy but have little to show for your efforts. As Lao Tzu said, "It's better to do nothing than to be busy with nothing."

How can you attain the optimal experience of flow even under these circumstances? We explored the importance of finding tasks that are a match for your skill level, and tasks that challenge you enough to help you advance. We touched on the importance of setting clear goals that provide you with immediate feedback. Now it is a matter of creating parameters that allow you to dive in your task without distraction, providing you with the control you need over your actions and the opportunity to go deep into the task.

Having a large heap of laundry allows my husband to get into the zone, whereas a small pile would not have the same desired outcome for him. You need time to focus your mind. When you do so, your involvement in the task can seem effortless and your engagement will likely alter your sense of time, making it feel like it passed much more quickly.

Stretching yourself, no matter what you are working on, can help you increase your skills and you will feel more fulfilled as you accomplish greater and greater challenges. And as Csikszentmihalyi reminds us, "The purpose of the flow is to keep on flowing, not looking for a peak or utopia but staying in the flow."[3]

The main difference between *flow* and *absorption* is that when you are in flow, you have short term peak experiences. In contrast, absorption is a more pervasive and persistent state of mind that is independent of any specific task.

GETTING INTO A STATE OF FLOW

Set clear goals that are suitable for your skill level.

For boredom:
- ☐ Identify more challenging tasks that are completable, given your abilities and current knowledge.

For overwhelm: identify what about the task is most challenging.

❑ If it is the size of the task, break it down into manageable chunks.

❑ If it is the time frame in which you have to complete it, estimate how long you will need and ask for an extension or ask to delegate out aspects of the task.

❑ If the work itself is beyond your scope, get mentoring or ask to exchange the task to a more fitting one given your expertise.

❑ Create a plan about how you will attain feedback about the task.

❑ Eliminate distractions for a set period.

Conclusion

It is important to know that even when you do not have control over which tasks you are given, you can enjoy your experience and feel a sense of control in the task itself. Giving yourself ample time to work without distraction is a way of controlling your environment. The rest is about controlling your internal state for an optimal experience. By matching task difficulty with your skill level, creating clear goals that provide immediate feedback, and concentrating on your task, you can reach a state of effortless involvement, one that is so enjoyable, you lose track of time.

Now that you see how attainable flow experiences can be, I will teach you two ways to increase your engagement at work, through increasing job resources and personal resources.

Job Resources

EVERY JOB HAS both demands and resources, and depending on their ratio, they can be in balance or bring about burnout. Job demands are aspects of the work "that drain energy, such as work overload, conflicts with others, and future job insecurity."[1] Job resources, on the other hand, include ways that help you achieve your goals, handle the demands, and increase personal growth.

To illustrate what is meant by job resources, we will examine criteria from Schaufeli's assessment, the Energy Compass, which is based on the Job Demands-Resources (JD-R) model (Figure 18.1).[2]

According to the Energy Compass, there are four categories of job resources: social, work, organizational, and developmental resources.

Social Resources

Social resources include social support, having clarity on your role and responsibilities, and getting recognized for your efforts.

Part of the reason why social support leads to higher engagement is because it sends a message that the company for which you work cares about your well-being. One basic premise in demonstrating this principle is keeping stress levels down and encouraging work-life balance. To achieve this, your company may need to increase staff size and allow you more flexibility in terms of work arrangements.

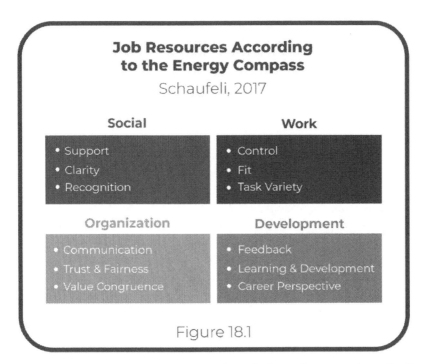

Figure 18.1

When it comes to social support such as informal mentoring, findings point to insignificant results that do little to protect you from burnout.[3] However, when provided formal mentorship, so long as there is a good fit between the mentor and the mentee, the relationship can act as a buffer for stress.[4] Mentoring reduces fatigue, increases confidence, and thereby improves self-efficacy, a primary factor for engagement.

As an example of how mentoring can make a huge difference, I refer back to Julio, the worker who is trying to keep up with the heavy demands of his job by working around the clock. Perhaps one reason Julio is overly-engaged or engaged-exhausted is because he feels alone in the pursuit of his work. Maybe he is focused on tasks that are outside his scope, which is why it takes him longer to complete them. If Julio were provided mentorship by his company, his mentor might help him to understand his strengths and weaknesses and how to align his tasks accordingly. He could learn to focus on his skillset and as a result, new opportunities might become available to him.

Julio's mentor may also have far-reaching connections to experts that can help Julio hone in on specific skills of interest. By having a mentor or role model, Julio will feel that the work he is doing is more meaningful, which will not only be beneficial for his company but will also improve his professional development.

When Julio feels overwhelmed by stress, his mentor might help him use different and more effective coping mechanisms. By learning how to adapt to challenging situations and by feeling like he has a sounding board in his mentor, Julio will feel supported which will lift up his mood, his energy, and his focus, and help him engage with his work even in the face of stress.[5]

If you are like Julio, you need to be clear about expectations related to your role. Too often, organizations go through management changes where such details fall through the cracks. When workers get promoted or start a new project, they may also experience a lack of clarity. Taking the time to define your role and communicate about it can have a significant positive impact.

Lastly, it is best if your employer has systems in place for you to attain recognition from your boss and colleagues about your work. If your place of work lacks feedback structures, consider what would help you feel more recognized for your efforts and suggest the adoption of these supportive new practices.

Work Resources

Work resources include how much control you feel you have over your work or how well you fit with your work environment. In the introduction to this book, I discussed the importance of control in minimizing burnout, especially when demands are high.

We will examine "fit" from the perspective of personality and skill level.

One common personality trait that researchers have studied with relationship to burnout is the introversion-extroversion dimension. An introvert is someone who turns inward to recharge. Samantha is an introvert and after a long day at the office spending time in meetings, interacting with coworkers, and dealing with customers, she is ready to plop down on the couch with a glass of wine, listen to some relaxing music and decompress from her day. Being around others is energy-depleting for Samantha. She seeks ways to recharge that reverse this equation.

Part of the reason Samantha becomes drained at work is because she needs to spend time alone to think. When she is in meetings having to make decisions, she has to participate in an extroverted world. Being in a leadership position requires Samantha to be introspective, but this is exhausting because she would prefer to be in the background rather than at the forefront. Because she is subject to overstimulation, she will more likely procrastinate to avoid additional stress.

According to a 2000 study, psychosocial stress negatively affects the introvert's body much more so than it does extroverts.[6] This means that being around others not only decreases introverts' energy levels, it also takes a toll on their physiology.

An extrovert is someone who requires contact with others to feel an energetic charge. Whereas Samantha wants to turn down the noise, Eric, who is an extrovert, prefers to reach out to a friend to talk things over. When Eric sits alone on the train on his way to work or sits at his computer for too long, he suffers because what he needs most is human interaction.

Extroverts like Eric are outgoing and talkative. They enjoy the fast-paced job environments, the type of work that will lead introverts to more easily burn out. During meetings, extroverts do well in brainstorming sessions because they think out loud. It is just how their brain processes information. When extroverts are in a leadership position, they relish in being center stage.

In addition to control and fit, a third work resource is your task variety. If you engage in a singular activity or in several tasks that are not varied from each other, you are likely to feel bored and become disengaged.

Organizational Resources

Your employer has additional resources by which to promote engagement, the antithesis to burnout. These resources include communication, trust and fairness, and values that are congruent with your own.

Communication and clarity are essential for the company goals to be understood and achieved by their employees. You need to clearly understand the expectations put upon you, what you need to do to achieve your goals, and how your part contributes to the overall vision of the company.

Companies create trust in their leadership by implementing strategies that tackle potential conflicts, providing a safe and nurturing environment, and bringing team members together. Christine Porath, Associate Professor at the McDonough School of Business at Georgetown University, found that when you feel respected at work, your focus and engagement increase.[7] She encourages companies to provide friendly work environments, including amongst coworkers. She says this can be achieved by "thanking people, sharing credit, listening attentively, humbly asking questions, acknowledging others, and smiling."[8]

Since unfair treatment is one of the factors associated with a job-person mismatch and, ultimately, burnout, it follows, then, that fairness on the job would lead to engagement. Fairness can include the work environment, flexibility of work schedules, diversity of staff, as well as decisions about pay and advancement.[9]

Another job-person mismatch is related to values. Ensure your values are similar to that of the organization so you can feel committed to your work.

Developmental Resources

Developmental resources include feedback, opportunities for learning and development, and career perspective.

Feedback is essential for you to be able to fine-tune your performance. While it is true that you came to the job with a particular skill set, you must fit into the company culture and need guidance about how to tweak your actions accordingly.

It is advisable for the company to provide opportunities for you to grow, not only to help you develop new skills that can enhance the company's success, but to hold onto you as an employee. Without challenge, there is a risk of under-engagement.

For you to meet goals more efficiently and effectively over time, the company can invest in programs that tackle common skill-related deficiencies (e.g., time management and Emotional Intelligence). The benefits of this are two-fold. The company will get better results and keep you there longer while you will attain personal and professional growth on the job and be less negatively affected by stress.

You must have a roadmap for your career, and this is something the company can develop as a way of motivating you to stay working there and move up the ranks. Research conducted for the book *Good to Great* demonstrates that building leadership from within the organization is better for business than searching for outsiders to lead.[10]

Each organization needs to assess its various job resources to determine which ones to improve upon to tackle engagement and burnout.

OBTAINING JOB RESOURCES

Check the boxes of any of the items that are currently true. Then note areas for improvement and consider ways to achieve them in your current position:

Social resources

❑ I have a mentor

❑ I am clear about my role expectations

❑ I get recognized from customers and colleagues

Work resources

❑ I have control over aspects of my work

❑ My work fits well with my personality and preferences

❑ I have a variety of different tasks to engage in

Organizational resources

❑ I am clear on the company's vision and goals

❑ I understand what the expectations are of me

❑ I know how my role contributes to the company's vision

❑ Conflicts are tackled as they arise

❑ The company provides a safe and nurturing environment

❑ The company creates opportunities to bring team members together

❑ I feel respected at work

❑ My work environment is friendly

❑ I have some flexibility in my work schedule

❑ There is a diversity of staff in my place of work

❑ I believe decisions about pay and advancement are fairly made

❑ My values match up to those of the organization

Developmental resources

❑ I get feedback about my performance and how to fit into the company culture

❑ My company provides me with opportunities for growth

❑ I have a roadmap for my career

Conclusion

Demands are part of any job. To avoid being drained by them, you need to have access to resources. Social support, control, communication, and feedback are examples of different types of job resources that can help you get the job done. By accessing social, work, organizational, and developmental resources, you will ensure you are clear about your role, well-matched for the job, and have a roadmap for continued growth.

Personal Resources

WHILE YOU HAVE little control over job resources, I will explain how personal resources are ways you can increase engagement by developing yourself. Mindset plays a big part in mitigating stress. Personal resources, also known as Psychological Capital, describe the within-person capacities, or the four pillars: hope, efficacy, resilience, and optimism (HERO).[1] These pillars correspond with increased life and job satisfaction, and by focusing on them, you can augment your personal resources. Having Psychological Capital can help you feel confident to take on challenges, persevere, and bounce back. Developing even a single one of these pillars will likely increase the other three.

Hope

Hope is a form of positive thinking based on realistic optimism and includes expectations that good things will happen. Researchers suggest that hope is linked to goals as well as to plans to meet those goals.[2] In other words, when you want to accomplish something, you maintain your motivation through the belief that your goal is attainable by seeking pathways to that goal.

What differentiates hope from optimism is that plain optimists only have a positive attitude, but hopefuls are action-oriented, anticipate obstacles, and plan around them.

The more informed you are about situations, the better you can assess your ability to make headway. Alternatively, you may choose to remain ignorant or dismiss relevant information. Depending on your outlook and grasp of reality, your way of thinking about a challenge will shift.[3]

You may feel hopeful but have a distorted sense of reality, in which case you are just wishful. This sort of hope is not action-oriented and is, therefore, similar to plain optimism. It is false hope.

If you have a distorted sense of reality and your outlook lacks hope, you will not only feel hopeless, but you will also feel helpless. This is often the case when you do not understand or want to know the truth about a difficult situation. You feel disempowered, dismiss the information, and even shut down internally. You remain static rather than take action to problem-solve.

You might also feel hopeless when faced with reality. This is often the case when you know what you are facing and believe that the situation is beyond your control. This, too, is a passive stance where you surrender to the situation. You become resigned, as is case when you are burned out and feel worn out.

In the book *Good to Great*, Collins shares the paradoxical story of Jim Stockdale, a United States military officer who, although he was held captive for eight years during the Vietnam War, never lost faith that he would prevail.[4] Stockdale made it out alive, but not all of his prison mates did. What is paradoxical is that, according to Stockdale, those who felt most optimistic were the ones who did not make it out alive.

The optimists in Stockdale's group kept imagining they would get out by a specific date. When time and time again that did not come to pass, they reportedly died of a broken heart.

The lesson from the Stockdale Paradox is that to be truly resilient, you have to face your challenges, not wish them away. You must remain realistic and focus on aspects of the challenge over which you have control. In Stockdale's case, he focused on lifting the morale of his fellow prisoners and by focusing on something he had control over, he persevered.

Whether you are feeling more and more hopeless or have lost your hope entirely, it is essential to find a way out. Sometimes, you may opt for a passive stance because you worry about disappointment, but this is dangerous territory that can lead to depression. Instead, remember that when situations are outside of your control, you need to focus on acceptance and on managing your emotions.

Do you tend to catastrophize when something goes wrong? Do you tell yourself that "things will never change" or that "this always happens"? Pay attention to extreme language. Usage of words like "always" and "never" makes you believe that you have less control than you do and that difficulties are permanent. Instead, think of exceptions to the rule, times when this challenge either was not present and circumstances were better, or when you were able to overcome it. This helps you remember that even when there are obstacles, they are temporary, and when barriers are permanent, the way you think about those obstacles may still shift.

HOPE DEVELOPMENT

To develop real (as opposed to false) hope, you need to have something exciting to look forward to in the near or distant future. This goal is something that you believe you can accomplish due to your agency (efficacy) and pathway (resources). I will reference the book, *Psychological Capital and Beyond*, in which the authors highlight several ways to develop hope at work.[5]

Having goals is an essential criterion to develop hope because it highlights where you are currently, where you want to go, and how to get there. When you are clear on why you have your goals, your involvement takes on more meaning and increases your motivation to work.

When developing your goals, ensure they are specific rather than generic. For example, if you want to make more money, stating your intent in this way does not specify how much more you want to make, and therefore does not let you know when you have reached that goal. If, instead, you specified you want to get a ten percent raise in salary, now you have a set number in mind that you can work toward.

Goals must also be measurable. How will you know, otherwise, when you have succeeded? By being clear on ways that you can track your progress and what the end outcome will look or feel like, you increase your chances for success.

Stretch goals are goals that are challenging, allow for growth and increased engagement, but are still achievable. In addition to the simple goals you might be working toward, you want to incorporate goals that stretch you beyond your limits. Referring back to the goal of making more money, a simple goal might be to make an extra thousand dollars while a stretch goal might be to double your income.

When you formulate your goals, state them in ways that are positive in terms of what you will do rather than about what you will refrain from doing. Instead of saying, "To save money, I will not go out to eat during the week," you will have more success if you say, "I will cook my meals during the week and invest the extra money that I save in my retirement account."

Sometimes goals feel overwhelming, especially those stretch goals. To maintain your hopeful framework, break your goals down into smaller milestones and focus on the little steps you can take to make progress toward your bigger goals.

When a car drives over a patch of grass in the exact same location day after day, it creates a visible path. The same happens in your brain when you do something over and over again, whether you do it outright or only in your mind. The latter technique is called mental rehearsal and has been shown to light up the same parts of the brain as actually doing the activity.

While it is true that your past experiences can be useful lessons of how to accomplish your future goals, it is best to think about new possibilities rather than just limiting your solutions to ones you have already tried. Try mentally rehearsing the steps you will take to achieve your goals. This improves your pathway thinking.

Even when you are excited about a goal you are working toward, there are times when you can lose momentum. To this end, it is helpful to build habits that sustain your motivation. For example, create a morning ritual that you do when you wake up. Start each day by visualizing your goal and meditating on the next steps you need to take in order to achieve it. By habituating a specific behavior that you want to engage in at a particular time, you create a sustainable practice for success.

When you work for someone else, creating goals is not enough. There are additional pieces to the puzzle for which you will need cooperation from your company. Because you do not operate in a vacuum, you need the support of upper management. They can empower you by giving you increased autonomy to make decisions and delegate out tasks so you have more time to participate in new opportunities. They can provide recognition and positive feedback that explains how your actions are directly tied to the outcome of the company. Often employees do not get to see the direct results of their hard work, so having this feedback can be very motivating to continue on your course. When you are setting goals, your manager can help align your strengths and talents with appropriate resources. Lastly, the leadership team can provide you with hands-on training focused on developing your talents into strengths.

No matter where you are currently on the burnout spectrum, you can develop hope through these methods. Aim to have a realistic grasp of the situation in front of you and maintain a hopeful outlook that leads you to anticipate obstacles, create plans around them, and attain your goals. Make sure your goals are clear, challenging, and attainable and that you enlist the support and resources needed for success. This can quickly improve your outlook and experience.

Believing that change is possible directly ties into your belief in your ability to make the change. The latter is your self-efficacy belief.

WAYS TO CULTIVATE MORE HOPE AT WORK

In your notebook, answer the following questions to set yourself up for success at work. This planning session will help you be more prepared and identify areas to target to increase engagement.

- ❏ How can I think about my situation realistically and optimistically?
- ❏ What are my specific and measurable goals that I hope to accomplish?
- ❏ What are my achievable stretch goals?
- ❏ What plans do I have about how to accomplish those goals?
- ❏ What obstacles might I encounter in pursuit of these goals?
- ❏ Do I have a contingency plan in place of how to tackle obstacles?
- ❏ What aspects of the work do I have control over?
- ❏ What aspects of the work don't I have control over? How is this affecting me? (Remember to focus on acceptance and emotional management).
- ❏ Instead of catastrophizing or giving up, what are exceptions to the rule or more helpful ways of thinking about the situation? (Remember that obstacles are usually temporary).
- ❏ Am I focusing on what I will do rather than what I will avoid?
- ❏ What are the identifiable milestones for my goals?
- ❏ Have I mentally rehearsed the steps I will take?
- ❏ Do I have habits in place to sustain my motivation?
- ❏ Do I want to ask for more autonomy to make decisions, delegate, and participate in new opportunities?
- ❏ Am I getting recognized for my actions?
- ❏ Am I getting positive feedback about my work?
- ❏ Do I understand what the expectations are of me?
- ❏ Are my strengths and talents aligned with available resources?

Efficacy

"If you really do put a small value upon yourself, rest assured that the world will not raise your price."

— Anonymous

FROM PERCEIVED FAILURE TO EXTRAORDINARY SUCCESS

At the age of 28, Joanne saw herself as a failure. After her marriage fell apart, she was an unemployed single mom, and so poor that she had to receive welfare benefits. She fell into a deep depression.

Joanne could have stayed stuck in a negative state of mind, thinking about life's disappointments, comparing herself to more successful friends, or telling herself that she will never climb out of the pit in which she found herself.

But Joanne was determined to be a writer. She would spend her days pushing her baby's stroller, and once her infant daughter fell asleep, Joanne would sit in a cafe and write. It took her two years, but she ultimately finished her first book.

With her manuscript in hand, Joanne then faced rejection after rejection. In total, twelve publishing houses turned her down. Two years after the book's completion, one publisher finally agreed to print a limited run of only one thousand copies of the book. That decision changed the course of history.

Within five months of publishing, Joanne's book earned several awards and was picked up by a major multinational publisher who paid her $105,000. Joanne now had recognition as a writer and the financial security to continue her craft.

Joanne's success started with an idea and was attained through determination, patience, and a strong belief in her abilities despite the odds. She is widely known as J. K. Rowling, the author of the Harry Potter book series, whose brand is now worth an estimated $15 billion.

THE POWER OF BELIEF

It is one thing to believe that change is possible and another to make it happen. If you want to change your financial situation, you might buy a lottery ticket and hope to win a lot of money. There is a minuscule chance that you will find success with this strategy. Alternatively, you can ask yourself, "What can I do to create financial increases in my life?" This is a more powerful approach over which you have control.

The belief in your ability to succeed, which drives you to face challenges even when you may have failed in the past, is called self-efficacy. Your efficacy belief determines the amount of effort you invest. The more you invest of yourself, the higher the chances that you will be successful.

Multiple factors affect your belief in your abilities. If, for instance, you are asked to give a presentation at work in front of your entire division, your response may vary greatly depending on your past public speaking experiences. If you have never spoken in front of a group or have tried it before but feel you had failed miserably, you will see yourself as less competent, which will negatively affect your efficacy in this task. Alternatively, if you have mastered public speaking in the past, you will likely believe that you will succeed at this task, thereby increasing your efficacy. Therefore, it is not the task itself that determines your belief, but your associations with that task based on personal experiences that influence how you perceive it.

Even if you are new to your position and have no prior experience, you can increase your efficacy by watching other people perform the task at hand. Research has shown that when we observe people who are similar to us engaging in a particular behavior, we overcome our fears more rapidly and believe that we, too, can be successful.[6]

A less powerful influence that can alter your efficacy is verbal persuasion. If you are feeling doubtful about your ability to succeed in a task, sometimes all it takes is encouragement from your boss, coworker, or friend to give you the boost you need to get started. The reason this method is not as reliable is that it can also work against you. If you are not highly efficacious and someone discourages you by pointing out the likelihood of failure or the difficulty ahead, your belief in your ability to succeed will likely diminish further.

Had J. K. Rowling not believed as staunchly as she did in her writing, she might have felt hopeless about being able to change her depressing life. Had she internalized the dozen rejections she received when trying to publish her manuscript, she might have given up entirely. Even though Rowling had never published a book before, she did not let this challenge frighten her. She was able to sustain her energy no matter what the outside world presented because of her strong self-efficacy. Like Rowling, if you believe enough in yourself, you will be able to attain your goals with determination. By pushing yourself to achieve tasks that are unfamiliar and challenging, you can reach even greater heights.

In addition to history, vicarious learning, and verbal persuasion, there is another factor that can influence your belief in your ability. When you are faced with challenges, your body might experience physical arousal. If you interpret that arousal as unfavorable, you will be filled with fear and either avoid the project or sabotage your efforts. Alternatively, when you reframe your arousal as excitement, you can use the momentum of your inner state to delve into the task.

As you can see, low efficacy beliefs are associated with threats to be avoided while high efficacy beliefs are linked to challenges to be mastered. Because of these associations, it is easy to see how your beliefs can lead to self-fulfilling prophecies. Self-discouragement leads to avoidance, which prevents you from experiencing success and reinforces the belief that you are unable to successfully tackle a particular task. Conversely, self-encouragement leads to an investment of effort and higher chances of success, which furthers your belief in your ability.

Your self-talk can either lead you to spiral out of control or into a state of flow.

HOW BELIEFS AFFECT PERFORMANCE

Sometimes in life, you will be faced with extreme challenges. These challenges may be external (e.g., high demands or a shortage of resources), or they can be internal challenges, including a negative state of mind. Regardless of the source of your main challenges, remain aware of how they affect you and take control of your reactions.

If you have ever had a "bad day," you might recall how you experienced one bad thing happen and decided that it was going to be "one of those days." You began anticipating more negative outcomes and perhaps this is what transpired. The more you focused on negative outcomes, the more you found yourself attracting adverse events to you.

On the flip side, you may have had the experience of a "winner's streak" in which you experienced something favorable that put you in a very optimistic mood. For the rest of that day, you anticipated winning and consequently found a parking spot right in front of the grocery store, found money on the street, or got promoted at your job.

Sometimes these streaks last more than a day. We see this in people who experience clinical depression. They can stay stuck in a negative thought pattern for weeks, months, or even years. They become so convinced they cannot win that their mood becomes part of their identity.

Even throughout your day, you might have ups and downs, not only in your mood or way of thinking but in your perception of your ability to be successful. Reflect on this scenario: Equipped with your existing skills, you enter into your place of work where you have specific resources. Given your view of yourself based on past experiences and that of your

200

environment, you form an initial judgment of your ability to complete the task at hand.

You notice anxiety forming. This happens whenever you feel less confident about what is asked of you, usually when the task is unfamiliar, complex, or one where you have failed in the past and have not yet learned from that failure. Whenever you experience anxiety, you cannot help but feel wary about taking action. Despite this hesitation, you plunge ahead but are ultimately unsuccessful.

Should this scenario happen without you either figuring out what you did wrong so you can self-correct or without specific, accurate, and timely feedback from your manager, you will be left guessing. Given the little information you have, you may come up with an incorrect explanation for your failure.

With each repetition of this scenario, your confidence decreases, which directly affects your performance. If you continue experiencing failure after failure, you might conclude that your lack of success is due to your inadequacies, bad luck, or to not having enough control over the situation. You might start labeling yourself as a loser and become increasingly anxious or frustrated. This will further decrease your belief in your ability to succeed.

A streak of poor performances despite your efforts can lead you to process information automatically about failures and lack of successes and, perhaps, to expect future failure. This can cause such strong anxiety that you might procrastinate to avoid the pain of another anticipated disappointment.

This scenario describes a "downward spiral." Beliefs play a significant role in your performance, and without adequate information in the form of feedback, it is tempting to fall into the trap of wrongly attributing your failures to your inadequacies. This only further complicates the situation and you perpetuate a sense of despair. Knowing this, you can be mindful of your self-talk and seek out objective data that can help you analyze the challenge, giving you a different perspective, as well as point to new directions to tackle. In Self-Efficacy Spirals, you will learn more about how to break down your experience so you can gain insight into what starts and maintains a spiral, as well as how to stop and reverse it. These insights can increase your chances of success and decrease your failure rate.

WAYS TO CULTIVATE INCREASED EFFICACY

Use the checklist below to create patience, determination, and a strong belief in your abilities despite any odds.

☐ Watch others perform the task to learn vicariously from them.

☐ Talk to your manager to attain verbal persuasion that you can successfully tackle this task.

☐ Interpret physical signs of arousal as excitement rather than fear.

☐ Ask for specific, accurate, and timely feedback.

☐ When you aren't successful, make accurate conclusions about the reasons behind it.

☐ Avoid labeling yourself as a loser.

☐ Maintain a positive mindset even in the face of failures.

☐ Stay in action mode. Confidence is not built from passivity.

Resilience

"Our greatest glory is not in never falling, but in rising every time we fall."

– Confucius

Part of what makes jumping on trampolines so much fun is the fact that when you apply pressure, the springs help you shoot up. Resilience is like a spring. It is your ability to bounce back from adversity.

We are all resilient to a point. Think about all the disappointments, failures, and defeats you have encountered in your life. If you were not resilient, you would not be able to keep going. So when you come across a disappointment or a harsh reality, how do you get past it? What is the process you go through that allows you to bounce back? As it turns out, the keys are in your biology and your mind.

THE BIOLOGY OF RESILIENCE

Charles Darwin highlighted a theory to explain why some people thrive while others wither away, which he named the "Survival of the Fittest." In this evolutionary theory, Darwin described the process of natural selection. When the going gets tough, the tough get going, leaving the not-so-tough in a cloud of smoke. He attributed the differences between these two different types of people to their genes.[7]

Research and history have demonstrated that there is truth to this theory. People with family histories of mental illness are more likely to experience mental illness themselves. People with family histories of medical illnesses like Type 1 diabetes, cancer, or heart disease, are more likely to experience such diseases in their lifetime.

That being said, with the advancement of science and medicine, we have been able to give never-before-seen advantages to the biologically predisposed. Even if your father and his father suffered from lifelong depression, when you struggle with depression, there are more medications and treatments today than ever that can help you overcome this battle. The more we know about the brain and the mind, the more we have come to realize that there is also a lot you can do to help yourself.

THE PSYCHOLOGY OF RESILIENCE

Psychologist Carole Dweck made popular the notion of a growth versus a fixed mindset.[8] According to her, when faced with an obstacle, people with a growth mindset can counterbalance negative events by focusing on their positive aspects. If your company suddenly announces major layoffs and you lose your job, if you hold a growth mindset, you will likely stay optimistic and focus on finding a new one. If, however, you have a fixed mindset, you might attribute the loss to a personal attribute and, consequently, feel depressed and unmotivated to pursue another position.

There are multiple layers to your mind. Like an onion, the core of your mind lies in the center and is hardest to change. This core determines the direction of the layers that come after it. That innermost layer is comprised of your *schema* or *core beliefs*.

The lens through which you each see the world makes up the core beliefs you hold to be true, even in the face of evidence to the contrary. These beliefs lead you to attribute causality to internal, stable, and global factors, also known as attribution errors.

Like the child who blames herself for her parent's actions, we as adults might attribute events to three factors that make us less resilient. The first is an *internal factor*. If you have a fixed mindset, you are likely to attribute the layoff to something deficient in yourself. This often stems from a core belief that you are inadequate. When you believe this, you tend to look for evidence that demonstrates you are right. Therefore, when something happens, like losing your job, you are more likely to blame yourself.

The second factor that reduces our resilience is the *stability* factor. When you believe that your flaw is permanent, you are less likely to feel optimistic about your ability to bounce back. Not only do you see yourself as inadequate, but you feel hopeless about being able to change that inadequacy.

Finally, the third factor that makes people less resilient in the face of stress is a global one. When you have shortcomings, you can see them as a weakness. If, instead, you think of yourself as the problem, you are taking a local problem (the shortcoming) and making a global issue out of it. When you do this, every failure reinforces your belief that you are a failure. This belief is not only accompanied by feelings of shame, but it makes you less likely to keep trying. This is sometimes why people become stuck.

Do you believe you are not enough? This limiting core belief is part of a fixed mindset that can lead you to misattribute your inadequacies to everything that goes wrong, especially if you believe you cannot overcome your limitations. Instead of feeling guilty when you make a mistake, you feel ashamed of yourself. In this case, work on rewiring your brain to change your limiting belief. Affirm that you are enough often and with consistency until you build the habit and neural pathways in your brain to believe it is true. Doing so will help you put events into perspective and recognize that when something falls short of expectation, it is a specific rather than a global aspect that went awry. Remember the adage, "Don't throw out the baby with the bathwater."

IN SEARCH FOR MEANING

If you were one of Jim Stockdale's prison mates in the Vietnam War, what would allow you to accept your harsh reality when what you want most is to be free? As previously mentioned, the way you think about your situation can mean the difference between life and death.

Viktor Frankl was also a prisoner; he was imprisoned in a Nazi concentration camp during World War II. Frankl survived and subsequently wrote a book entitled *Man's Search for Meaning*. In it, he explains about what allowed him to survive. For Frankl, it was about finding a purpose and imagining his desired outcome. By doing so, he could feel positively even in the midst of his dire circumstances.[9]

According to Frankl, all prisoners experienced shock which, over time, led to apathy and eventually to depersonalization. This is not all that different from the cycle of burnout. The stress experienced over the high demands of your job leads you to overexert yourself. Over time you become worn out and cynical.

What is so radical about Frankl's philosophy is that he contends that there is meaning in everything, even in suffering and death. This is in line with the HERO dimensions of Psychological Capital. Without meaning, you lose all resilience of mind.

MALADAPTIVE COPING

Coping is the way we respond when faced with a situation. There are three maladaptive ways of coping. I will teach you how to classify your behaviors based on these coping styles so you can focus on adaptive and more balanced ways of coping instead.

Imagine that you believe you are not lovable. If your preferred coping style is one of *overcompensation*, you might find yourself becoming a people pleaser. Deep down, you think that people will only love you if you make them happy, so you dance circles around others' needs while ignoring your own. From an energetic perspective, when you overly exert yourself, you are over-utilizing your energy.

The second type of maladaptive coping is *avoidance*. Rather than doing or feeling too much, you run away from the problem. If you find yourself saying, "I just don't want to think about it," you are avoiding your reality. The issue with this model is that the problem will not just go away. You might be able to distract your mind for the moment and opt for immediate gratification, but sooner or later, the problem resurfaces. Often when you face a problem that you believe is out of your control and one that may be too painful to focus on, you try to cover it up. This can lead to developing bad habits (e.g., addictions).

The third type of poor coping you want to be aware of is *surrendering*. This coping happens when you believe your flaws are global. You think there is nothing you can do, so you give up trying. You accept that you are doomed for failure. From an energetic perspective, this represents an internal collapse or deficiency. Returning to my previous example, if you believe you are not lovable, rather than try to win people over, you might isolate yourself and fall into a depression.

ADAPTIVE COPING: TIPPING THE SCALE OF RESILIENCY

To some degree, your genes and learned behaviors affect the way you respond to stress, but this does not mean there is nothing you can do to help yourself. You can focus on learning skills that help you face challenges and override your ineffective automatic responses so that you can be more in control. You can appraise situations more accurately rather than blame yourself when you are not exclusively responsible. When you become highly emotional, you can ground yourself and think through the situation once more when your mind is clear. Rather than revert to sugar, drugs, alcohol, or any other vice to change your state, focus on healthy alternatives. Ultimately, the goal is to face your challenges, not run away from them, but when emotions run high, find effective ways of managing them first; then come back to problem-solving.

Instead of looking at your deficiencies, improve on your weaknesses, or accept them and look to your strengths. Effort counts. Focus on what you want more of, not on what you don't want.

SOCIAL SUPPORT

Your relationships also help your resilience. Who are your cheer-leaders? When you are struggling, is there anyone who will give you encouragement to keep going even when it seems all the odds are stacked against you? Build your support team. This can consist of friends, family members, teachers, therapists, or coaches. You may also feel inspired by fictional characters in a movie you saw or a book you read. Your support person may be a celebrity or someone you admire. Once you have located your squad, know that you can rely on their support in tough times, even if only in your mind. If your support team consists of deceased individuals or people you cannot contact, internalize their voice, and when faced with a challenge, ask yourself what they would say. Remember, being vulnerable is not a sign of weakness. It is much more beneficial to have the courage to know your limitations and ask for support when you need it.

If you do not feel you have a support team, even having just one person on your side can make you more resilient. If you need to increase your circle, look for like-minded individuals. Consider volunteer opportunities or a place of worship to create community. Call people who do not live close to you. Technology is helping us break distance and financial barriers to communication. And, if being around others is too overwhelming, you can gain similar benefits from having a pet.

Knowing what affects you most and preparing for it in advance can help you stay grounded in the presence of stress. Reflect on past mistakes and the lessons you have gleaned. Try to visualize what happened, and rather than seeing yourself respond the same way, replace your response by applying these lessons learned. Notice how different the outcome will be with these new applications. By visualizing a positive outcome, you are prepping yourself for a more favorable one the next time around.

According to Dr. Phil Zimbardo, author of *The Time Paradox*, individuals who are positive about past events tend to be more resilient. When they bring to mind memories from the past, they think of those events in an optimistic way. Zimbardo notes a correlation between the way these individuals think about their past and their current mental state. They tend to experience less anger, anxiety, and depression.[10]

While resilience is about maintaining your integrity during a big change, adaptability allows you to adjust to the situation or at least have a different perspective.

ADAPTABILITY

When I was growing up, my family did not have the same financial means of many of my friends. While kids in my class focused on certain clothes or shoes that were fashionable, as an eight-year-old, I had to contend with more significant issues. I was a recent immigrant who arrived in the United States without any English language skills. I was put in a classroom with American students and primarily expected to fit in. But fit in, I did not.

For the majority of my first year, I could not even understand what people around me were saying. Eventually, I was able to formulate sentences in English, but I still felt so inadequate and shy that I tried to blend in rather than stand out. I desperately wanted to feel normal. Even if mimicking the behaviors of others made no sense, it was my attempt at being like everyone else.

So in the years following my arrival to the States, when my classmates were fashion-conscious and keeping up with the Joneses became their favorite pastime, I had to rationalize to myself that having knockoffs was a good alternative. I convinced myself that being different is part of what makes me unique.

I will be the first to admit that being an outsider was not easy at the time. It led to of feelings of loneliness and inadequacy, but it also provided me with something else that contributed to my character.

Because at a young age I had to jump through hoops, face difficult challenges, and think about who I was in comparison to those around me, I became resilient. I could not take many things for granted. I had to redefine normal. I had to make up my own rules. I had to rediscover myself.

After attending the same elementary school for five years, I attended a summer camp with entirely different kids. That summer I had a serious wakeup call because the kids at the camp greeted me with sincere interest. I felt weirdly popular for the first time in my life. That was when I realized there was nothing wrong with me and I could embrace my uniqueness. It was simply a change in the environment that allowed me to have this new positive perspective.

I notice my resilience in my attitude toward challenges now as an adult. My childhood experiences, which forced me to think for myself and learn to survive by adapting to my environment, helped build up my resilience muscle. My attitude of hope when faced with failure or disappointment, belief in my abilities even when faced with new tasks, coupled with an optimistic framework, allow me to persevere and, ultimately, reach great heights.

BUILDING UP YOUR RESILIENCE

Authors Nan Henderson and Mike Milstein describe two ways in which you can build resilience into the work environment.[11] The first way is to build resilient surroundings that provide opportunities for meaningful participation, that set and communicate high and realistic expectations, and that provide care and support. The second method for increasing resilience is to mitigate risk factors by increasing social connectedness, setting clear and consistent boundaries, and teaching life skills.

Given that you likely do not have control over your work environment, when you are job searching, try to find a position that promotes collaboration, provides you opportunities to progress, and supports you through feedback, rewards, or other forms of recognition. While in your position, create bonds with your coworkers, learn to work within the boundaries of the organization while setting your own boundaries, and develop your interpersonal skills to reduce conflict and increase cooperation.

"I was always looking outside myself for strength and confidence, but it comes from within. It is there all the time."

– Anna Freud

Resilient people believe that things happen for a reason. They find meaning in everything rather than fixating on a specific ideal. They view setbacks as temporary and reframe them to mean an opportunity for growth. They think of themselves as stronger with each adversity they overcome rather than as a helpless victim.

Resilience is a self-perpetuating cycle. The more resilient you are, the stronger you become after a negative experience. Your resilience becomes evident when you face challenging situations, not only in the way that you interpret and react to the challenges, but also in your ability to adapt to change.[12]

As in the tale of *The Tortoise and the Hare*, resilience is not about speed.[13] Resilience is about having the mindset and skillset to continue the journey. Arrogance is what led the hare to get off course and lose the race to a tortoise who persisted even with the knowledge of how unlikely it would be to finish ahead of a much faster animal.

When you boil it all down, the heart of the matter is trust in yourself. You have to be able to trust yourself to problem-solve and to know that even though you are imperfect, you can improve over time with the right intention and mindset. By focusing on what you can control, you can regulate your emotions and behaviors and make good choices to navigate the terrain.

According to Dr. Brené Brown, cultivating a resilient spirit is about letting go of "numbing and powerlessness."[14] This is in line with the idea of changing your coping from avoiding and surrendering to adaptive coping. Know that you are stronger than you think, and with effort and hard work, you can build your resilience. By embracing vulnerability, you will surround yourself with people who support you. By embracing yourself as a flawed and valuable human being, you will realize that no matter how bad things get out there, inside, there is strength and goodness.

> ## CHECKLIST TO INCREASE YOUR RESILIENCE MUSCLE
>
> ❑ View setbacks as temporary and reframe them to mean an opportunity for growth
>
> ❑ Think of yourself as stronger with each adversity
>
> ❑ Find meaning in everything
>
> ❑ Face your challenges
>
> ❑ Override automatic negative thinking
>
> ❑ Improve areas of weakness or accept them and focus instead on your strengths
>
> ❑ Internalize the voice of your social support team and ask yourself what those people would do in your situations
>
> ❑ Increase your social circle
>
> ❑ Connect regularly with supportive people who live at a distance
>
> ❑ Know what affects you most and prepare for it in advance
>
> ❑ Review past mistakes and visualize yourself implementing new lessons
>
> ❑ Focus on adapting yourself to new situations
>
> ❑ Set clear and consistent boundaries

Optimism

If you have ever done the trust exercise in which you are blindfolded and allow yourself to fall with the hope that you are caught in time, you know that it can feel scary. In essence, you have to learn to fall, to take risks that may not pan out, and remain optimistic that you will be able to handle whatever comes your way. Optimism protects you from burnout. But as I mentioned, you still need to know how to face reality.

Optimism is not about being an idealist. Optimism is about taking a long hard look at the reality and not making more of it than is there. It is about trusting your ability to adapt while focusing your mind on the more positive aspects of a difficult situation.

There are many benefits to being optimistic. For one, optimists vary their coping methods.[15] You can view circumstances from various angles, and the perspective on which you focus will largely determine how you are affected. Optimists tend to focus on the more positive aspects and avoid dwelling on problems.[16] Being optimistic allows you to find meaning in negative events, stretch yourself, and therefore adjust better to adversity.[17] This does not mean that you are oblivious or in denial. Researchers have found that optimists are more knowledgeable about their health conditions and mindful of how to live a healthy lifestyle.[18] Pessimists tend to experience more depression, anxiety, and stress than their counterparts.[19] It seems that the optimist's fluidity of thought and adaptability in behavior lead to greater satisfaction, self-esteem, and psychological well-being.[20] The good news is that optimism, like many of the skills mentioned in this book, can be developed.

FOCUSING THE MIND

I remember after buying my first car, a Honda, that I suddenly saw Hondas everywhere. After I had my baby, I saw people wherever I went with strollers. When I walked hand in hand with my husband, I saw lots of other couples together. These are not coincidences.

The reason we see evidence that confirms our experience is because we are focused on it, whereas beforehand, we were not. This is called the confirmation bias. We cannot possibly take in all the information around us. Doing so would overwhelm us. The brain is designed to help us survive, so it limits the input it takes in. What if there was a way to program your mind so that it could pick up on the information you deem necessary rather than the status quo? Well, there is.

Mindfulness is a practice that helps you develop the skill to focus the mind. Like any new skill, it needs to be learned and practiced over time. One way to build this muscle is to practice mindfulness meditation. You close your eyes, and rather than let your mind wander, you set an intention to focus on one thought. You can focus on a word or phrase, on your breath, or on being neutral. The latter entails noticing whenever your mind drifts in any direction and then bringing it back to neutral. Each time you notice and return to center, you are practicing mindfulness. The more you practice refocusing your mind when circumstances are calm, the more this skill will serve you when chaos ensues.

Your brain is a magnet for negativity. When you are negative, you have no trouble noticing when something goes wrong: you get stuck in traffic, you spill your coffee, you cannot fall asleep even though you are exhausted and know you have a big presentation the next morning. However, we tend to overlook when positive things happen. Pay attention when you wake up if the sun is shining, when your burger comes out just the way you like it, or when a stranger smiles at you when you pass him on the street. Even when we get feedback, we seem to focus on the one area for improvement rather than on the nine things we did right.

Mindfulness helps focus the mind on the present. Through this process, you can let go of the past and your expectations for what will be. Mindfulness looks reality right in the face and rolls with the punches rather than allowing you to overthink the situation. You can choose to focus on the things that go well around you so you, too, can reap the benefits of optimism.

GRATITUDE

Being grateful is about feeling thankful for a benefit you have derived from someone or something. It is another example of how you can train your mind to focus on the positive aspect of a situation. Even on your toughest days, you can choose to find something to feel grateful about and focus on that. You can be thankful when the sun shines because of its light and warmth. You can feel gratitude for the rain because it hydrates the plants and allows them to grow. You can find value in any situation.

When you are trying to develop an optimistic mindset, gratitude can serve as your gateway. It, too, has associated benefits including more positive emotions, greater personal well-being, and improved relationships.[21]

Gratitude, as a subject of scientific research, has only been studied since the year 2000. In this short amount of time, the evidence has strongly shown that adopting an attitude of gratitude and engaging in exercises that strengthen this sense of appreciation provide ample mental, physical, and social benefits.

Mental Benefits

In 2016, researchers conducted a study to examine the benefits of gratitude journaling on university students seeking mental health counseling.[22] They divided participants into three groups, each of which received psychotherapy services. What differentiated these groups is the following: The first group had to write one gratitude letter weekly for three weeks to someone they know. The second group had to write about their thoughts and feelings related to negative past experiences. The third group did not receive instructions to write at all.

Researchers discovered that the group who wrote the gratitude letters showed significant improvements in mental health issues related to depression and anxiety, showing positive signs even four and 12 weeks after the experiment had ended.

What contributed to this significance of gratitude writing was the main finding that people who engaged in journaling about gratitude used fewer negative emotion-based words. The shift in focus from toxic emotions like resentment, frustration, and regret occurred because these participants had focused on how other people contributed to their flourishing. This shift took them away from what otherwise might have been ruminative thinking.

Gratitude not only improves your mindset, but it can also boost your self-esteem. This result was found in athletes who practiced gratitude.

Researchers believe that focusing on gratitude steers our mind away from social comparisons where we feel inferior to others who are more accomplished and allows us to appreciate them instead.[23]

Physical Benefits

A study conducted in 2012 found that more grateful participants experienced fewer physical aches and pains.[24] These individuals were more likely to engage in healthy activities such as a routine exercise regimen and regular medical check-ups. We might conclude that those who practice gratitude feel more positively about themselves and, thus, take better care of their bodies. Their self-care practices, therefore, result in better health.

Another study looked at the relationship between gratitude and sleep. The findings pointed to higher sleep quality and duration for grateful individuals. Due to the more positive mindset of practicing gratitude, they tended to engage in more positive thoughts before bed, which helped them attain improved sleep.[25]

Social Benefits

The authors of one of the measures of gratitude used in scientific studies, the Gratitude Resentment and Appreciation Test (GRAT), conceptualized gratitude with the following: (1) Abundance mentality: Rather than feel deprived when someone else has attained their goal, grateful individuals would see others' success as a joyous occasion and not harbor feelings of envy; (2) Acknowledge others: When they encounter success, grateful individuals take the time to acknowledge others' contributions to their accomplishments; (3) Appreciate small details: While it is easy for us to feel a surge of happiness when we accomplish great feats, grateful people can appreciate the simple aspects of day to day life.[26]

We can hypothesize that if you can rejoice in your success, acknowledge others for their contributions, and appreciate the small things in life, you will benefit from stronger social bonds. This is exactly what the research supports.

Researchers at the University of Kentucky found that gratitude correlated with decreased aggression toward others.[27] That is, individuals who scored higher on gratitude scales were found to have more empathy toward others and were less likely to seek revenge when something went wrong. This finding demonstrates both a social and emotional benefit in that grateful individuals are more likely to reduce interpersonal conflict and experience more social closeness with others because they are harboring less anger.

When we express our gratitude to others, it deepens our interpersonal connections.[28] And as the saying goes, "You reap what you sow." When you build close relationships, you have greater access to social support when you need it. Because having these relationships decreases your stress and improves your mood, you are also less likely to need support.

Ways to Be Grateful

Now that you are aware of the prosperity associated with a gratitude practice, I will explain how you, too, can reap these benefits.

According to researcher Sara Algoe of the University of North Carolina, gratitude is a three-step process:

- Step one is to *find* people with whom you are suitable.

- Step two is to *remind* yourself of existing social relationships.

- Step three is maintaining and investing in these relationships by forming bonds (*bind*) with these influential individuals.

As such, the Find-Remind-Bind theory demonstrates that gratitude is a practice that brings you into connection with other people and is an ongoing exercise that nourishes these interpersonal bonds.[29]

Consider your social circle. Are the people in it suitable to your personality and values? If you are content with the bonds you have, focus on engaging with these individuals on a deeper level. If, however, you want to increase your circle, if you want to find new and more fitting friendships, and if you want to feel less lonely and more connected with others, focus on finding the bonds first. Expand your community by joining local chapters of like-minded individuals. Consider neighborhood groups, religious organizations like churches and temples, meditation circles, or volunteer opportunities. You can join both leisure and business networking events in your area through sites such as Meetup and Eventbrite. Create a goal and take the necessary steps to see it to fruition.

You can also focus on your inner world to reap the benefits, a practice over which you have more control and can engage in more frequently. Here are three ways to practice gratitude:

1. Write a thank-you note to someone you appreciate. Simply the act of writing such a letter invokes positive emotions in you, whether or not you send it. That said, should you have the opportunity to share your letter with the person to whom you are grateful, this would be an exercise that can allow you to deepen your connection with that individual.

2. Start a gratitude journal. Everyday write in a notebook about what you are thankful for by focusing your mind on the positive. This will sharpen your attention to the small details of life, as mentioned above. This practice can be as short as a couple of minutes of writing, so do not let a lack of time be an excuse. Simply get in the habit of writing down three events from that day that you are grateful for and, as a bonus, consider writing your contribution to these events. If you are thankful for someone in your life, reflect on a recent occurrence that sparked this sense of appreciation in you.

3. Practice a loving-kindness meditation (Metta) daily. This type of meditation involves mentally sending goodwill, kindness, and warmth toward others by silently repeating a series of mantras, and fosters compassion for yourself and others. It replaces self-criticism with more positivity and helps you feel more socially connected. Furthermore, it can reduce pain associated with migraines and slow down aging.[30]

Research has shown that people who take the time to reflect on and write about the good things in their life were not only more optimistic, they felt happier and more satisfied.[31] To download your free gratitude template and to access a guided loving-kindness meditation, go to www.BurnoutToResilience.com.

No matter where you currently find yourself, you can always cultivate a more optimistic mindset. Practice mindfulness and gratitude daily, have trust in yourself and in what is possible, and pay closer attention to the positives that show up every day in your life. What you focus on will expand.

CULTIVATE OPTIMISM

Learn to trust your ability to adapt and focus your mind on the positive aspects of a difficult situation by following these guidelines:

- ❑ Vary your coping methods
- ❑ Be flexible in your thinking
- ❑ Use fewer negative emotion-based words
- ❑ Practice self-care
- ❑ Adopt an abundance mentality
- ❑ Celebrate other people's wins
- ❑ Acknowledge others' contribution to your success
- ❑ Appreciate small details

Practice the Find-Remind-Bind approach:

- ❑ Find people with whom you are suitable
- ❑ Be reminded of existing social relationships in your life
- ❑ Maintain and invest in (bind to) those relationships

Daily practices:

- ❑ Write down three things for which you are grateful and how you contributed to them
- ❑ Practice loving-kindness to maintain a positive mindset about others, even when they act out

Conclusion

The four pillars of Psychological Capital are your personal resources that can help you manage the demands of your work. These pillars are hope, efficacy, resilience, and optimism. Together, they encourage you to employ positive yet realistic thinking that is action-oriented, a belief in your ability to succeed, adaptability, and a sense of purpose regardless of the challenges you face or the number of failures you have endured.

By embracing these pillars, you can set yourself up for success. As a result of more exceptional achievement, you will increase your efficacy. The more you believe in yourself, the more you will embrace challenges and adaptively cope with them. The more trials you endure, the more resilient you will become. Your growth mindset will lead to continued opportunities and greater satisfaction. Furthermore, you will establish stronger social connections, improve your well-being, and appreciate life more.

Time Management

TO BE EFFICIENT so you can be effective, you have to consider how well you manage your time. One of the reasons people become so stressed out at work is that they feel there is more to do than there is time. This is not, by any stretch, a new dilemma. It's about how one deals with it that can make all the difference.

I've divided time management up into three different segments: Prioritization, Procrastination, and Perfect Attention.

Prioritization

All too often, we are swamped by the amount of demands placed on us. We might even take on other people's work because they ask. Realistically, we don't have an infinite amount of time or energy, so the amount of work we take on has to match our existing resources.

While the requirements of your job may not be entirely in your hands, you have to ask yourself, "What is something that only I can do?" They hired you for a reason. You have unique talents, experiences, and abilities that differentiate you from your coworkers. What makes you unique at work? Hone in on those areas to provide maximum value.

What happens to the rest of the requests, responsibilities, and demands placed on you? This is where prioritization comes in.

If you've ever used an organization system, you know that it's essential to divide items into piles. For instance, if you were organizing shoes, you might separate athletic shoes from dress shoes or closed-toed shoes from sandals. By placing items in categories, it is easier to identify them when you need them the most.

When it comes to your work, you need to segment as well. Imagine that you have a four-part filter through which all requests get funneled (see Figure 20.1). As a task comes in, rather than have it pile up in a single stack, ask yourself, "Which part of the filter does it belong in?"

The first filter is for urgent and important tasks. These are tasks that you need to get done immediately. Your attention should go to these so you can clear them out. The goal here would be that once those tasks are out of the way, you keep this filter empty as much as possible. One of the reasons we burn out is because we are in a state of constant crisis. We focus on putting out fire after fire, which readily depletes our internal fire.

Tasks that you deem essential, that only you can do, that allow you to contribute the greatest value, should go in the second filter. This is where, ideally, you spend the majority, if not all, of your time. By eliminating urgent tasks and focusing on non-urgent yet important tasks, you find higher purpose in your work without overexerting your energy. This is what allows you to enter a state of flow and feel engaged in the work.

The remaining two filters are ones to avoid as much as possible. They include tasks that are urgent but unimportant. These are tasks that someone with a lower skillset can do, such as an administrative staff person or a team member whom you are managing. They also include tasks that are non-urgent and unimportant. The reason you don't want to spend your time on these types of functions is that spending time on anything unimportant takes time away from more critical tasks.

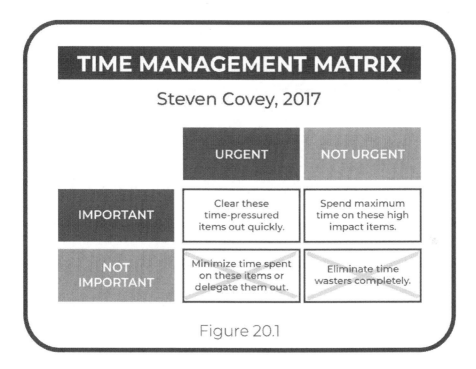

TIME MANAGEMENT MATRIX

Steven Covey, 2017

	URGENT	NOT URGENT
IMPORTANT	Clear these time-pressured items out quickly.	Spend maximum time on these high impact items.
NOT IMPORTANT	Minimize time spent on these items or delegate them out.	Eliminate time wasters completely.

Figure 20.1

Remember, the name of the game to being in your power, to feeling fulfilled, and to avoiding burnout is to make conscious decisions about what you are doing with your time.

Steven Covey, the author of the bestselling book, *The 7 Habits of Highly Effective People*, came up with this four-quadrant system for prioritization.[1] In his experience, people who focus on urgent matters become burned out, which leads them to spend time on tasks that are neither urgent nor important. As an alternative, he suggests, plan how you will spend your time on those tasks that are important and non-urgent.

WHAT YOU CAN LEARN FROM A SPIDER ABOUT TIME MANAGEMENT

We all have busy and demanding lives. Our biggest challenge can be how to increase productivity while keeping our sanity. One of the best time management lessons comes from a children's book.

In *The Very Busy Spider*, Eric Carle writes about a spider incredibly focused on a singular task: spinning a web. Throughout the book, different animals approach the spider and ask whether she would like to have a fun experience with them. In each instance, the spider doesn't answer them and continues on. At the end of that busy day of spinning, the web is complete, and the spider is so tired, she has fallen asleep.[2]

From this book, there are three lessons you can learn to help your productivity. First, you need to focus on one task at a time and make it your most important job. Work that only you can do demands your primary attention. Everything else can be delegated or outsourced.

Second, expect constant distractions and plan accordingly. When you have a plan of how to handle distractions, you will be more productive. Turn off devices. Let coworkers or family members and friends know that you are unavailable for calls, conversations, and hanging out until you finish your project.

Third, get good at estimating task length. If you're focused on a single project, ask yourself how long it will realistically take. You may just focus on a task that is a portion of the larger project. How much time do you have, and what can you achieve during that time? If need be, work with a timer to keep you focused and ensure you're taking breaks throughout the day. One such timer is the Pomodoro Technique, which reminds you to take five-minute breaks after each 25-minute period of work.[3]

If you follow these three tips, you too, will be able to pull off your to-do list productively and efficiently.

Too many tabs open on a computer or too many applications open on the phone make the system run slow. Imagine what it does to you when you have too many things you are trying to accomplish at once. To avoid overwhelm, dilute your to-do list. Prioritize the jobs that will have the most impact if you get them done first: the most critical tasks. Eliminate distractions. Instead of multi-tasking, have a singular focus on one task at a time, and you'll become masterfully effective. Like an elevator or an airplane, you have to know how much weight you can carry and, after that, start turning things down.

PRIORITIZATION GUIDELINES

- ❑ Focus primarily on important and non-urgent tasks
- ❑ Focus on tasks that only you can do
- ❑ Delegate or outsource out all remaining tasks
- ❑ Expect distractions and plan accordingly
- ❑ Work with a timer to stay mindful and take breaks
- ❑ Focus on one thing at a time

Procrastination

Sometimes, even when we need to work on a critical task, we may purposely put it off and engage in more mindless pursuits that are easier and less demanding. Why do we do this?

There are generally two answers to this question. The first is that we are burned out. When we feel energy-depleted, we try to conserve energy by engaging in tasks that require less of us. When we come home tired after a day at the office, we may opt for an evening in front of the television rather than going to work out. The same can happen in the office, and we see this with superficial office banter, time spent on social media, or mindless eating.

The second reason we procrastinate is that we are unable to cope with difficult emotions, especially a fear of failure. If you are a perfectionist or at least care very much about what others think of you, you'll be less likely to take risks. Unless you are fully confident that you can garner success, you will find excuses to avoid a task you've previously failed at or never attempted before. If you're frustrated with an assignment, you may prefer to engage in something less frustrating. And, if you're bored with your work, you might seek stimulation elsewhere.

Fear of failure is related to a fear of rejection. It comes from a belief that you are inadequate, and each failure, therefore, feels like a reminder about your lack of worth. No one likes to feel this way, so we try to prevent this situation from happening by shifting our focus to other safer ways to spend our time.

Procrastination may seem like a great strategy, and it's a survival mechanism. If there was a snake in your path, you would be smart to avoid it, but that's also how your brain functions in the office. The trouble is that avoidance keeps you stuck in a perpetual pattern. You never overcome your fears this way. To truly get over such obstacles, you have to face your fears. That means taking risks and trying something even if success is not guaranteed because the path to growth is through learning from mistakes.

Even with the best of intentions, you can find yourself getting stuck, dragging your feet, and inadvertently watching deadlines creep closer and closer. Matt was someone who tended to over-promise and under-deliver. He came to see me because he wanted to increase his follow-through so he could move forward in his career.

When Matt showed up for our first meeting, his energy struck me immediately. He was charismatic, enthusiastic, and ambitious. Matt had big dreams of what he wanted to accomplish and how he wanted to contribute but had fallen short in his delivery, which led to him being fired from jobs time after time. While losing a job due to lack of productivity would be hard on anyone, it was especially hard on Matt because he felt stuck and unfulfilled. There was so much desire within him to be productive, yet he didn't know how to overcome this invisible hurdle.

The first thing that made a difference in Matt's productivity was the use of the app Rescuetime[4]. If you're not familiar with this tool, it tracks your online activity, thereby giving you insight and motivation to improve your performance. It does this by helping you decrease the time you spend on distractions and focus more on the essential aspects of your job. It provides one of the key ingredients in helping you be successful: accountability. And it does this by increasing your self-awareness.

This brings us to the second element for follow-through success: self-efficacy. When you believe you are capable, you are more likely to feel confident, take more risks, and achieve more. Your accomplishments will then continually increase your self-efficacy.

Conversely, when you lack a belief in your ability, you experience more self-doubt, use avoidance as a coping strategy to protect yourself from your projected failure, and accomplish less. You then fall into the trap of believing that the reason you didn't achieve what you wanted to is that you weren't capable when in truth, it was because you didn't try.

Matt understood that by changing his belief in his ability, he would be able to get things done. His lack of follow-through stemmed, for the most part, from his insecurities and self-doubt. Once he was able to see his self-limiting belief as an obstacle and reshaped it to align with his desired outcome, he became unstoppable.

The third and last nugget that drastically improved Matt's success was when he started valuing his effort, not just the outcome. Many of us get overwhelmed by all that we have to do. It can seem like our lists are never-ending. The more expectations others have of us, the less we will get done and, of course, if we value outcomes and are not getting as much done as we would like, we can start to feel bad about ourselves.

When you invest time and energy into a task, sometimes it will flop, and other times, it will work out well. When things don't go your way, you are put to the test. How do you talk to yourself? By appreciating your investment of resources, you are focusing on the journey, not just the destination.

This is also essential when a task is large and may require you to work on it for several days. Just because the entire mission isn't complete after one day doesn't mean you didn't get anything done. Be realistic in your expectations, given the resources at your disposal. According to Matt, "Doing small tasks builds up the ability to do bigger tasks."

If you find yourself struggling with procrastination, work to increase your personal competency skills, especially emotional management. One way of managing difficult emotions related to a task is by forgiving yourself. Researchers found that when students forgave themselves after procrastinating on studying for a first exam, their procrastination subsequently went down when they needed to prepare for a second exam. The reason these students cited for this shift was that self-forgiveness helped them to regulate their negative emotions.[5]

In every situation, we can find positive and negative aspects. Tasks on the job are no exception. The next time you are feeling negative about a task, ask yourself what aspect of that task is positive. If you lack confidence in performing well on this task, consider what tasks you've worked on in the past that were similar and on which you did well.

You might also think about what positive outcomes may come from completing this task. By shifting your perspective from a negative to a more positive aspect, you can bypass procrastination and get to work.

You might be wondering, "If I've struggled with procrastination my entire life, will it take me another lifetime to make these changes?" The answer is no. Most people believe that it takes about 21 days to create new habits. From my experience, this is usually true for small habits, especially habits of mind (i.e., self-efficacy beliefs), but for behavioral change, it can take longer.

The good news is that while it may take longer than three weeks, it doesn't have to take a lifetime. Matt, who had struggled with a lack of follow-through for over three decades, was able to become productive in just under three months.

So if lack of follow-through is something you struggle with, take note, as you too can have a renewed experience, feel better about yourself, and do so in about ninety days.

It is too easy to run away from aspects of work deemed unpleasant, too challenging, or boring. But if you want to be productive and give yourself a real chance to succeed, you need to implement emotional management skills and embrace the task.

For you to easily remember the three aspects you need to incorporate into your routine, think of the ABC method:

1. Accountability: Find an accountability system that keeps track of your activity and sustains your motivation to improve with continual feedback.

2. Belief: Work on your belief in yourself to make your self-fulfilling prophecy a positive rather than a negative one.

3. Credit: Give yourself credit for your efforts, not just your outcomes. With this compassionate approach, you will build up your confidence, get more done in less time, and feel good about your accomplishments.

INCREASE YOUR FOLLOW-THROUGH

- ❑ Track your activity or have someone keep you accountable.
- ❑ Work to increase self-efficacy and eliminate insecurities and self-doubt.
- ❑ Value your effort, not just the outcome.
- ❑ Have realistic expectations. Just because the task isn't completely done doesn't mean you didn't get anything done.
- ❑ Forgive yourself for any mistakes you make.
- ❑ Identify the positive aspects of tasks, even when they feel negative.
- ❑ If you lack confidence on a task, consider past tasks that were similar on which you did well.
- ❑ Identify the positives that would come from completing this task.
- ❑ List out the risks you might be taking if you overcome the problem and the prices you'll continue to pay if you don't achieve your goal.

Perfect Attention

One of the most significant ways we lose time is when we are distracted. It's easier than ever in today's workplace to become distracted from essential tasks we intend to accomplish.

We have computers, phones, meetings, papers, people, and objects all around us. Emails stream in constantly. Texts and calls come in sporadically. Just when you get into the groove of your work, something takes your attention offline.

To be excellent at work, you have to have perfect attention. If you were the CEO of the company, you could make executive decisions about what you say "yes" and "no" to. Similarly, you are the CEO of yourself. You need to make executive decisions about how to manage your time, and one of the best ways to increase engagement is by decreasing distractions.

Decide to turn off notifications and check your emails, voicemails, and texts during breaks rather than throughout the day. Decide to avoid small talk with those around you so you can focus on your work. Decide to spend your time on your most important tasks while your energy is high so you don't have to cram and stress over your to-do list once you're exhausted and coming up on a deadline.

Making these types of decisions comes from a place of empowerment. And while eliminating distractions can help anyone be more efficient at work, it is especially crucial for those who have less flexibility of time.

An interesting phenomenon happens when you have less time but more purpose. Rather than feeling overwhelmed and stressed, you become focused, and get more done in the same timeframe.

This phenomenon is common amongst working moms. Their efficiency tends to increase because they know they have a hard cutoff time when they have to leave the office. They zero in on what they need to do.

They speak up more against taking on big-sized projects or helping coworkers with their work. These moms work as if at the end of every workday there is a deadline. There is no procrastination. There is no distraction. They have to be somewhere else at a specific time to pick up their child or to release their child's caretaker. Having a double load is now part of their reality, and they kick into gear daily so they can carry their responsibilities in both their professional and personal worlds.

Consider what purpose awaits you outside of the office. If you don't have a family, perhaps schedule an exercise class, a dinner date with a friend, or engage in a leisure activity after work. Knowing that you have a definite cut off time will help you focus on your work and enjoy the benefits of increased work-life balance.

Perfect attention results from eliminating distractions and creating boundaries around your time. Be intentional about how you engage in the workplace because this will determine not only how quickly you finish your work, but how much time you have to engage in more personal matters.

PERFECT YOUR ATTENTION

1. Decrease distractions

   ❑ Turn off notifications

   ❑ Check messages during breaks

   ❑ Avoid small talk

2. Find purpose outside the office and create a hard cut off time to leave work.

3. Protect your time and say no to taking on projects you can't realistically afford to take.

Conclusion

There are three essential ingredients to proper time management. The first is prioritizing your most important tasks and focusing on them one at a time. The second is creating engagement in your work.

Rather than avoid what scares you, face it head-on. Take risks and follow through on tasks. Be kind to yourself and work to build up your confidence.

Lastly, create a supportive environment for your mind to get tasks done by eliminating distractions, protecting your time, and finding purpose outside the office, so you have a hard stop to your work. These techniques will keep you focused and make you more efficient.

E#3: Empowering Exercise

To build on what you have done so far and take the next appropriate action, follow these three steps to increase your engagement:

Step 1: Now that you are clear on your needs and feel empowered, it's time to find ways to increase engagement. In the table below, list your needs in the first column. Next, fill in the job resources (e.g., mentoring, increased control, task variety, communication, fairness, value congruence, feedback, opportunities for learning and development, career perspective) you may require to align your needs with your tasks in the second column. Finish the table by including ways that you believe will increase optimal engagement and ways to improve productivity in their respective columns. This will serve to organize your thoughts and clarify your message before you ask for what you want.

Needs	Job Resources	Ways to increase engagement	Ways to improve productivity

Step 2: Communicate to your manager about the information in the table above clearly and concisely utilizing the skills you learned about assertiveness in Relationship Management.

Step 3: Elicit feedback for your contributions. Feedback allows for both professional growth as well as a feeling like the work you are doing is meaningful, and this knowledge increases engagement.

E#4: EFFICACY

When you lack belief in your ability, you are more at risk for burning out, especially if your efficacy has been stripped away by work conditions. On the flip side, high self-efficacy correlates with engagement and follow-through.

According to Albert Bandura, a psychologist who wrote a lot about the construct of self-efficacy, your beliefs shape your expectations and affect your goal setting, the amount of effort you put into a goal, and how persistently you cope with obstacles when pursuing that goal.[1]

In this section, we will delve into the nature of three types of efficacy spirals. The first type is a downward spiral, as described in Personal Resources. The opposite spiral, of course, is an upward spiral in which you experience success in place of failure. The final spiral is what is known as a self-correcting spiral. By examining how these spirals work and how your thinking and performance are intertwined, you can learn how to take back your power.

Self-Efficacy Spirals

IN OUR BUSY and demanding world, we seek to find ways to become more efficient (get more done in less time) and effective (focus on activities that yield the greatest outcomes). While we know about efficiency and effectiveness, a third concept to consider is efficacy. It can make or break your success because it affects the tool you need most to help you move ahead: your mind.

While we've already mentioned that downward spirals are associated with failure and upward spirals are associated with success, we need to understand the basic tenets of these mechanisms. In the psychological literature, these phenomena are called self-efficacy spirals. The reason there is a relationship between your efficacy beliefs and either success or failure is because of the interdependent nature between self-efficacy and performance (see Figure 21.1). The more you believe in your ability, the more likely you will pursue a task. The more successful you are in accomplishing a task, the more you will believe in your ability to do so in the future.

When self-efficacy beliefs match effort levels, you might end up in an upward spiral where you experience successes after successes, which heightens your self-efficacy. Alternatively, you might experience a downward spiral as a result of a series of failures that decimates your efficacy beliefs. You can also experience a self-correcting spiral where your performance and self-efficacy initially parallel each other, but then either one changes direction. How does this happen?

Efficacy-Performance Relationship

(Figure 21.1)

Imagine you attempt to write code, but you don't get the results you want. You try again and again, and disappointment follows each attempt. If you expected your knowledge and efforts to translate into success but they don't, this may affect your belief in your ability to get the project off the ground. You may then procrastinate working on it or just give up. But perhaps after a cooling-off period, you review your steps, realize your mistake, and take a more successful approach. Your self-efficacy just increased, so you sit back down and try again, hence increasing your performance (see Figure 21.2).

Self-Correcting Spirals
Masuch, 1985; Weick, 1979

take a risk

failed attempts

lowered self-efficacy

procrastinate/give up

increased self-efficacy

successful attempts

realize mistake

review steps

Figure 21.2

The same situation can happen in reverse order (see Figure 21.3). You attempt your code and find that it works time and time again. This builds up your self-efficacy but can lead you to become overly-confident and complacent. You decide that since you're so good at what you do, you don't have to try so hard. You are less motivated to figure out what is leading to your continued success. The result over the next succession of tasks reflects this change in effort and ends up leading to some failure as you experience a ceiling effect. Once again, your self-efficacy decreases, as does your performance.

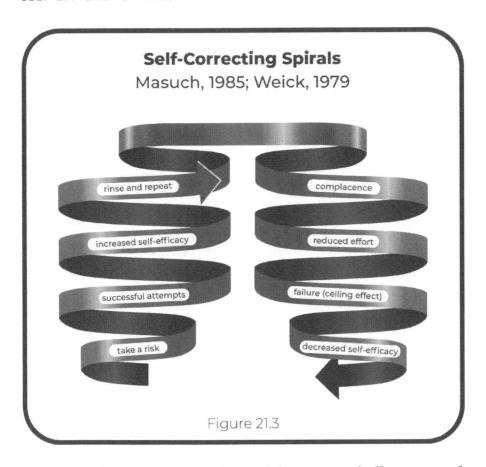

Self-Correcting Spirals
Masuch, 1985; Weick, 1979

rinse and repeat

complacence

increased self-efficacy

reduced effort

successful attempts

failure (ceiling effect)

take a risk

decreased self-efficacy

Figure 21.3

The name of the game is to understand the cause-and-effect nature of task performance. When you recognize why your efforts lead to either success or failure, by keeping your finger on the pulse, you are increasing your chances of future successes. Otherwise, you are at risk of becoming overconfident. Therefore, one purpose of the self-correcting spiral is to promote learning, which keeps you moving in a vertical direction to achieve greater success over time.[1] Also, if after a chain of successes you become complacent, it helps turn that complacency into a downward spiral that keeps you in check.

Conclusion

Your beliefs can affect your success and failure rates. When you experience an outcome associated with your effort, you can enter into an upward spiral if you are successful or a downward spiral if you've failed. Additionally, when you become complacent after attaining success or when you learn from your mistakes after a failure, you might find yourself in a self-correcting spiral that takes you in the opposite direction. Be mindful of your beliefs and keep your attention in your work sharp.

How Spirals Get Started

TO STOP OR REVERSE a downward spiral, we first have to understand what constitutes a spiral, what gets spirals started, and what keeps them going.

Researchers cite three general rules to self-efficacy spirals:

1. You must have attempted a minimum of three tasks.

2. Spirals are not dependent on success or failure, but rather on your efficacy beliefs.

3. Optimal learning and performance result when you learn from your mistakes.[1]

The researchers also discuss three factors that lead to spirals: feedback, task uncertainty and complexity, and task experience. Some of these we discussed in Personal Resources, but to better understand their contribution to a spiral, let's break them down.

Feedback

Feedback is a necessary element for continued success or for preventing a downward spiral. It requires us to look at what we have done, whether or not it is working, and why. In a traditional work context, feedback refers to information received from a manager or supervisor whose job it is to examine your work and share their expertise and knowledge about your performance. To be effective, feedback needs to be accurate, timely, and specifically address the cause-and-effect nature of your performance. Feedback that misses the mark on any of these three factors is ineffective and can start a spiral.

If you work on tasks, especially challenging ones where you have less knowledge or experience, it is crucial for you to receive effective feedback. Assert your needs and focus on clear communication between you and your boss in asking for effective feedback.

Task Uncertainty and Complexity

When you are trying out a task that is completely new to you, your boss, or your organization, even the person to whom you report will not know the causal relationship of your performance to the outcome.

This ignorance means you are unlikely to receive the feedback you need. Similarly, when tasks are complex, there could be more than one cause-and-effect factor, which translates into less clarity and possible confusion. The less you understand about what leads to success, the higher your chances of failure, and the greater the likelihood of a spiral starting.

If you are working on an original project, keep expectations realistic. Expect to ride the wave of self-efficacy spirals and know that they are there to promote your long-term learning. Rather than becoming attached to your immediate results, stay focused on the big picture and prepare yourself for turbulence. If, however, your task is only new to you but has been done before, consider consulting with someone who has experience with it, even if it means finding a mentor outside your place of work.

Task Experience

When experience is low, if you are successful in your attempt, you may make mistaken attributions for your success. This misinformation can lead you to take a wrong turn, or as mentioned earlier, to become overconfident, which can start a spiral. During this early period, the focus is on increased learning. You are learning about causality, what leads to success, what leads to failure, and why these relationships exist. Note that your self-efficacy is strongly affected by initial successes or failures. So the more you fail initially, for example, the weaker your self-efficacy beliefs and the lower you can expect your performance to be. With this in mind, avoid the trap of being too quickly influenced by early results. Focus instead on garnering more experience on a given task to prevent a negative spiral from starting.

Conclusion

After attempting a task at least three times, you might enter a downward spiral if you meet any of these conditions: You receive inaccurate, untimely, or unspecific feedback; you are uncertain about the cause-and-effect nature of a task or the task is complex; or you lack experience related to the task at hand. The opposite of these conditions can contribute to an upward spiral. Given this knowledge, you can be mindful of how to handle yourself at work and what to ask for to perform to the best of your abilities. By focusing on learning rather than on the outcome, you can increase your overall performance over time.

What Keeps
Spirals Going

FOUR FACTORS KEEP spirals going: attributions, automatic information processing, emotional arousal, and expectations and labels.[1]

Attributions

In a similar fashion to the importance of feedback being accurate, attributions (or the causality you assign to your task performance) are essential. Proper attributions can help correct behaviors when you are making errors. Otherwise, you are at considerable risk for making an attribution error.

Different attribution errors affect performance. If you attribute failures or successes to yourself, that is an internal attribution. While, at times, you might contribute to a task's failure, its failure alone does not necessarily mean you are at fault. Often there are external factors that contribute to a lack of success. Alternatively, you might attribute all the blame to external factors and not take any responsibility for mistakes you have made. This is an attempt to conserve your self-efficacy because when faced with failure, if you attribute the failure to yourself, you will become anxious.

A second attribution error relates to stability. Because spirals occur after three or more consecutively stable wins or losses, you are likely to attribute the win or loss to a stable factor such as your ability. When you've failed multiple times in a row, and you associate that failure with your inability, this can lead to discouragement. Conversely, when you attribute the win or loss to instability with statements like, "I didn't invest adequate effort in this," the loss is less likely to decrease your self-efficacy because you acknowledge you are capable of more and can invest more effort in next time. Adopt Thomas Edison's approach. After experiencing more failures than most people you'll likely ever meet, Edison said (as quoted by Elkhorne), "I have not failed. I've just found 10,000 ways that won't work."[2]

Lastly, when you attribute success or failure to a controllability factor, you are making a third type of attribution error. When you see yourself having control over the process, you are more likely to self-correct. Even when you have no control over some aspects of the process, search for aspects over which you have control and focus on those. For instance, when you experience anxiety, if you focus on regulating your breathing, you can change your state even in the face of an event that feels scary and is out of your control. It is when you believe you have no control that you end up feeling frustrated, anxious, or helpless and continue a downward spiral.

When you attribute your success or failure to factors that are internal, stable, and over which you lack control, you are more certain to remain in a spiral. Consider what external, unstable, and controllable factors may have contributed to your performance and take these into account to get the full story of what's transpired.

Automatic Information Processing

When your performance outcomes repeat, you are more likely to process information related to those outcomes automatically, which is quicker and more superficial. For instance, organizations that year after year yield success often stop analyzing and learning. Instead, they focus on maintaining stability, and over time, they start to decline due to the belief that they are invulnerable.

Blockbuster was a sensational business, renting the latest releases of movies to customers from their many brick-and-mortar locations. But as consumer needs began to change and folks wanted digital access to media or to have films shipped to them for greater convenience, Blockbuster fell behind the curve. Only six years after Netflix launched its services did Blockbuster begin to test-drive the new model, but by then, they had missed the boat.

The recommendation, then, is that you continue pursuing in-depth forms of feedback even when you are successful. Consumer needs change over time, so what leads to success today may not be enough moving forward. Don't let what happened to Blockbuster happen to you. Stay vigilant and curious.

Emotional Arousal

We are emotional beings, and our experience at work is no exception. Our performance affects how we feel, and how we feel can impact our performance. We've already mentioned the importance of attributions (the meanings we give to our results). The next step in the chain is to consider how the way that we think affects how we feel at work. When we make attributions that are internal, stable, and uncontrollable, we are more likely to feel a sense of despair, which will negatively affect our efficacy, and thus our performance.

If you're feeling discouraged or frustrated, your negative mood may lead you to interpret information through a more negative lens associated with low self-efficacy. If you experience intense fear, your arousal may interfere with your performance. When emotional arousal is high, spirals become more prominent.

Be mindful of your mood. Staying in the task with negativity does you no good. When you feel negative, either take time out to recalibrate or reframe your anxiety as "excitement" to shift the energy and your potential downward spiral.

Expectations and Labels

"We don't rise to the level of our expectations, we fall to the level of our training."

– Archilochos

The Pygmalion effect is when your expectations become your reality.[3] High expectations lead to high performance, while low expectations lead to poor performance. This is not only true of your expectations of yourself, but other people's expectations of your performance have just as much of an impact. When you have a stable outcome over time, you may start adopting a label for yourself as a "winner" or a "loser."

Remember that what's important is your mindset and your effort. Whether you succeed or fail at a task is irrelevant. So long as you are learning, you are winning. Avoid labeling yourself. The outcome does not represent who you are; only your efforts do.

Conclusion

Once a self-efficacy spiral starts, it's essential to understand what keeps it going so that you can intervene correctly. To this end, you must correctly attribute what leads to success and failure. Avoid processing information on autopilot and, instead, stay analytically-minded. Be conscious of how your mood affects your performance. Pay attention to performance-related expectations. And, avoid labeling yourself regardless of the outcome.

How to Stop a Downward Spiral

WHILE IT MAY be easier to avoid a spiral than to stop or change it, there are two ways to end a spiral. These techniques are both cognitive and behavioral.

Redefining Success and Failure

One of the main reasons we experience lowered self-efficacy is because we are attached to the idea of success as a reflection of our ability. Researchers suggest that "...success is not based on the outcome, but it comes from the information gained via the task attempt."[1] By redefining your success as what you've learned as opposed to what you've accomplished, you can stop a downward spiral and help preserve your self-efficacy. When you define success in this way, you only fail if you do not learn. Even when you obtain the results you set out for, if you do not learn something new and simply rely on what made you successful in the past, you are not truly successful by this new definition.

Given what we know about what leads to downward spirals and what keeps them going, by seeing your successes as opportunities to experiment, attain high-quality feedback, reduce arousal, and decrease automatic processing of information, you are helping to stop the spiral.

Small Wins and Losses

As mentioned earlier, one of the factors that can prompt a spiral to start is task complexity. When the tasks you are going after are too big, focus your efforts on small chunks. Break tasks down to simplify your mission. Doing so will reduce the risk of massive failures, provide more opportunities for learning, and help you build up your self-efficacy when you have small wins. Besides, this will have a positive effect on your emotional arousal.

While James Watson and Francis Crick worked on discovering the structure of the DNA, which eventually led them to win the Nobel prize, they observed that their attitude largely contributed to their progress. This was later called the "Progress Principle."[2] That is, when you make progress in meaningful work (small wins), you feel most accomplished.

Your progress might feel insignificant in comparison to the total project and what needs to get done. To change your view of it, keep a list of your small wins so you can reflect back on them and see how the list has grown over time. By keeping each small victory in perspective with your total wins, you will see how you are making meaningful progress.

Conclusion

As we've already seen, spirals can be corrected. So, if you find yourself in a downward spiral, don't panic. You can stop it by redefining the meaning of success and failure. You can also chunk tasks down to manageable bits, so your failures don't seem overwhelming. By accumulating small wins over time, you will feel like your work is shaping up to have meaning.

Reversing the Spiral

J. K. ROWLING STARTED in a downward spiral, even labeling herself as a "failure." Somehow, her self-efficacy in her writing never wavered, and she was able to not only reverse the spiral but has been in an upward spiral ever since.

If you find yourself in a downward spiral, here are nine strategies you could use to reverse it:

1. Break down your complex task into smaller chunks to reduce your losses, increase your chances at small wins, and correspondingly, increase your self-efficacy.

2. Request specific, accurate, and timely feedback from your manager. If you know when you'll finish your task, schedule a meeting with your manager for the deadline or just beforehand to review your performance and elicit detailed information about the causal relationship between your performance and the end result.

3. To avoid attribution errors, focus on which internal and external factors contributed to the outcome. Try to stay objective and share your conclusions with your manager during your meeting to see if, based on their experience, they agree. This can help you consider additional factors when taking your next stab at a task.

4. If your manager is unsupportive or even critical, let them know you need them to change their tune. Assert your right to get your needs met so you can perform at your best.

5. Avoid labeling yourself. You can accomplish this most easily when you focus on learning rather than achieving and when you redefine your successes and failures.

6. Manage your emotions. High emotional arousal (excitement or intense anxiety) can negatively affect performance.[1] Because there is a relationship between your thoughts and feelings, when you avoid self-labeling or associating your worth with your production, you are more likely to stay even-keeled.

7. Pursue an in-depth investigation of what led to your outcome rather than resort to automatic information processing.

8. Manage your expectations. To avoid a self-fulfilling prophecy, even in the face of failure, you need to stay positive. Focus on what you want rather than what you don't want. Incorporate positive self-talk and a growth mindset when approaching challenges and when facing defeat.

9. Use adaptive coping. We all face obstacles and stressful situations, but what matters most is how we cope. Adaptive coping includes focusing on solutions when faced with a problem or as a first step, managing emotions so that eventually you can problem-solve. Maladaptive coping is, simply, avoidance. When you avoid, you may sidestep stress at the moment, but long-term, you have not solved the problem. It will continue to come back and haunt you.

Conclusion

It is inevitable that you will face challenges, obstacles, and failures on the job, but rather than have unrealistic expectations for perfection, recognize that you make mistakes and that they serve as lessons on how to improve your future performance and help you avoid a downward spiral.

The key to success is to focus on learning. When you experience both failures and successes, the goal is to understand which specific performance behaviors lead to which specific outcomes.

While the journey can be emotionally grueling at times, seek out encouragement and effective feedback. Remember that no one result defines you. For every failure you experience, there were likely several past successes as well. Be prepared to self-correct (even when you experience success) to avoid a ceiling effect. When the latter is upon you, you'll be able to prevent a negative spiral from starting.

If downward spirals bottom out and you cannot perform any worse, focus on self-correcting your performance or on increasing self-efficacy beliefs. Otherwise, no increases will take place, and you will be more likely to experience apathy or quit.

E#4: Empowering Exercise

Individuals who have successful experiences and who attribute that success to themselves have higher self-efficacy. Below, list your past successes that resulted from your efforts:

_____

_____

_____

_____

_____

_____

_____

_____

_____

_____

_____

_____

PART III:
NON-DOING

E#5: ENERGY

Every day as you come across life's challenges, tasks, and responsibilities, you exert energy. When you expend energy without replenishing it, you rapidly burn out.

In Time Management, we talked about prioritizing time on the job. That said, prioritization is something you must do in every aspect of your life. You must prioritize your personal life to have some balance.

One of the biggest hurdles busy professionals point to when it comes to taking care of themselves is a lack of time. In this section, we will tackle time management as it relates to self-care.

Time, however, is rarely the real reason why we don't prioritize ourselves. Usually, there are mindset obstacles. Mindset Obstacles for Self-Care will show you how to overcome these before you dive into your self-care practices.

Once your thinking aligns with your desire to recharge, you will need to find what self-care practices work best for you. In Managing Your Energy, we will delve into ways to protect and recover your energy. If you notice that even when you are taking measures to fill up your energy tank, you are just not feeling energized enough, not to worry. To address this, I will discuss recovery strategies customized to your personality.

Part of managing your energy is about creating healthy boundaries. I will share with you the price that having poor boundaries can have on you. I will debunk the myths you might hold that prevent you from having better boundaries, and provide you with some suggestions on changes you can make.

Finally, Transitioning Out of Work Mode focuses on transitioning out of work in ways that help you create balance, increase your happiness, and energize you to continue doing your job effectively.

Mindset Obstacles to Self-Care

INCORPORATING SELF-CARE INTO your life may not be a new concept, but if you still haven't weaved it into your routine, there is a reason.

For some people, focusing on themselves can be challenging, especially if they believe their needs are not very important. If this is the case for you, you might notice that anytime you do something for yourself, you feel guilty. This is a mindset issue and resolving it will lead you from martyrdom to self-gratification.

Perhaps you pride yourself on the fact that you always serve other people. This satisfaction might be how you derive purpose in life. While there is nothing wrong with providing for others, it becomes problematic when your approach is one-sided. Does doing something for yourself really eat at you? If so, pay attention, because we're going to unlock two notable concepts to help change the way you feel.

I work with many people who experience burnout, and one of the reasons they get to that place is because they don't take care of themselves adequately enough. Shawna was a client who found herself in that role. Doing anything for herself seemed really decadent, even when it came to cleaning out her closet. Most people probably wouldn't see cleaning out their closets as a selfish act, but because it was something that was for her and her alone, it felt indulgent.

Shawna strove to be like Mother Teresa, always taking care of others. What she didn't realize was that this put her into the role of a martyr. No matter how much she did, she felt like it was never enough, leading her to apologize for herself, even when she did not need to.

Even if we were to come up with a plan for how to incorporate every great self-care strategy into your life, and even if you bought into the idea that self-care is important, the bottom line is, so long as you believe you don't deserve it, you're not going to successfully implement it. That is why the first step to changing this predicament entails changing your beliefs. What do you currently tell yourself? What is it that you believe? What do you see as your role and what does that mean about taking care of yourself?

When you identify the belief blocking you from engaging in self-care, reflect on the fact that it is not serving you. To change your behavior, you'll need to change your belief. One of the best and most effective ways of doing that is through affirmations or mantras. With your limiting belief in mind, consider what you would rather believe. Take note of someone you know that engages in regular self-care and what they must believe about themselves to act accordingly.

Shawna recalled listening to other moms who play tennis mention that they went out and bought a camera. This camera, however, was not for their kids. It was not for taking pictures of the family. It was to record their own tennis game. This blew Shawna's mind because, as she said, "That's never something I would do." But when she was able to think about the kinds of beliefs these moms must have, she said, "Well, they must really believe that they're important." As a result, she was able to come up with her own mantra which was, "I am worth it." Shawna's mantra can be a mantra for anyone who struggles with prioritizing themselves.

You may not believe that mantra at first. The second step is to practice saying it until you get to a place where it feels true. Ask yourself, "How much do I currently believe my mantra on a scale of 0 to 100 (if 0 is 'not at all' and 100 is 'absolutely true')?" Shawna started out believing the mantra only 30 percent, but as she practiced it day in and day out, it significantly changed.

As soon as your beliefs start to change, you can align your behaviors with those beliefs. The third step is to come up with ideas of self-care activities with which you would like to fill your life. What sort of activities bring you joy? Several of my clients mentioned how much they enjoy dancing, so they joined a dance class. If you feel really good when you exercise, consider what kind of exercise you like most, as well as the setting and frequency. Do you prefer jogging outdoors or working out in the gym? What will you do to relax your mind? Meditations are great self-care rituals to incorporate, and research has demonstrated the myriads of benefits associated with this practice.[1] What about ways to relax your body? Perhaps you would like to schedule a massage once a month or make it a habit to take a hot bath once a week. Figure out what it is that you want to do for yourself that can help you manage your stress. This, in turn, will help you be a better provider for other people and keep you from burning out.

OVERCOME YOUR MINDSET OBSTACLES TO SELF-CARE

- ❑ Pride yourself on taking care of yourself so you will be able to continue to serve others.

- ❑ Identify the underlying reason why you might believe you don't deserve self-care.

- ❑ On a 100-point scale (0 = not at all; 100 = completely true), how much do you believe this limiting belief now?

- ❑ Practice the mantra, "I am worth it" multiple times a day and check weekly to see if the believability factor (0-100) has gone up.

- ❑ Once you believe you are worth self-care, align your new belief with self-care strategies.

Conclusion

Self-care is essential to prevent burnout, but a negative mindset can get in the way. To overcome this obstacle, start by identifying your limiting beliefs. Create mantras that help you prioritize yourself and practice them until they feel true. Once you believe you are worth it, you will easily align your behaviors with your new-found belief and start taking proper care of yourself.

Managing Your Energy

ONCE YOU'RE ONBOARD that self-care is non-negotiable, the next obstacle on your path might be finding the time to incorporate it into your day. It's easy to get caught in a catch-22. Sometimes, when you have a lot on your plate, you might think you don't have time for yourself. You work hard to push through and get things done. But when you don't take care of yourself in the process, you might notice that you enjoy the work you are doing less, that you have less energy, and that you are less efficient in getting it done. The formula for success is scheduling your self-care first and then everything else around it.

Create a red velvet rope policy around your time. Make yourself a VIP. This alters your perception of what is truly important and makes sure that you attend to your needs before anything else.

If you are an entrepreneur, this is even easier to execute because you have more control over your schedule. Find time during the day to work out because your chances of doing so diminish after a long day. If you are employee, negotiate to have an extended lunch break to work out or work from home at least one day a week. Perhaps use a coworker as an accountability partner and go together to the gym after work. If there is a class you like, by committing to a specific day and time, you are increasing your chances of continued attendance.

It's also crucial not to over-schedule yourself. I recently heard someone say that before she schedules a meet-up with a friend, she asks herself if she anticipates being less busy next month. If the answer is no, she refrains from committing to a future engagement. You know what happens when an event you committed to shows up on your calendar. You feel obligated to go. But if you have too much on your plate, you will either go grudgingly or cancel at the last minute. Be realistic about what you can do in the time you have.

One of the biggest mistakes we make is underestimating how long tasks take. I used to do this all the time. I would have three plates spinning at once with the overly-optimistic notion that I could prevent them from crashing down. When you take on too much, you stress yourself out and are always on the run. By taking on less, I learned that I could be on time or even early to a meeting with someone, and that extra time gives me breathing room, especially when the unexpected happens. If there is traffic, if parking spots are limited, or if I want some time to gather my thoughts before I meet with a friend or colleague, having a few extra moments can make a big difference in the quality with which I present myself. Now, I ask myself how long it might take to get somewhere or complete a task, and then double my estimation to leave additional time for the unexpected.

By prioritizing your self-care, you make sure that there will be time for it. By keeping your future commitments realistic, you ensure that you won't run yourself ragged. And by giving yourself ample time around your engagements, you minimize any potential stress.

Recovering Your Energy

Scheduling your self-care practices is a great way to have time carved out to re-energize. Now you just have to incorporate the types of activities that will help you recover your energy, especially if you're starting from a place of burnout.

Every car has a gauge that tells you when it is low on gas. To continue driving it, you have to fill up the tank. Similarly, you need to gauge your energy level and find ways to refuel, especially when you feel yourself dragging.

Some people seek out instant energy boosts in the form of sugar, nicotine, or caffeine or ways to quickly relax and take the edge off (alcohol, marijuana, or a benzodiazepine). These methods can calm your nerves and allow your brain to slow down and take a break from worrying thoughts.

The problem with these approaches is that they are short-lived. Not only will they not sustain energy levels for long, but you will experience a crash, requiring you to refuel over and over again. They don't dramatically change your pattern either. They are quick fixes that provide momentary relief. But when you wake up tomorrow, you'll be back in the same boat.

Managing emotions is much easier to do when you routinely take time to de-stress. Creating healthy habits is a great way to recover from daily events and prevent overwhelm. Structure these ten self-care practices into your week and then find a way to fit the rest of your world around them.

1. *Sleep*. Research has shown the implications of sleep on our mood,[1] not to mention our motivation and ability to focus. Most people require eight hours on average. Know your body's requirement and get to bed on time rather than waste time in the evening mindlessly checking your social media accounts, email, or flipping through television stations. If need be, set an alarm to remind you to start winding down your activities and get into bed.

2. *Physical activity.* We spend many of our waking hours sitting in transit, at our jobs, or in front of a screen at home. Our bodies start to hurt when we don't move enough. Build-in time each day to stretch and take walks. Several times per week, find time to exercise your muscles, build up strength, and increase flexibility. Moving your body helps exert energy and provides you a physical outlet to release anxiety and stress. It gets your mind out of the future and into the present.

3. *Nutrition.* When we are busy, we sometimes forget to eat. This can mean that we fall out of a scheduled routine and eat later than usual or skip meals altogether and then notice a shortage of energy or a headache coming on. Alternatively, we might over-eat, eat out of convenience, or eat to avoid feeling an unpleasant emotion. Food is your fuel. You need to make good choices, plan your meals, and use food appropriately as nourishment.

4. *Water.* In addition to minding your food intake, your body needs plenty of water throughout the day. Many of the popular beverages people consume, particularly coffee, can be dehydrating. Even when you aren't physically active or exposed to the blistering sun, you lose liquids sitting in air-conditioned or heated environments. You also wake up dehydrated each morning after hours of sleep. That's why it's important to drink water first thing each day as well as throughout the day and minimize substitutions that contain caffeine, sugar, or other additives. Water helps with digestion and can keep you working at a more optimal level.

5. *Meditation.* Meditation has several uses. You can get into a routine of daily meditation, which acts as a vitamin to protect your immune system. You can also take a timeout when you're stressed and meditate for a few minutes as a way to get back to center. In this way, meditation serves as a tool for emotional regulation as it slows down your reaction time. It's an opportunity to sit quietly, train the mind to let go of worries, stressors, and plans, and to be present.

Meditation allows you to tune into your body and notice any tension or pain. It's a time to focus on breathing, relaxing, and just being without doing.

6. *Media.* Adverse events indeed happen around us and the world all the time. That's what the media focuses on the most. When you take in lots of media, you become influenced by what you hear and see. The cumulative effects of negativity can compound the stress you already feel from your daily responsibilities and life events, so limit your media intake and spend that time on more helpful self-care and relaxation habits.

7. *Nature.* Spending time in nature is a very grounding experience, which can help regulate anxiety and fear states. It's an opportunity to breathe fresh air, to reconnect to your roots, and to relax without the bustling noises of modern society. Exposure to sun rays is vital to absorbing Vitamin D, without which you are more vulnerable to experiencing depression in the wintertime; yet another reason to be in the outdoors.[2]

8. *Journaling.* A habit that produces a more positive mindset is gratitude journaling. Just ask yourself what in your life you are grateful for. The answers can be as simple as the sun shining, your partner's smile that greeted you upon awakening, or even a good night's sleep. Furthermore, researchers have found that 20 minutes of daily writing about positive emotions helps reduce stress and anxiety.[3] By spending time writing about what's going well, you can improve your mood and build resilience to face future challenges. Once you've written about your day, you can go back and review your writing through a different lens. This helps you identify thinking traps, like mind-reading, overgeneralization, or prediction, and reframe your thoughts so they are more helpful to you.

9. *Breathing.* Breathing is something you must do to survive, but your breathing tends to be very shallow. Spend time mindfully taking

deep breaths throughout the day during times of meditation as well as times of stress. The breath allows energy to move throughout the body and regulate your emotions. The more mindful you are about what's happening in your body, the more aware you will be when you hold your breath. Breath awareness serves as a reminder to release any tension.

10. *Social support.* Because you are wired for connection, when you share your feelings tactfully with others, you are happier. Social support is considered not only a positive experience but a coping strategy that helps you get through difficult times. The alternative is isolation, which leads to depression and loneliness. Ask for help when you need it. Getting support from others will create bonds and help you achieve more of your goals.

To top it off, practice the Taking Down the Flame technique by Donna Eden to ground your energy. You can find a demonstration of this exercise on www.BurnoutToResilience.com.

CUSTOMIZED RECOVERY STRATEGIES

Stress is about perception. What might be stressful to one person may not affect someone else at all, or can lead to entirely different results in a third individual. When considering recovery strategies, you need to consider individual differences and, in particular, how you obtain your energy.

In Job Resources, we talked about how introverts turn inward to recharge because being around other people takes a toll on their energy levels. Extroverts, on the other hand, need to be around others to restore their energy. Given the distinct differences between introverts and extroverts, it's essential to implement recovery strategies that fit your personality.

Typically, introverts benefit from being alone or with one other person. Coping strategies that can help introverts recover their energy include taking a long walk, journaling, or exercising. These are all forms of grounding that anchor frantic energy and release stress from the mind and body.

Introverts need to find ways to reduce stimulation. This can include being proactive in how they conduct themselves both at and outside of work. While at work, they may opt for periods during the day where they limit verbal contact and, instead, use email and text as their primary means of communication. When possible, it can mean working from home to get away from the crowds. During a commute home on public transit, they might consider using noise-canceling headphones. If they live with other people, they may want to retreat to their bedroom and close the door. These ways of isolating are healthy means of recharging for introverts and must be looked at as something an introverted person needs to do to prevent burnout. That said, if you are introverted and you want to seek balance in life, recognize that you may also benefit from social support, albeit in smaller doses.

Extroverts may not be as affected by stress as introverts in the first place simply because of their personality. This is mainly due to their perception of stress and ability to function in a stimulating environment without feeling overstimulated. Also, their coping incorporates more social contact, which can positively influence emotional well-being. That said, engaging in extroverted behavior can be "mentally depleting" after three consecutive hours, according to a 2016 study.[4]

Extroverts may have so much enthusiasm for getting the job done, that they become workaholics and burn out in the process. Extroverts may also be less likely to pick up on signs of stress or find it hard to talk to others about their emotional state, which can bring on burnout. In consideration of all these factors, extroverts can benefit from incorporating self-care, grounding, and relaxation for a more balanced approach, and pay more attention to their emotions.

Protecting Your Energy

Once you've taken the time to incorporate self-care and focus on ways to energize your body, you'll need to be mindful of how to protect that energy. To do so successfully requires being conscious of how you feel energetically. Based on your energy level, rather than on how many more items are on your to-do list, decide when you need to stop for the day. Those items will still be there tomorrow. And when others are asking you to do something, if you're tapped out, learn to say "not today." Maybe you'll take it on tomorrow or next week. Perhaps you will say no altogether.

Another way of protecting your energy is by having self-compassion. When you set unrealistic expectations of yourself, you are setting yourself up for failure because you end up feeling bad for not living up to those expectations, especially if you value being productive.

It's tempting to see faults in yourself and attribute the failure to your inadequacy. In truth, being critical of yourself is not helpful. It doesn't get you to be more energized or get more done. Realize that the problem is not about what you lack, but is more about being out of touch with what is realistic. Re-adjust your expectations. Accept yourself for where you're at, and if you have big goals, give yourself time to reach them. Slowly.

CHECKLIST TO MANAGE YOUR ENERGY

- ❑ Schedule time in your calendar for self-care
- ❑ Create a red velvet rope policy around your time
- ❑ Avoid overscheduling yourself

CHECKLIST TO RECOVER YOUR ENERGY (continued)

- ❑ Gauge your energy level
- ❑ Avoid quick fixes
- ❑ Create healthy habits (sleep, physical activity, nutrition, water intake, media consumption, nature, journaling, breathing, social support)

If you are an introvert:

- ❑ Find activities where you are either alone or with one other person (e.g., taking a long walk, journaling, exercising)
- ❑ Limit verbal contact and use email and text to communicate
- ❑ Work from home
- ❑ Use noise-canceling headphones on your commute and in a noisy office setting
- ❑ Get social support in small doses

If you are an extrovert:

- ❑ Surround yourself with others
- ❑ Focus on grounding and relaxation
- ❑ Notice what triggers you
- ❑ Pay attention to your emotions

CHECKLIST TO PROTECT YOUR ENERGY

- ❑ Be aware of your energy levels
- ❑ Take breaks as needed rather than focus on your to-do list
- ❑ Practice self-compassion
- ❑ Readjust expectations to be realistic

Conclusion

Managing your energy begins with self-awareness. By being aware of your energy levels and needs, you can implement self-care strategies that help you recover when energy is low. You can protect that energy from becoming depleted. You can maintain your energy by implementing daily practices and by remaining mindful of whether you should commit to future obligations ahead of time.

Boundaries

"People are able to achieve extraordinary accomplishments if they are able to meet their own self-fulfilling needs while pursuing the goals of the organization."

– Abraham Maslow

WHILE IT IS HELPFUL to recover your energy when you are exhausted, you must take a preventative approach to protect it. One way to do this is to set appropriate boundaries.

We've established the importance of self-care and uncovered some of the main obstacles to implementing it, including poor time management, believing you don't deserve it, and overwhelming job demands. Yet, despite everything going on in the external world, self-care and overall boundary-setting are not optional. Setting boundaries is the primary way to maintain your energy and well-being so you can be effective in your work and relationships.

In this section, we uncover the underlying beliefs, fears, and behaviors that lead to poor boundaries as well as ten strategies for creating healthy ones.

Lack of Boundaries

If you are a giver, it won't surprise anyone much to find you in a helping profession. Perhaps you're a doctor, nurse, teacher, or therapist. You work hard all day providing care for others. You might stay at work until late, skip meals due to the high demands of your job, and even take your work home.

Maybe your career choice is less indicative of your giving tendency, but the way you relate to others in your life is more telling. Are you someone who gives away your time? When someone asks you for help, do you feel compelled to say "yes"?

The issues surrounding a lack of boundaries include control, fear, and low self-awareness. When you are so agreeable that you take on tasks you don't really want, you are letting other people control you. The reason behind this might be that you fear they will become angry or disappointed otherwise, and you care very much about how others feel. You may even consider it your job to make others happy. You might have a fear of rejection and try to please others so they stay close to you.

If you believe that your needs matter less than those of others, you will feel guilty about tending to your own needs and therefore prioritize other people's needs ahead of your own. The clearer you are about what you value and what you need, the more authentic you can be in your relationships and decision-making, and the more balanced you will be in your life.

When it comes to setting healthy boundaries, knowing yourself is key. Once you have clarity about what's important to you and what makes you tick, you can better manage your life and relate to others in a meaningful way.

THE PRICE OF OVER-GIVING

It's 4:35 pm on a Friday. Joanie approaches your desk. She asks if you could take a look at her report. She is nervous about meeting with the boss and hopes you can go over it with her and give her some pointers. You still have a lot of work to do yourself and you're looking forward to the weekend. You've worked hard all week. But how can you say no?

You give and you give. In fact, you give with all your heart because it feels good. So, where does it go sour, and why?

Giving is a beautiful act. It allows you to contribute to the world and create connections with other people. Over-giving, on the other hand, is a sign of poor boundaries. We've already mentioned why you might be an over-giver, but what are the implications of this behavior?

Over time, you start to notice a shift. You feel depleted. You might even feel resentful when the sentiment isn't reciprocated. But there is a glue that keeps you coming back to give more.

The increase in positive feelings and the decrease in guilt are the two mechanisms that contribute to the perpetual cycle of over-giving. But this cycle is not sustainable (see Figure 28.1).

The story that exemplifies this scenario is *The Giving Tree* by Shel Silverstein. In it, a little boy and a tree have a beautiful relationship. The tree loves the boy and wants to fill his every desire. As the boy matures and grows into a man, his needs change and increase. The tree doesn't want to let the boy down. He continues to provide him with everything that he has. And as the book states, "The tree is happy." But eventually, the tree is left as a stump, having given away all its fruit, branches, and trunk to the boy. The story ends when the tree has nothing left to give and is "happy...but not really."[1]

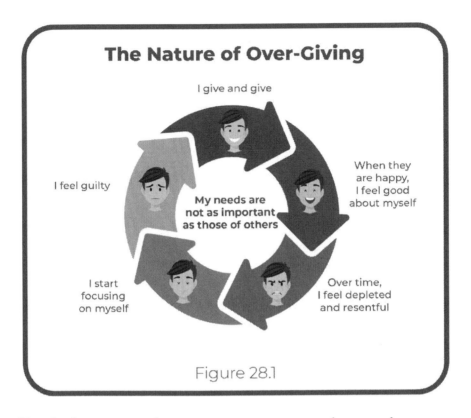

The Nature of Over-Giving

I give and give

When they are happy, I feel good about myself

My needs are not as important as those of others

I feel guilty

I start focusing on myself

Over time, I feel depleted and resentful

Figure 28.1

You don't want to end up a tree stump no matter how much you care about others. At that point, there won't be anything left to give, even if you want to. To break the cycle, you need to change your underlying belief about your worth. Recognize that over-giving is a source of self-neglect that can deplete your resources. Each time you need to decide about doing something for someone else, ask yourself, "What are the potential consequences to diverting my time and energy away from me?"

Set boundaries around your giving. Only once your own cup is over-flowing can you give the excess away. Don't operate from an empty vessel. It only leads to burnout.

Create a boundary around your energy. Learn how at www.BurnoutToResilience.com.

Debunking the Myths About Boundaries

There is a reason why you may not have good boundaries in place. It is essential that you examine your underlying beliefs and feelings. Here are some common myths about boundary-setting and what keeps people from putting boundaries into place:

If I decline other people's requests, they will be angry with me.

While it may be true that some people will be angry with you some of the time, if you are dealing with reasonable people, they will likely understand that you cannot always comply with their requests. Remember, people ask because they have nothing to lose, but just because they ask does not mean you have to say yes. And, if someone is angry with you for setting a boundary, they are not respecting your needs. This is not the type of relationship you want to cultivate anyway.

People won't like me if I don't do what they want.

The hope is that people will like you for who you are as a person, not for the favors you do for them. Be careful whom you attract into your life. Doing for others may be a way of pleasing them, but they won't necessarily like you for it. This conditions them to keep coming back and asking you for more favors because they know they can rely on you. While this is admirable, it does not necessarily lead to a reciprocal relationship. When you have unmet needs, you build up resentment.

Confrontation is scary. It's easier to say yes.

If you are scared by the idea of confrontation, this is part of your self-awareness. It's a first step to recognizing an area of weakness you need to work on continually. By improving your ability to stand up for your rights and negotiate what you want, you will overcome the fear and establish motivation to forge ahead. The rewards will speak for themselves.

Sacrificing myself for others makes me a good person.

Your deeds define part of who you are and it's important to be generous and helpful. However, there needs to be a healthy limit around how much you give and how much you take for yourself. Self-sacrifice does not equate to being a better person. Instead, it is what leads to burnout over time.

If I put myself first, people will think I'm selfish and uncaring.

When you ask for a favor, do you always expect the other person to say yes? If they don't, do you consider them selfish? It's time to reassess expectations of yourself and others. Perhaps you are a very empathic person, and when others struggle, you want to take care of them so much so that you lose track of your own needs. This is very selfless of you, but the opposite doesn't necessarily make you selfish. Remember, being focused on yourself is part of self-care. Without self-care, you are less capable of helping others in the long run.

Consider this definition of boundaries by psychologist David Gruder: "[A boundary] is any limit you need to honor to collaborate with another person without resentment and with integrity."[2] With these parameters as guidelines, you can make good decisions about when to say yes.

How Boundaries Decrease Drama

When we don't have good boundaries in place, we fall into what Stephen Karpman calls "the Drama Triangle" (Figure 28.2; as discussed in Johnson's article on the BDP family website).[3] We take on one of three roles: the Victim, the Persecutor, or the Rescuer.

The role of the Victim is not for someone who receives poor treatment, but someone who acts as if they are a victim. In this role, you recognize how desperately needy you are for not having met your needs for too long. You become passive and wait for someone else to step up to the plate and take care of you. When no one does, you either become angry and transition into a Persecutor or attempt being a Rescuer to someone else with the hope that the other person will eventually reciprocate.

As a Persecutor, you are finally releasing all your pent up anger. The reason this role creates drama is that the person blames others for his problems rather than taking responsibility for himself. Following this release, you are likely to experience guilt, an indication that your belief about your importance hasn't changed. The guilt then moves you back into the Rescuer role where you get to compensate for lashing out.

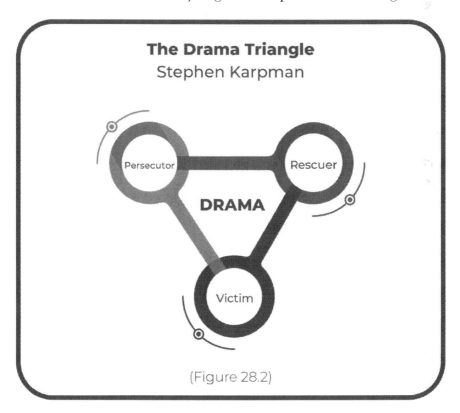

The Drama Triangle
Stephen Karpman

Persecutor

Rescuer

DRAMA

Victim

(Figure 28.2)

The Rescuer believes their role is to rescue others. You put other people ahead of yourself, tend to focus on giving and, consequently, don't ask for what you want or turn down other people's requests. The imbalance with which you approach others creates co-dependency because you approach relationships with a lose-win attitude. To have one of your needs met, you believe you need to give up something else. But no one can last forever in this depleting role. Over time, you build up resentment and may lash out as you transition into the role of the Persecutor. When abandoned, you may turn into a Victim.

This cycle continues, endlessly driven by feelings of anger, fear, and guilt. It never gets resolved, and the person continues to suppress their needs and suffer because of it. The only way out is to set boundaries.

If you think your life could benefit from putting boundaries into effect, here are ten suggestions on how to set healthy boundaries with yourself and others:

1. Put a time limit on your work, whether at the office or home. Working late into the day does not allow you to recover from stress and can negatively affect your sleep. Give yourself a time cushion before bed to relax and unwind. This practice will help you feel more energized the next morning so you can give the work your all.

2. Decide when to stop receiving phone calls or checking emails. It's so easy for us to get carried away and think each notification from our phone is an urgent matter that needs immediate attention. Remember that although someone might reach out to you at all times of the day and night, you don't have to respond right away. When you need to focus on your tasks, turn off all notifications. When it's time to relax, turn off your devices.

3. Does your job expect you to work until the work is done? If so, consider how frequently you are willing to sacrifice your day off and for how long. When you decide ahead of time, you can set expectations with others and relieve yourself of the idea that you have to keep working regardless of your resources. The demands on you rarely ever end, but your weekends do.

4. You might be worried about letting your customers down if you don't respond to their every wish. Focus on reading their demands as requests. As in any relationship, it is feasible for you to be able to fulfill some requests and not others. Set realistic expectations with both yourself and others on what you can and are willing to do.

5. If you are dealing with difficult personalities in your work or personal life, ask yourself how you want others to treat you. Sometimes our fear of losing out on a relationship pushes our boundary off the map. This only confirms to others that we have no limit in place and that they can get away with manipulating us to do what they want. Don't let your fear outweigh your values. Stay true to yourself. This will allow you to attract the right people rather than desperately attach yourself to the wrong ones.

6. When you're interacting with others, aim for respectful communication. Keep calm and excuse yourself if you need space rather than let your anger build. Similarly, don't engage with others who disrespect you. By setting clear expectations, you send a firm message that you will not tolerate yelling, blaming, or shaming.

7. Be clear on your values. This will allow you to make decisions more easily, especially when considering which tasks to take on. When someone makes a request of you, this sense of purpose that stems from your values can guide your decision on whether you accept or decline the request.

8. Before you take on a new task, let the other person know how much time you have. This sets a clear expectation of how long you can dedicate to the project and when you will stop. If it isn't a sufficient amount of time, this upfront clarity conversation can prevent you from taking on something you cannot realistically complete.

9. Assert yourself to protect your resources. If your boss or partner is asking you to take on a new project, share with them what you have on your plate already and prioritize together what this new project

will replace. This ensures you don't overload yourself while providing support to new priorities that pop up.

10. Express your feelings appropriately. If someone else oversteps your boundary, you are likely to feel angry. Learn to express that anger in a way that describes the facts, connects their behavior to your feelings, and requests a change in approach from the other person. You will meet your needs more effectively in this way.

Conclusion

Setting boundaries may not be in your practice yet, but it is something you can put into effect with time. To be successful with boundary-setting, you have to believe that you matter. Recognize that you have needs much like anyone else and that it is your responsibility to get your needs met. Also, realize that you have limited resources, and you need to protect those resources from depletion by being strategic about how much of them you give away and how much you keep for yourself.

When you believe you matter, you can side-step guilt. You can tune into your values and make purpose-driven decisions about what you do with your time and how you interact with other people. You feel empowered to ask for what you do want and to say no to what you don't.

We place white picket fences around our homes to protect our property. It's time we recognize the need to do the same with our resources so we can have more balance between our internal needs and the external demands placed on us.

Transitioning Out of Work-Mode

WHEN WE TALK about energy, self-care, and setting healthy boundaries, we need to focus not only on what happens at the office but what happens in our personal lives. As you transition out of work, you need to consider what practices will help you do so most effectively so you can maximize your recovery time.

Creating a Transition From Work to Home Life

Each day, you have to transition from work to your personal life as you leave the office. If you have a family, the additional responsibilities at home might instantly bombard you, making it difficult to take time for yourself. Additionally, it might be challenging to let go of all your work duties, meaning you bring work home and don't truly get a break.

To overcome these hurdles, we will examine how to create a transition from the office so that you can mentally switch work off and recover.

When you work in a high pressured environment, you might have a hard time cutting the cord. If you do not transition out of your work mode, you will bring all the stress from your job into your personal life. This can negatively affect your relationships, health, and emotional life.

Here are five suggestions to help you create a transition out of work so that you can protect your energy and your space:

1. Walk off any excess energy and come home refreshed. If you take public transit, consider getting off a few stops before your home and walking the rest of the way. If you drive, drop off your belongings and take a walk around the block before officially arriving at your front door.

2. When you come home, have a routine that helps you to shift over from your work life into your personal life. An easy ritual to help you feel like you're stepping out of your work mode is to change out of your work clothes. When you get home, take out clothes that feel comfortable, especially if you work in an environment where you wear a suit or an outfit that feels stifling. This change starts to make a shift in your mind and body.

3. Take some time out to ground yourself. Sit down, close your eyes for a few minutes, and take several deep breaths. This doesn't need to take very long. Taking ten deep breaths can make a big difference in releasing all the tension from the day that you've accumulated.

4. Do some journaling, especially if you have a lot on your mind. There might be ongoing projects that you need to come back to the next day at work. Writing them down is a way of downloading the information from your brain and onto paper so you can focus on your personal life. Once you've closed up your journal, you are shutting down your work brain.

5. Get into a relaxed state. If meditation is in your practice or if you'd like to create such a practice, I would recommend that you sit down in the same place and at the same time each day to build a habit. Take a minimum of five minutes to close your eyes and meditate as

a way to transition out of work. If you are cooking dinner, put on some relaxing music to help soothe you. Enjoy a hot beverage or consider slipping into a warm bubble bath. Diffuse essential oils such as lavendar or lemon that have a calming effect as you breathe them in. Getting into a more relaxed state can allow you to be more present.

These are daily habits that can help switch off your mind as it relates to work and enable you to maximize your personal time. In addition to engaging in such behaviors daily, you might also consider longer stretches of recovery time.

WORK TO HOME TRANSITION CHECKLIST

❑ Walk off excess energy before coming home

❑ Change out of work clothes

❑ Ground yourself with 10 deep breaths

❑ Journal about anything related to work that is on your mind

❑ Get into a relaxed state

How to Take Vacations From a Busy Job

Even if you are aware of the benefits of taking a vacation from work, there may be real obstacles that make it challenging to step away. According to Project Time Off, a study conducted most recently in 2018 by the U.S. Travel Association, over half of American workers are not using their paid vacation time.[1] Employees accounted for three main concerns that led them to forfeit much of their time off. Many worried about appearing "less dedicated or even replaceable" if they took a vacation.[2] This reflects the work culture and the employees' sense of stability in their job. Some workers decided to stay and work because they felt their workload was too big. The third barrier to taking time off was when workers felt there was no one to cover for them while they were gone. Given the demands of many jobs, it is understandable if you worry about the impact of work piling up while you are on vacation.

Despite these barriers, you need to think strategically about how to last in your career as opposed to burning out. Let's examine some options that can tackle these barriers and allow you to reap the benefits.

"Workcations" have become a solution for many of these obstacles above. This is when workers travel and work remotely from a new destination. It allows them to experience a change of scenery while continuing to plug away at their work. Workcations are a step in the right direction for some people. That said, there are greater benefits to completely unplugging from work.

The average American worker takes 17.2 days of vacation per year. Of those three and a half weeks, Americans use just eight days for travel. When comparing these "homebodies" to "mega-travelers" or workers who use most of their days off for travel, we see a dramatic difference in levels of happiness (see Figure 29.1). Mega-travelers report significantly more happiness than their counterparts. This finding demonstrates that traveling during your time off significantly increases your happiness and wellness meters.

To counter burnout, you need to seriously consider the impact your decisions make long-term on your ability to sustain your energy and levels of satisfaction for your work. The study shows that mega-travelers were also significantly happier with their company and their job than those who opted out of travel.

If you are someone who has resisted taking time off, consider this: mega-travelers not only reaped benefits related to happiness; they were much more likely to receive a promotion.

It's true that when you step away from your work, it might pile up, or you might appear less dedicated to those who stay behind. But think about what you are missing out on when you don't take a vacation.

Some benefits homebodies miss out on include a chance to recover from stress, to have fun, and to make lasting new memories.

Figure 29.1

To maximize your vacation days and reap all the benefits associated with taking time off, take a proactive approach. Plan when you will take your vacation in advance. Planning increases happiness with personal relationships. It gives you something to look forward to. In addition to having your actual time away, your mental planning time extends the benefits of the vacation in your mind.

Besides planning when you'll be on vacation, you need a plan of action for your work. When possible, find someone to take on some of your workload. Set expectations with customers so they know when you are out of town and to whom they can reach out in your place. Often, people think that their customers are going to be very upset if they are not available to serve them. While that might be true in certain industries, your customers might be happy to know that you are getting away, especially if they take a long term view of the relationship with you.

Sometimes, it's hard to get away because, as mentioned, you might worry about peer pressure and what people around you will think. You might even have colleagues who say, "Wow, she's never around. She's always going on vacation!" While that may not be true, fear of their perception may keep you from being able to get away.

It's important to live with your values in mind and not take to heart too much what other people think. They might have different values than you. They might value work a lot more than you do or maybe you value a balanced lifestyle while they are really focused on honing their craft at their job. Don't let those factors get in the way. Make sure that you take the vacation you need so that you can stay in the game doing the craft that you love to do for the long term. Having an opportunity to disconnect allows you to connect back more effectively.

Now that you see the benefits of taking a vacation, make the most of it.

How to Make Your Next Vacation Count

Going on vacation is often our way of getting away from everyday stressors, but vacationing can also be very stressful. To avoid this mistake, make sure that what you're doing and how you vacation meets your needs.

While advanced planning can increase the chances of attaining your travel goals, keep in mind, there are often stress-related scenarios associated with flight delays, weather conditions, and conflict with your travel partner. To make your vacation as stress-free as possible, set realistic expectations. Realize that you will get to your destination, but not everything will turn out the way you planned for. Pack weather-appropriate clothing to maximize your comfort. Make sure that the person you take on vacation is someone you get along with (you don't want to spend your vacation time quarreling). Being away from your routines can be stressful enough.

According to a recent online survey, professionals in business services and health care industries cited travel as a way to avoid burnout.[3] If we consider that some of the biggest contributors to burnout are high demands and low autonomy, traveling can be a stress-busting option for these individuals because it is a decision they get to make for themselves and is a time set aside with little to no demands.

One of the traps you might fall into when on vacation, however, is trying to see everything. If you are someone who wants to take in all of the sights, you might find that instead of feeling rejuvenated, you feel completely drained. I've done this in the past and then found myself saying, "I need a vacation from my vacation!" Don't pack in too much on any particular day. Pay attention to your energy level, and make sure that what you're doing is exhilarating but also refreshing. Plan for some days where you have adventures and other days when you do something more relaxing.

Lastly, consider your accommodations. Depending on who is in your party, this can really affect the quality of your vacation. Nowadays, there are so many options with home-sharing that you can stay in a full house or an apartment. The extra room this affords you can make a big difference, especially when you are traveling with children.

Everyone can have their own room and, if you prefer not to eat out three times a day, you can have a place to cook your meals. Staying in a hotel room can feel constraining, so opt for a suite instead. That way, if your children go to sleep early, you are not confined to an early bedtime. Having a dedicated time and space for yourself helps you make that vacation count even more.

CHECKLIST TO MAKING THE MOST OF YOUR VACATION

- ❑ Set realistic expectations
- ❑ Wear weather-appropriate comfortable clothing
- ❑ Travel with someone with whom you get along
- ❑ Don't pack in too many plans on one day
- ❑ Plan for days of adventure and days of relaxation
- ❑ Stay in accommodations that afford you space

Conclusion

Repairing your energy requires that you recover from work. Find ways to restore your energy levels by psychologically detaching from your job once you leave the office, engaging in relaxing activities, and socializing with family and friends. Take vacations to new and exciting places to reenergize before returning to work, but make sure you plan accordingly so that your vacation addresses your needs away from home. By doing so, you will avoid burnout, experience greater happiness, and even move your career forward.

E#5: Empowering Exercise

The goal of this two-part exercise is to increase your energy. The first part is to overcome mindset obstacles. The second is to commit to implementing aspects of your self-care regimen.

Step 1: If you don't have self-care incorporated into your life, it is likely that you aren't making the time for it and that you don't believe you are worth it. On a scale of 0-100 (if 0 = not at all and 100 = absolutely true), how much do you believe you are worthy of self-care? _____

If you scored 69 or below, practice the affirmation, "I am worth it" every day throughout the day and come back to re-rate your belief on the 100-point scale once weekly until you've reached a score of at least 70. Then move on to Step 2.

Step 2: Consider which self-care activities you would benefit from incorporating in your life now that you believe you deserve it. Start with the basics (e.g., getting a full night of sleep, eating healthy meals, exercising your body several days a week, taking breaks throughout the workday). When you're ready to upgrade, you can start to implement meditation, massages, hot baths, or other relaxing and fun activities as well as plan for future travel.

I commit to implementing these self-care strategies:

_____

_____

_____

_____

_____

_____

_____

This is my plan on when and how I will incorporate these into my routine:

_____

_____

_____

_____

_____

_____

_____

_____

E#6: EFFORT

"Productivity is never an accident. It is always the result of a commitment to excellence, intelligent planning, and focused effort."

– Paul. J.Meyer

Effort, according to Oxford Dictionaries, is "a vigorous or determined attempt."[1] It's easy to become misled about what effort really means and what is required. In this section, we are going to uncover two ways of thinking about effort. The first is related to the concept of "work smarter, not harder," which indicates that there is a way to attain results without overexerting your  energy. The second relates to the concept of Right Effort, which is part of the Buddhist Eightfold Path to enlightenment.

Smart Effort

WHEN YOU THINK about it, effort is something that requires motivation. You put your energy into tasks because you are either moving toward something you want or away from something you wish to avoid. So when we talk about effort, keep in mind the rewards that are swaying your decisions.

Once you have a clear understanding of the rewards you seek, you must know how to focus your efforts to be balanced. Weak attention means a lack of effort, which is likely to keep the status quo at best. Too intense an effort will drain you. Instead, the goal is to engage in your work and find joy in it. You may have to challenge your beliefs about what is possible for you to achieve without overexertion.

What Motivates You to Do a Good Job?

Suppose a stranger approached you with this proposition: "I will assign you tasks that I would like you to complete. I want you to spend, at minimum, one-third of your day on these tasks, and in return, I will compensate you."

How would you respond? You might have several follow-up questions such as: What are the tasks expected of me? What is the maximum time you expect me to work each day if the minimum is eight hours? How much would I get compensated?

These questions examine whether there is a good effort-reward balance because your time is your most precious resource. You want to spend your time on optimally rewarding tasks. To help you understand what you find motivating, you need to examine the different types of rewards associated with work and identify which rewards are most essential based on your values.

Before we jump in, let's take a look at what motivation is and what is behind it.

What is Motivation?

Each of your actions has a reason or "motive" behind them. You have desires or needs that cause you to behave in a certain way. Whether you move toward a target or away from it will depend on your motives.

You are faced with choices each day, even if you don't recognize them. The reason you often overlook this fact is that you have fallen into a routine, but completing a set of tasks or doing nothing at all is still a choice. The question is, what leads you to continue doing something and, similarly, what can get you to change?

We are creatures of habit. When we are used to doing something, it takes less effort. There is less of a learning curve and only a bit of focus required. This is what we call "keeping the status quo." If you are satisfied with what you have based on doing what you are doing, you will continue in your routine. The motivation here might be satisfaction, avoiding your fear of change, or a desire to protect your energy and exert less effort.

It is when you want something more that you are required to change. If you want a raise at work, to expand your social circle, or to lose weight, you need to focus your efforts on what will get you the results associated with your goal.

And while attaining the goal is sometimes the reward for your efforts, there are several other ways you can feel rewarded for your work.

Types of Rewards

Motivation is what leads you to behave in a certain way with the anticipation of a particular outcome. This intentional practice is what gets you off the ground. For example, if you are unemployed and you want to make money, by searching for jobs you are focusing your actions on tasks that can help you attain your monetary goal.

But once you're in that job and you have a guaranteed paycheck, different motivations are needed to do the work. If you've experienced intense stress on the job or even burnout, you need to take a step back and think about what you're doing and why you're doing it.

Beyond the paycheck, you chose this line of work and continue to choose it each day by showing up. There must be more keeping you there. By getting clear on your motivations and how they align with your values, you can take inventory of whether you are in your power or need to redesign your work life.

There are two types of rewards that keep us motivated to work: external and internal.

EXTERNAL REWARDS

Returning to our earlier example, often, what we focus on initially is external because it is central to our survival. We seek work, especially early in our career, that will pay the bills. When we are more advanced in our careers, we may want a promotion in title and pay.

Other rewards that keep us motivated to do our work every day include feedback, acknowledgment, and recognition. As humans, we have a need to feel seen. If we work hard on a project, we want to know that our efforts are noticed. When we receive praise or even some direction on how to improve, we feel like we are making an impact and that our hard work amounts to something.

In the movie Hidden Figures, Katherine G. Johnson works relentlessly at her NASA job. Her brilliant mind focuses on manually calculating orbital mechanics necessary to perform a successful spaceflight. No matter how hard or long she worked, she was often unable to stay ahead of the curve. As soon as she handed in her documents, she was told that the team was moving in a different direction.[1]

If this were your reality, perhaps at first, you would feel frustrated for having wasted your efforts. But if this were a pattern at your job, chances are that the pay would not be enough to keep you there because once you've met your basic needs, what drives you is internal.

INTERNAL REWARDS

What kept Ms. Johnson working as hard as she did was the knowledge that she was part of something monumental. The meaning she derived from NASA's mission was so great that it allowed her to keep forging ahead.

It took a while for all of Ms. Johnson's efforts to amount to anything concrete, but when the first American astronauts completed their roundtrip flight to space, she felt an immense sense of pride.

Despite many roadblocks, Katherine G. Johnson's determination paid off in many internal and external rewards. But not all work obstacles are solved by effort alone. So how do we know when to stick it out and when to move on?

When the Rewards Aren't Motivating Enough

If you were making half a million dollars a year in your career in your early thirties and had a VP title, would you quit your job? It may sound counter-intuitive, but as demonstrated in the story of Greg Smith, external rewards are often not enough.

Greg Smith was vice-president of the investment firm Goldman Sachs. After twelve years, he decided to leave despite his title and high compensation. The three main reasons he cited for his departure included the company's declining "integrity," a "toxic" environment, and the company's culture of "ripping" off clients. While the external rewards were motivating, on the one hand, the lack of alignment between the company's values and his own took their toll.[2]

My cousin also worked for Goldman Sachs in the 2000s. During one of my stays at his New York apartment, I watched him wake up very early and leave for work, not to return until 10 or 11 p.m. He described using his apartment only for sleeping and showering on weekdays because he would be working all day at the office and then dining out with clients each night.

While he was being compensated well for his time, the pressure to perform was even higher. The company had high expectations, and as happens when one is in sales, the ultimate decision to buy lies with the prospective customer. The stress was mounting, and I found my cousin resorting to pills to deal with his anxiety and slow mental deterioration. Eventually, he realized the external rewards were inadequate when compared to how the demands of the job affected him, and quit.

Why Rewards Are Important

We've already mentioned that rewards motivate us to work, but there is more to it than that. My research has uncovered seven answers to the question, "Why are rewards important?"

1. *Self-efficacy.* In her article *Burned-Out*, Maslach mentioned that the most prominent factors associated with efficacy on the job were control and reward.[3] In other words, for you to believe you are capable of doing your job well and actually doing it well, you need to have some autonomy over your decisions at work, and you need to have some reward for your efforts.

2. *Engagement.* According to researchers, employees who were engaged in their work experienced significantly more rewards than their exhausted and less engaged coworkers.[4] It makes sense that we are more likely to see our work as meaningful, for example, when we have the energy to do it well and can get into a state of flow. The reward is a consequence of our engagement initially, but it also keeps us coming back for more.

3. *Feeling valued.* Whether the reward is internal or external, when you work hard, you want to be compensated for your efforts. When you are acknowledged verbally, financially, or otherwise, you feel like others respect and value your work. This motivates you to keep going.

4. *Intrinsic satisfaction.* We know how rewards make us feel. But it is also important to note what happens when we aren't rewarded. We've already mentioned that rewards motivate us. It stands to reason, then, that without proper rewards, we lose our sense of satisfaction and the motivation we need to do our work. We may feel invisible or unimportant. These feelings can lead us to lose our stamina or look for more rewarding work elsewhere.

304

5. *Self-worth.* When you receive adequate rewards for your efforts, not only does the recognition justify the work, but it elevates your sense of self. Success comes from putting your efforts toward a task and learning from your failures. Once you have an accomplishment, you feel good about yourself, and this motivates you to keep learning and striving.

6. *Trust.* As you probably already know, trust is critical in any relationship. The relationship you have with your organization is no exception. For that to happen, you need to feel like it fulfills its promises. If the higher-ups in your organization recognize your work and reward you accordingly, you build trust, which continues to motivate you to do good work for them.

7. *Inspiration.* One source of reward is positive feedback. When you put your energy toward accomplishing a company goal, getting feedback on your work can be empowering. It helps build up your self-efficacy, and it inspires you to continue on your journey because someone is watching and supporting you.

Rewards are essential for a variety of reasons. Regardless of what those reasons are for you, the most important aspect to keep in mind is that they are adequate for the work you are doing. You may be making a half a million dollars as Mr. Smith did, but if there is a misalignment between your values and that of your company, the pay alone won't likely keep you there. That said, while rewards don't lessen the workload, they can help stave off burnout because of the motivation they instill in you.

With that in mind, let's consider what is needed for you to have effort-rewards balance.

Balanced Rewards

When we seek balance, we look for ways to engage without too much or too little effort, and to have our efforts amount to meaningful rewards. We already know that too much effort can lead to burnout. Let's now take a look at what happens when there is too little reward.

Researchers conducted a study whereby students were asked to screw bolts in for one hour. At the end of that inordinately tedious task, the researchers offered students money to recommend the task to other prospective participants. Some students received one dollar while others were paid $20 for their recommendation.

Those who received $20 thought that while the task was boring, they got well-compensated, so it evened out. There was sufficient justification for their lie, and they did not feel internally conflicted about it. The students who received only one dollar experienced cognitive dissonance when asked to recommend the task to others. They felt a tension between their belief that the task was monotonous and their decision to support it. Because their compensation was too small to justify lying, they had to change their perception of the task to eliminate their inner conflict.[5]

If you are giving your job your all and aren't getting the rewards you desire, you might convince yourself that the job must be worth it. Alternatively, you might take matters into your own hands to seek fairness.

In a study on the "interplay between job demands and job resources," researchers found that employees whose job required high effort but provided low reward called in sick more often than any other employees.[6] We can interpret their absence as a result of being sick, as a lack of motivation to come to work, or as a way to reward themselves for their high effort by taking time off. The former factor may relate to burnout, especially if the sickness is psychosomatic or a result of job-related stress. The latter factor might be an attempt to balance the relationship between effort and reward.

Rather than have to explain away your reasons for staying in a dead-end situation or sabotaging your career, consider some ways to balance the equation:

Increase rewards. Approach your employer for higher rewards. Remember that rewards come in a variety of colors, so while you may not always be able to get increased monetary compensation, you can probably attain additional sources of reward (e.g., a promotion in title, more vacation days, a work-from-home day, stock in the company).

Recognize if you are not being compensated fairly and address this with your hiring manager. If they are unwilling or unable to rectify the situation, take proactive action and start your job search. It's a good idea to know what the market will bear and get what you are worth.

Decrease demands. Employers are in the business of making money and their biggest cost is employee salaries. It is natural for them to try to get as much as possible from their hires, but they need to recognize there is a limit to how much they can get away with. Aim to turn down anything that doesn't align with your long-term career goals so you can produce quality work on fewer items rather than have your hand in an overwhelming number of tasks that are half-baked.

Become empowered. In the book *The Truth About Burnout*, the authors recommend systematizing your autonomy, finding ways to keep yourself accountable, and creating relative rewards for your work.[7] This gives you the ability to address issues as they come up. If your manager tends to micromanage, talk about how this negatively affects you and what would better allow you to do your work.

Balancing rewards is not only relevant when you feel undermotivated. It is also applicable when you are overmotivated or motivated by fear.

One of my coaching clients made it her mission to rebalance the effort-reward equation. Catalina, a female physician and researcher, had a tendency of taking on too much for fear of missing out or of being perceived in a negative light. She came to see me because she felt overwhelmed with work demands and resented her predicament.

As a result of our work, she was able to establish helpful criteria of when to say 'no' to others' requests and reward herself in the process. For each request she turned down, she paid herself $100—money she could use on a shopping spree. Very quickly, the motivation to say 'no' outweighed the motivation to say 'yes' and Dr. Catalina not only had less stress, but also more downtime.

She also established a checklist of when to say 'yes' to requests. This list reflected her values and priorities. If the effort was low (e.g., if someone requested her to give a talk she'd already given and therefore didn't need to spend a lot of time preparing for), she would be more likely to take it on. But only if she got paid and didn't already have more than three other travel commitments for the year.

By establishing clear guidelines for how to handle incoming requests, you too can avoid feeling overwhelmed, guilty, or resentful. Be clear on your values and available time before you commit yourself to anything extra.

Focus on meaning. Rather than trying to get more rewards by taking on excessive amounts of work, focus your efforts and find value by going more in-depth with the projects you already have. By becoming engaged, your job starts to feel more meaningful. If the work you are doing is not challenging enough, communicate your needs to your supervisor. By focusing on meaningless work, you lose out on an opportunity to increase your professional development.

Recover your energy. If you are burned out, you may be attempting to conserve your energy by neglecting responsibilities. Focus on recovering your energy and then figure out whether you can re-engage with your work in a different, more effective way that maintains your vitality.

Being aware of the effort-reward model can help you assess whether you are in balance, and if not, it can serve as a reminder to rectify the situation. As Abraham Lincoln once said, "The probability that we may fail in the struggle ought not to deter us from the support of a cause we believe to be just." Remember, you always have a choice, and it's up to you to design a life of balance.

Once you've secured adequate rewards and have garnered the motivation to work, it's time to consider the effort side of the equation.

Balanced Effort

It takes effort to make things happen, and putting too little or too much effort into your work can take you out of balance.

Previously, we said that too little effort could be a way of compensating yourself when you feel under-compensated. You might also find that with too little effort you are under-performing. You need to understand why you engage in your work in the way that you do and figure out how to become better aligned with your inner rewards.

When your attention is weak, your performance will suffer. What leads to poor attention is external distractions, inner attachments, fears, and desires. To improve your attention so your efforts amount to the desired outcome, it's important to eliminate distractions.

External chaos (emails, alerts on your phone, or a messy desk) can break up your concentration and prevent you from focusing your efforts. Take the necessary steps to minimize notifications, set expectations about your availability, and clear out any clutter.

Even with a perfectly controlled environment, chaos can ensue internally. You might be overthinking your decisions, be filled with doubt and skepticism, or feel afraid of what the future might hold. If you find it difficult to pay attention, it might be because there is something you are avoiding. Practice controlling your mind through meditation to bring your best self to your work. Focus on gratitude for everything that's right in your life now rather than worrying about what is to come. This will keep you in the present and improve your attention at work.

The problem may not lie in your attention, but in your beliefs about how much effort you need to exert. You may feel exhausted by all the responsibilities you are already carrying and overwhelmed by the prospect of taking on anything else. But consider this: life doesn't have to be difficult.

Your beliefs are what drive your behaviors and if you believe it has to be difficult, you may either find yourself struggling or resisting it altogether. By using the power of the mind, you can focus on attaining what you want and perhaps making it easier than you would otherwise estimate it to be.

If you've ever experienced a state of flow, you know that you can exert a lot of effort and not feel drained. Optimal engagement enables you to gain confidence, feel grateful, and come into harmony with your efforts.

There are tools like visualization that can be helpful to manifest goals more smoothly. Once you see yourself having the success that you want, going through the motions in real life is less daunting. Moreover, there have been countless reports from people who have used their spirituality to manifest goals in less time and with less effort. The Law of Attraction states that when you focus on what you want with appropriate effort and action rather than on what you don't want, you can attract the right things to you.

CREATING EFFORT-REWARD BALANCE

Consider which part of the effort-reward equation lacks balance and use the table below as a guideline of how to increase balance on either side.

Balance Your Efforts	Balance Your Rewards
Become aligned with inner rewards	Increase rewards
Eliminate distractions	Decrease demands
Declutter	Become empowered
Overcome negative thinking, doubt, fear	Focus on meaning
Manifest through visualization and inspired action	Recover your energy

Conclusion

Smart effort is all about a balanced relationship between effort and rewards. Rewards are what motivate you to work and are important because they drive you to do your job. The more engaged you are, the more likely you will accomplish great results, which increase your efficacy and encourage you to keep striving. Rewards, when adequate in relation to your efforts, make you feel valued. Without them, you can quickly burn out.

While work ethic and being action-oriented are necessary ingredients for success, more effort doesn't always equate with more productivity. To get the most out of your efforts, create conditions that allow you to stay attentive to your work. Focus on increasing task engagement and getting into a state of flow. Doing so will allow you to get more done in less time. Additionally, attending to what you want rather than what you don't want can help you manifest your desired outcome with less effort. By letting your mind work for you rather than against you, you can smartly manage your energy while working toward your goals.

Right Effort

IN BUDDHISM, EIGHT guidelines can lead to enlightenment. They are known as the Eightfold Path.[1] While our focus here is more on getting through the workday with balance rather than on reaching enlightenment, there is wisdom in the way Buddhists conceptualize effort.

Right Effort is one of the concepts in the Eightfold Path. What is meant by Right Effort is mental discipline: the ability to prevent and release negative thoughts and feelings and, instead, cultivate and strengthen good thoughts and qualities. By being aware of your inner experience, you can establish habits that transform, empower, and strengthen you.

Any growth takes time and effort, whether it's personal, professional, or spiritual. If you are impatient with the process, you will become frustrated. Recognize that while you think you want the transformation to happen quickly, you may not be able to handle it all at once. When it unfolds slowly over time, you have an opportunity to adapt. The ultimate reward that comes from this transformation and growth is freedom.

Relative Motive Strength

There is a continuum between achievement motivation (AM; moving in the direction of your desired goal) and failure avoidance or fear-of-failure (FF; running away from your desired goal as a result of fear). This is known as Relative Motive Strength (RMS), shown in Figure

31.1. When you are closer to the achievement end of the spectrum, you are more likely to associate your efforts on demanding tasks with positive outcomes such as "dedication," "concentration," "commitment," and "success." When you are more fearful of failing, you are more likely to associate effort on demanding tasks with negative outcomes like feeling "overloaded," "stressed," "obsessed," and burned out.[2]

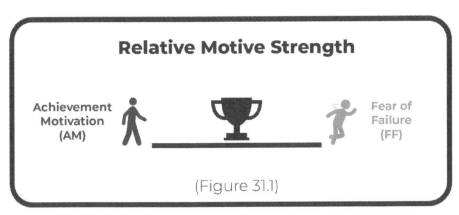

Relative Motive Strength

Achievement Motivation (AM)

Fear of Failure (FF)

(Figure 31.1)

When you think about what is behind the difference between these two extremes, it's the way you see yourself. Self-efficacy is the belief that you can be successful. Your self-efficacy can be affected by your over-arching core belief about personal adequacy or can be task-specific. Either way, it's an illustration that when faced with demands from the external world, your thinking can shape how you perceive those demands and yourself.

When you see yourself as adequate, you don't allow your failures to define you. You understand the importance of your long-term goals, and that failure is part of the learning process. This keeps you motivated and unafraid. Alternatively, when you fear failure to the point of short-changing your efforts, you see yourself as inadequate and will want to avoid this pain point, which will confirm your beliefs. In short, it's about your inner dialogue, your self-judgment.

Both the AM and the FF individuals have a goal. The former is more focused on achievement. The latter is more focused on avoiding failure.

Their actions will be different because of their varying focal points, and their success rates will, therefore, vary as well. It's easy to see why FF individuals enter into a self-fulfilling prophecy when their lack of success becomes attributed to their inadequacies. This wrongful attribution reinforces their avoidance of demanding tasks, thus linking their past, present, and future (see Figure 31.2).

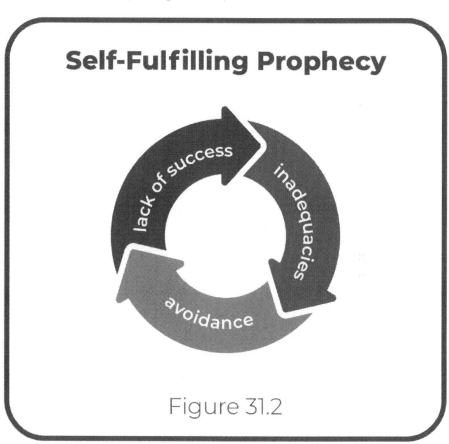

Self-Fulfilling Prophecy

lack of success

inadequacies

avoidance

Figure 31.2

Most individuals fall somewhere in the middle of the RMS continuum. But if you are a perfectionist, you can end up on either end. That means that you may be able to reach great heights, but it will be at a cost, namely, to your state of balance.

So how can you achieve greatness and still be balanced? How can you attain success without burning out in the process? One answer to this dilemma lies in ancient philosophy.

The Art of Non-doing

Over 2,500 years ago, in present-day Nepal, a monk began teaching what came to be known as the Middle Way. This monk, now known as Buddha, taught that the Middle Way was how one could be free from living in extremes.[3] His teachings challenge much of how Westerners run their businesses and their lives.

Many of us, including high aimers and perfectionists, focus on what we can do. We busy our days with lists of tasks to accomplish and seem never to have enough time to get everything done. Living in this way is very stressful. We can feel buried by our work, so we start to multi-task with the hope that we will get more done. Working on multiple tasks at once only makes us fall out of balance, and because it entails distraction, we can become confused about what's most important. It's better to do less at once, attain mastery, and then move on.

According to *Buddhism*, doing is the way of limitation. It's filled with our thoughts and judgments and creates a world of pleasure and pain. Instead, Buddhism proposes *action without doing*. We have to get beyond our thoughts, and that will make our actions perfect.

There are two targets in this art of non-doing. First, we look at what not to do. This helps us eliminate tasks from our list rather than continually add more. It helps us focus on what's most important rather than multi-task and lose our integrity. This also includes not thinking and judging which prevent us from acting. This philosophy is in line with the saying, "less is more."

Secondly, we focus on how to do without doing. So, rather than swimming against the current, allow the current to lead you. Every sailor knows that using the power of the wind can move the boat more forcefully in the direction they want rather than opposing the wind's strength. This translates into being flexible in your thinking and actions and building momentum on the existing structures around you.

Recall the first time you learned how to drive. There were so many aspects to think about. You may have wondered, "How do people make it look so easy?" You had to be very focused to avoid making mistakes, to make sure you were safe, and to follow all the rules. It may have felt overwhelming to simultaneously think about signaling when changing lanes, about slowing down with adequate space to not hit the driver at the stop sign in front of you, or about merging onto the highway when there were fast-moving cars flying by. But with lots of practice, your mental focus lessened. Now that you've mastered driving, you likely have days that you get to work and don't even remember how you got there.

There are two lessons in this example. The first is that mastery comes with time and consistent practice, but until then, you need much mental energy. You may need to focus on a strategy to get things done. With mastery, you can get into the flow and engage in the task without being overly-focused on it. You become one with the action.

The second lesson is that when you fall into habits, you can end up engaging in tasks mindlessly. However, this is quite different from non-doing. The main difference is awareness. Non-doing is doing with consciousness, which is different from unconscious action. It is intentional and comes from letting go of your thoughts and feelings, which cloud your awareness.

According to spiritual teacher Samvara, you can achieve perfection through a formula:

"Tremendous Attention + Extreme Abandonment = Perfect Action"[4]

He refers to being very mindful and focused rather than having mere thoughts. It is about taking action without focusing on the outcome. It's like aiming your arrow at a target, pulling back the bow, and then letting the arrow go. You can't hit the goal unless you release the arrow. Similarly, you have to be hyper-focused on what you want, take action, and then let go so you can move on to the next perfect action without judgment, worry, or fear about the outcome of the previous action.

It's about turning off the struggle. When you're faced with a problem, head into the solution, rather than looking for excuses or for someone to blame. Problem-solving in this way differs substantially from obsessing over details, ruminating and becoming paralyzed, and from staying stuck in your mind. This is a way of doing but having little to show for it. As Samvara said in his lecture, *How to Do Buddhism*, "When you're doing, the shadow of the self is cast over everything."[5] By this, he is referring to the ego. This is when we get caught up in what it means about us when we accomplish or fail and how others might perceive us. "When you're not doing," he says, "everything you do exposes the light of truth."[6] In essence, with perfect action, you are authentic, in the moment, and whatever happens is a direct result of your mindset.

You might be wondering how you can accomplish this art of non-doing. I will share two ways. The first is the essential practice of meditation. This is a tool that "trains the mind and reshapes the brain."[7] It's a continual practice of clearing your mind and going beyond your thoughts. When you direct this mindfulness to your actions, you can get in the zone, become one with the action, leave behind all judgments, get out of the way, and achieve perfection.

In 2017, Alex Honnold climbed El Capitan, a vertical rock formation of 2,900 feet at Yosemite National Park, without ropes and in under four hours. The New York Times quoted his climb as being, "one of the great athletic feats of any kind, ever."[8] What is so astonishing about this accomplishment is that most people would not even attempt it, let alone be successful. One misstep and you tumble to your death. This can easily bring up intense fear, which serves as a distraction. It seems Honnold was able to focus his mind, become one with the rock, and focus on where he was going rather than whether he might fall.

Your work may not be as treacherous, but it may bring up fear when you have to take risks. Develop tremendous attention. With extreme abandon, avoid thoughts about success or failure, like "I'm going to flunk this" or "I'm going to ace this." These are future-based thoughts that take you out of the moment.

The second way to accomplish non-doing, according to Samvara, is that, "When you are impeccable and selfless, there is power in everything you do."[9] Taking perfect action to help others rather than focusing on what success or failure means about you, makes you more powerful and allows you to derive more meaning from your efforts.

According to the theory of karma, your intentions and good deeds today contribute to your future happiness. As the saying goes, "You get what you give."

Hard Work and Success

In What Leads to Burnout, we defined the term "high achiever" and saw that it is a combination of hard work and the success that follows. There are some truths to this definition and some myths to it as well.

TRUTHS

To be successful, you need to work hard, but this is less about putting in endless hours, taking on copious amounts of work, or pushing yourself beyond a state of balance where your work interferes with your health and personal life. Hard work, as it is defined here, is about directing your mind and moving beyond self-judgments, fears, and the tendency to avoid. You are a high achiever when your mind is not cluttered, and you can attend to the task, take action with "tremendous attention," and let go of any attachment to the outcome. This is associated with achievement because your perceptions affect your efforts. Your perceptions are how you focus. Your efforts are how you act. Your mind shapes your success.

MYTHS

This section has demonstrated that you can work hard and not have success. When you hold yourself back with your limiting beliefs, it leads you to sabotage your efforts. This can result from having diverted focus that attempts to get too much done without mastering anything or being clouded by your thoughts so that you take less action. The fact that you are busy does not mean you are effective with your energy.

To be successful, all that is required is intention of mind, acting with attention, and removing thought. This eliminates the need to work as hard as you otherwise do, alleviates the pressure of having a certain outcome, or the attachment of meaning you assign to your self-worth. You can have perfect action without perfect results, but the former will lead to success in the long-run, not the latter.

Conclusion

The demands of the workplace can certainly lead to burnout, but the demands you place on yourself can change your experience. You have more control over your mind and the quality of the effort you put forward than over your environment. Therefore, it is in your best interest to harness your power from within, to train your mind to work for you rather than against you, and to understand what leads to real success, not just moment-to-moment, but also long-term.

E#6: Empowering Exercise

If you've never intentionally manifested anything before, here is your opportunity to try it. Engage in these five steps as a behavioral experiment with open-mindedness and see what happens.

Step 1: Decide what it is you would like to manifest. It might be a raise, to connect to someone of influence, or to come up with your next big idea. Write down exactly what you want to see happen in specific detail.

_____

_____

_____

_____

Step 2: Create an affirmation about your vision coming to reality and write it down. If, for instance, you want an extra $5000, say "I am experiencing increase right now. I favor $5000 coming into my bank account."

_____

_____

_____

_____

Step 3: Practice your affirmation each morning when you wake up and each evening before you go to sleep. Keep your eyes closed as you would in meditation. As you say this phrase to yourself, visualize your desire manifesting as if you were watching a movie.

Step 4: As you meditate on this vision, ask questions about what you need to do to make it come true.

Step 5: Journalize your downloads. Any answers you receive to your posed questions are items on which you need to take action. Write these down and then go into immediate action mode.

_____

_____

_____

_____

E#7:
ENLIGHTENMENT

"When you have everything, you no longer see yourself in the world.
You see the world in you."

– Dana Gibson

Once you are managing yourself well, have your needs met, are focused on getting things done, and have the right mindset in place, this final solution is about helping you create practices for resilience. This entire book has been a build-up to this very moment where you find out how to bring it all together and elevate yourself to higher grounds.

In discussing this final solution to burnout, we will uncover what enlightenment is all about, why it's essential, and what it takes to reach it. I explain the importance of mindfulness and meditation, amongst other positive practices.

What is Enlightenment?

CONSIDER HOW YOU feel in your body when you are mentally and emotionally exhausted. There is a heaviness that makes it hard to get through the day. Your brain is in a whirl of cynicism and negativity. You feel hopeless about the possibility of change or that things can turn around.

In contrast, enlightenment is a lightening of your load. This occurs when you free yourself of the inner dialogue that brings you down and of the despair you feel that impairs your ability to perform.

Enlightenment is something that happens as a result of training your brain to focus impeccably. It is the ultimate control that allows you to feel free and in charge no matter what you are facing.

Keep in mind that enlightenment is the result of advanced skills. That is why it is the final of the seven steps to overcoming burnout.

This does not mean you have to wait to start your brain training until you've mastered your emotions, empowered yourself, gotten to a state of flow, or watched your efficacy soar. Instead, it's a skill you can start to develop alongside these other feats and which can increase the speed with which you experience success.

Inner Resources

Much of what we discussed in the early part of this book is about external circumstances that lead to burnout, especially high demands and low autonomy. Remember, there will always be aspects outside of your control, but looking within can help you stay afloat.

We all experience some degree of stress, but what is it that enables some people to survive extremely stressful situations while others burn out? That is the question that medical sociologist Aaron Antonovsky wanted to answer. He researched Holocaust survivors to uncover the mystery. Antonovsky found that when people have a strong "sense of coherence" (SOC) about themselves and the world around them, they are more resilient.[1]

SOC is characterized by the confidence that you can make sense of your experience, that you have the resources to manage external demands, and that you can assign meaning, and consequently, become committed to the challenges you face.

While your situation at work is by no means life or death, there are lessons to be learned about coping from this extreme example that can help prevent burnout. Because stress results from the perception that the demands exceed your resources, by challenging yourself to look for alternative and more positive interpretations of a difficult situation, you can increase efficacy and resilience. Your mind is designed to create a story around your experiences. So be aware of the story you are telling yourself and make sure that it is one that empowers you.

Journey to a Meaningful Life

"When you change the way you look at things, the things you look at change."

– Wayne Dyer

The journey toward a meaningful life is about using intention to guide your behaviors. It's about declaring what you want and going after it. And it's about seeing the big picture. You have to live in the present with an eye out for the future. You can always climb higher, but it's the road in front of you that determines your experience.

It is an accepted fact of life that when we reach adulthood, we work to support our lifestyle. For most of us, this entails waking up every morning and heading to the office for a day of at least eight hours, where coworkers, managers, bosses, and customers surround us. So if we fill up over one-third of our day with work, it might as well be meaningful.

The Holocaust survivors in Antonovsky's research created meaning of their dire circumstances, which allowed them to withstand extreme hardships. We arrive at meaning through the stories we tell ourselves so that we are resilient enough to cope with challenges. Therein lies the need to focus on perception.

Take a snapshot of your life. When you look back at the most difficult events you've endured, what impact have they had on you? Can you see patterns of how you've reacted during stressful times? And when you think ahead, what concerns you the most knowing what you know about the way you've been handling stress?

It is said that it's not what happens to you that leads to stress, but your interpretation of what is happening. Your reaction is very much tied to your perception, which is associated with variables like your mindset, self-efficacy, sense of purpose, personal values, desire for control, coping style, personality, and recovery habits, to name a few. In short, your style of thinking, the way you feel about yourself, and your personal preferences lead you to process information uniquely.

If it's true that your interpretation of events is what matters the most, then your way of thinking about external events is your ticket to making dramatic and desired changes. And if you want to withstand stress, to

327

manage your emotions well, and to create healthy habits that lead to success, you need to understand the psychology of the mind and its connection to your feelings and actions.

Imagine you're in a concert hall with thousands of other music lovers. You're happy to be there, spending time pursuing an enjoyable activity. Suddenly, the ground starts to shake. The music abruptly stops, and you realize that you're in the middle of an earthquake.

Your reaction to the earthquake will likely be quite different from the response of others around you. Some of the concert-goers, after getting over the initial shock, may become anxious and scream in terror. Others may lie on the ground to get closer to the vibrations and experience the quake more fully. Certain folks may feel sad, thinking that their life is ending and that they won't have a chance to say their final goodbyes. And while all those people have their private experience, you may be exhilarated because you've never been in an earthquake and find it fascinating!

How is it possible that people in the same space are experiencing the same event, but coming out feeling and behaving entirely different?

As you now know, people have different reactions based on the lens through which they see the world, shaped by their early life experiences. If mom and dad get divorced, many children think it's because they caused it. When an adult yells, children tell themselves that they're bad or not good enough the way they are. If only we were smarter, funnier, skinnier, or in some other way better than we are, our parent would love us, would never scream at us, and we would live happily ever after, just like in the storybooks.

When we're young, we think we are the center of the universe. If anything happens, it's because of us. We don't yet have a concept of others. When mom raises her voice, we don't stop to think that maybe she's had a stressful day at work. When our peers don't want to share their newest toy with us, we believe it's because we're not cool enough.

Fast forward to adulthood. You are now old enough and experienced enough to understand that what happens to you is also a result of other factors outside of yourself. If you get in a fight with a friend, you may fault the friend, you may blame yourself, or you may consider how each of you contributed in a certain way.

Keeping this in mind can help you be more coherent in your thinking about yourself and others, and lead you to mindfully interpret events in a way that boosts your inner resources rather than depletes them.

When all else fails, remind yourself that if meaning can be found in the Holocaust, it can be found anywhere when you search hard enough.

LEARNING FROM YOUR PAST

What are the 3 most difficult events you've endured in your life so far?

_____
_____
_____
_____

What impact have these events had on you?

_____
_____
_____
_____

How did you react in each of these situations?

_____
_____
_____
_____

What patterns do you see in your reaction to stressful events?

_____
_____
_____
_____

What concerns you the most knowing what you know about the way you've been handling stress?

_____

_____

_____

_____

What can you apply from this book that can lead you to more optimal outcomes?

_____

_____

_____

_____

Conclusion

Enlightenment is an advanced skill that results from having ultimate control over your mind. By eliminating negative thinking, you lighten your load and can achieve outstanding outcomes without burning out. Having a strong sense of coherence can help you be more resilient to the effects of stress. Acting with intention and a sense of purpose can increase your coherence and help you avoid the pitfalls of the mind.

Why Enlightenment is Important

ENLIGHTENMENT CAN DO more than just help you survive highly stressful circumstances. It allows you to thrive as you create your reality. As a result, you can have peak experiences, live up to your full potential, and lead a purposeful life that brings fulfillment.

Peak Experiences

When you follow the steps in this book, not only do you avoid and recover from burnout, you learn how to function at an optimal level, which is known as a "peak experience." Such extraordinary moments are ones in which you feel profoundly alive, aware, and euphoric. These are also moments where you are simultaneously self-sufficient and integrated in the world, have a greater awareness of truth, and are living in harmony.

Recall that when you are in flow, time seems to slip away. You immerse in the task to the point of losing track of time. Similarly, while having a peak experience, you are free of the confines of time and space, are fully present and functioning to your fullest potential without effort or strain. Your fears and doubts vanish, allowing you to think flexibly and be creative.

Self-Actualization

Refer back to Maslow's hierarchy of needs (Figure 4.1). The needs that correspond to the first four levels of the pyramid (Physiology, Safety, Love and Belonging, and Esteem) are considered Deficit Needs. When one of these needs is not fulfilled, you feel a sense of *deficit*, which leads you to pursue it. However, once those needs are met, you feel content. They do not motivate you to reach your full potential.

The ultimate goal, according to Maslow, is to be self-actualized. You reach the top of the pyramid when focusing on higher-level needs. In striving to always better yourself beyond the basic foundation, you create a state of harmony and understanding and realize your full potential. The values Maslow associated with this state include ones of integration, self-regulation, self-sufficiency, playfulness, effortlessness, and simplicity. [1] In short, a balanced, happy, and easy life. It's what we all want deep inside, but what so few of us ever experience.

CREATING A BALANCED LIFE

When people hear the word "balance," they automatically think about an even split between work and personal life. Given the demands of the workplace, this is impossible to achieve. But balance is not about an equal quantity between the two camps.

You already know that you have a whole slew of needs. When you focus on work, you may be taking care of your physiological, safety, and even esteem-related needs. But when work takes up too many of your resources, you end up not having the time to pursue meaningful relationships or the energy to take care of yourself properly.

I've heard many people say that although they know how important it is for them to exercise, for example, there just isn't enough time in the day. And even when there is time, they don't have the energy for it. On the surface, all these claims seem valid. But there is another way.

You know how when you really want something, you find the time, the energy, or the money for it? A coach I worked with once said that we all have resistance and make excuses. He used to share with prospective clients that if presented with an opportunity to buy a $100k car for only $70k, they would somehow find the money. Why? Because they would see it as a deal they could not refuse. They could easily turn around and sell the car for an instant profit.

How can you think about your health and relationships as that profitable investment? Instead of thinking of the resources you're lacking, ask yourself how you can muster the energy, the time, and the money to do what you really want.

We think that if we had more time, we would be able to get more of what we want done, but this is not necessarily the case. There was a time when I worked from home for part of the week and from my clinic for the other part. While it may seem logical to think that I went to the gym during my work-from-home days, the exact opposite was true. Why? Because of proximity, not because of time.

I purposely positioned my office close to my gym. I created breaks in between seeing clients when I would walk to my gym and work out. Because my gym is about a 20-minute drive from my home, I am less likely to work out on the days I work remotely.

How can you use the principle of proximity to accomplish your goals? Whether it's proximity to your gym or to the kinds of people you want to associate with, you have more control over your outcomes than you realize. You just need to be strategic in your planning and get creative in your thinking.

Even when you have proximity on your side, you might find that you have no time to engage in some of the activities on your wish list. I consider this backward thinking. You should start with what you want first and figure out how to plan the rest of your life around those activities. Want to join a meditation circle? Find out what nights during the week it is being held and put it on your calendar. Want to eat home-made meals when you come home from work, but feel too mentally exhausted that you end up eating take-out? Consider meal planning in advance, especially if you can find healthy and quick recipes you can easily assemble without too much mental energy. Want to get more sleep? Set an alarm to alert you of your bedtime so you can stay mindful of the time.

On the flip side, you may be spending too much energy on socializing. Do you have trouble saying no when someone asks you to hang out after work? If so, this may be taking up your remaining resources and not leaving much time for you to be able to rest or engage in other activities properly. Figure out what a more balanced picture would look like.

Recently a client of mine struggled with this exact issue. She found herself going out night after night and feeling drained from working all day and socializing every evening. Once she decided that she would like to cap her social outings to two nights per week, she was able to reserve her remaining time and energy for other opportunities and felt more rested in the process.

Outside of work, what is taking up more of your resources than you care to admit? Create boundaries around your time and you can find more of it for the things you want.

CREATING A HAPPY LIFE

Happiness. So much has been written on the subject. It is what we are all after, but we don't always go about it the right way. We seek immediate gratification because we don't want to wait to feel happy, but what greets us now doesn't always add up to joy. So how can you create a purposeful and happy life?

One of the regrets stated by the palliative patients mentioned earlier was that they wished they could have had the courage to be themselves.

Are you living for someone else's happiness or your own? Do what makes you happy. Be authentic and listen to your inner voice.

Lastly, ask yourself, "How can I let myself be happier?" You may come up with some ideas, but feel some resistance in pursuing them. If so, challenge the limiting beliefs that hold you back: beliefs that you don't deserve to feel happy, that it's not possible to have what you want, or that it is too scary to face change. Focus on how you will feel when you accomplish the items on your list and let the end result motivate you to take action.

CULTIVATING QUALITY RELATIONSHIPS

If relationships are a big piece of the puzzle toward happiness, consider the different relationships you have in your life. Who is in your inner-most circle? In the table below, rate the quality of your closeness to those individuals on a 10-point scale (1 = low quality, 10 = superior quality).

First-Tier Relationships	1-10 rating

How can you continue to foster those essential relationships, whether it's your spouse, your children, or your closest confidant?

_____

_____

_____

_____

Consider who is in your second- and third-tier circles.

Second-Tier Relationships	Third-Tier Relationships

❏ Are you investing your time and attention outside of work according to these tiers or do you need to rethink your paradigm?

❏ If you want to create new relationships, what are you doing about it? If you are seeking a romantic partner, are you out there dating?

❏ Are you investing energy in forming a community? Are you keeping in touch with old friends?

❏ Are you finding ways to spend quality time connecting to others outside of social media?

CREATING AN EASY LIFE

"Easy" is a subjective term and can mean different things to different people. For our purposes, we are defining this word according to Maslow's definition, which includes "effortlessness" and "simplicity."

Imagine an experienced ice skater who expertly maneuvers around the rink, performing difficult moves that would knock an amateur off their feet in two seconds flat. The skater makes it look easy and, in fact, it may be effortless for them if it is a peak experience and they are self-actualized.

The same is true for you. Surely there are tasks that you can do without much effort because of your expertise. But even more so than your experience, what leads to effortlessness is when you are working in a framework that allows you to reach optimal performance. This is when you are fully engaged in the work without distraction, when what you are focused on is meaningful to you, and when you are managing your energy to avoid depletion.

In his book *Barking Up the Wrong Tree*, author Eric Barker cites research that shows that people who relinquish unattainable goals feel happier and less stressed than those who keep working on such goals.[2] Exerting energy on impossible tasks prevents you from a state of effortlessness.

The other aspect of an easy life is when you employ simplicity in all that you do. What this refers to is monitoring your mind to ensure you aren't ruminating endlessly about your past mistakes or worrying about future ones. It's about letting your intuition guide you rather than overthinking your decisions or overriding what feels right with what seems logically correct. You might think of simplicity as the result of designing and then living your life on purpose. It becomes as easy as plug and play.

OVERCOMING INDECISION WITH EASE

Faulty learning can happen as a result of incidents through which you learned it's not safe to make a wrong decision or have a less than perfect outcome.

Follow these five steps to decide about an area over which you find yourself to be indecisive:

Step 1: Close your eyes and take a moment to ground yourself through several deep breaths.

Step 2: Bring to mind an area of your life where you tend to be indecisive.

Step 3: Tune into yourself. The truth behind this indecision is that you do know what you want, but you don't permit yourself to want it. Notice how this idea resonates in your body.

Step 4: Consider the alternative and notice how that resonates in your body.

Step 5: Decide to go with the idea that resonates as your truth.

Purpose

"Sometimes making a living and making a life point in opposite directions."

– Pico Yer

Living on purpose refers to aligning your decisions with your values. To accomplish this you need to have self-awareness about what you deem valuable. That said, when it comes to work, there are certain values we can all agree upon. From my experience of coaching professionals on their careers over the past two decades, I've aggregated a dozen such values.

It seems that one of our dearest work-related values is flexibility. We want the ability to flex our schedules to meet the needs of life outside of work. If you have to see a doctor during the day, you want to be able to make up the hours before or after your appointment. When you need to focus without distraction before a deadline, you want the ability to work from home so you can get more done. And when you are ready to go on vacation, you don't want your boss to say, "No, your coworker has already requested those days off," especially when you have a family event that is outside of your control.

As in any relationship, trust is a significant value. We all want to feel trusted and of course, we have to earn that trust. If you say you are working from home and are being productive, you don't want your manager to be suspicious of foul play. You also want to trust your manager. When you work as a unit and are outlining your goals for a promotion, you want your manager to provide feedback and help set you up for success rather than be passive-aggressive and skip your weekly meetings or cancel on you last minute. Trusting your coworkers is essential because you spend most of your time around them. You don't want to share something confidential with a teammate only to have that person tell their manager about it and have it come back to you. Lastly, you want to feel trust in the company you represent. If the company is either not following its stated values or if it is acting unethically, this can lead you to feel frustrated and even unsafe.

You want to feel the work you do serves a higher purpose. I've spoken with plenty of individuals who were unhappy with their job for any number of reasons. But one of the factors that made them hesitate to leave was that they really believed in the mission of the company. When a company's mission is aligned with your values, you feel like your work is meaningful and is serving the greater good.

While the top three values of flexibility, trust, and purpose are universal, there are many other values that you may want to hone in on in your search for a meaningful career.

THINKING AHEAD

Remember the regrets of the dying? They lamented working "so hard" because while they thought what they were doing was important, they realized at the end of their lives the missed opportunities.

When you think ahead to your last days, how do you want to remember your life?

_____

_____

Chances are you want to feel like you lived your life fully, that you felt loved by those around you, and that you left behind a legacy as a contribution to those who will live after you. So where can you be spending more of your time?

_____

_____

Who can you be investing in besides yourself?

_____

_____

How can you implement more relaxation and self-care into your every day so you don't burn out or end up living with regrets of your own?

_____

_____

Values can be looked at as intrinsic if they are qualities that live inside of you and extrinsic if they are benefits from the job that affect your life.

INTRINSIC VALUES

Autonomy is an example of an intrinsic value. Most people I've worked with state this is crucial to them, and given what we know about burnout, this makes sense. They want to be able to self-manage. They trust themselves to do a good job, don't want their manager looking over their shoulder and micromanaging their every step, and feel a sense of pride when they take on a project and see it through to its completion.

On the other hand, if you're an individual who struggles with self-induced structure, you may prefer less autonomy and more direction. You might really like routine rather than flying by the seat of your pants. In such a case, autonomy may be a less significant factor in your decision-making about a job.

Innovation and creativity are big factors to keep in mind when thinking about a career. If you're someone who feels stifled when told what to do and how to do it, you need to keep searching for a position that gives you the opportunities to experiment and create. This decision is not limited to your role, but also to the company for which you work. If you work for a company that is very hierarchical (e.g., a non-profit), you may not have the ability to infiltrate the established bureaucracy. You also need to consider who is on your team and how open they are to bouncing ideas off one another, to putting their ego aside, and to collaborating even when you're the one with the great idea. These values are some of the dominant reasons why people decide to become self-employed. They have an idea they want to bring into the world. They want to be the drivers of their vision because they believe in it and in the impact it can have.

What do you find valuable in the work that you do? What frustrates you about your job? When you turn your frustration into a value that isn't being met, you can identify the sources that can direct your search in a more meaningful direction.

EXTRINSIC VALUES

Extrinsic values include compensation, job security, balance, recognition, leadership, and travel. You've probably heard the expression, "Work to live, don't live to work." The idea is that work is a means to an end. It provides you with the money to live the life you want. Clearly, there can be much more to work than just money, and that is the point of this writing, but money is often a vitally important value that motivates us to work. This can be reflected in the salary you make, as you want to be compensated fairly according to your education, prior work experience, and your accomplishments on the job.

You also want to know that your job is not in limbo. When you work for a company that has big layoffs, even when your position is salvaged, it creates anxiety in you about the future security of your job. When you have a conflict with your direct manager or a coworker who is entrenched with the union, you feel scared that your job may not always be there for interpersonal reasons. A sense of security, both financial and in keeping your job, lets you focus on the work and not on whether it will be there tomorrow.

Referring back to the quote about working to live, you want to avoid having your job take over every waking moment. Today, more than ever, there is an expectation for workers to get the job done no matter what. Even if it is unspoken, you know that if you don't clear your plate today, more work will continue to pile on tomorrow. To avoid feeling overwhelmed, you stay at the office later and later, or attempt to get home to spend time with your family but then return to the computer and phone to work late into the night. Whatever hopes you had for personal care have taken a back seat due to the never-ending amount of work in front of you.

If you don't want to burn out, consider how and where you work. Are there ways you can get through tasks more effectively by delegating, setting boundaries, and avoiding distractions? If you are doing every-thing you can and still can't seem to dig yourself out from the demands of your job, perhaps you are in the wrong industry. Plenty of people are willing to forego balance because they value financial security or work status more. But if you're someone who is pining for more personal time to spend on yourself and your relationships, look for a career that gives you the lifestyle you desire.

When you work hard on a project, you want to be recognized. When someone else takes the credit, when the work you do goes unnoticed, or when your project gets shifted to someone else mid-way, you feel like the rug is being swept out from under you. This can be disorienting, feel like an injustice, and can lead you to feel angry and ignored. Whether it's at work or in your personal life, when you invest in something or someone, you want to feel seen. It's a universal desire because we are wired for connection. We want to know that our efforts count.

Consider how you like to operate. Do you enjoy helping people carry out their mission, like in the case of an executive assistant, or do you want to lead teams and be in charge? Leadership is a significant value to consider because if you enjoy being in a position of influence and mentorship, you need to seek out such opportunities. And, if it doesn't suit you, be sure to focus your efforts on a job that does not require you to lead.

Traveling the world may sound like a dream, but if you've ever traveled for work, you know that it can be less glamorous than it seems. That said, if travel is one of your values, you can bridge your personal and professional life passions. Flight attendants get to stop over in domestic and international destinations and spend their days off taking in the sights and sounds of a foreign city. Business executives use their flight time to get work done in preparation for a big meeting in a town hours away from home. Do you like traveling for work, or do you prefer sticking to your local routine?

By now, I hope you are considering your values and whether you are living a purposeful life. If there are values that are important to you which aren't being represented in your current scenario, don't despair. It is better to know what your values are and then design your life around them than to be oblivious and wonder why you are burning out. That said, you also want your values to align with each other.

When Values Are Misaligned: A Recipe for Burnout

Approximately one in two doctors experience burnout on the job. While fewer statistics about burnout exist for other careers, physicians often exhibit apparent burnout symptoms, including substance abuse issues.

High demanding careers can lead to burnout due to grueling hours and high expectations that emanate from both the industry and the high achievers in those industries. What we need to examine, though, is why individuals are drawn to those careers and what can be done to prevent burnout.

EXAMINING VALUES

As a coach, I often want to know about values. We all have them, but we're not always aware of how they drive us. We sometimes focus on a select few while we ignore the rest.

When we were playing M.A.S.H as kids, we likely didn't know much about any single profession, but we knew what adults had drilled into our heads: be a doctor or a lawyer. These were considered respectable jobs. It is what you did with your life if you were smart. There is prestige associated with these trajectories, not only for the work, but for the journey taken to get there. Besides, once you made it, wads of cash would apparently start falling on you from the sky.

As kids, we knew money was highly regarded. You could use it to buy most things. Those with money had more options, and options are good to have. You never wanted to be the kid whose family didn't have money because you couldn't allow yourself all the luxuries of life that your friends got to experience. And if you grew up without being able to afford what everyone else could, you wanted to make sure this trend didn't continue for the rest of your life. For many, there was an expectation to become accomplished—to make your parents proud.

Surely, everyone has a different reason for why they enter into the career of their choosing. But when we start the coaching process, we want clarity. And by focusing on values, we get a better understanding of what drives the individual's decision-making process.

Two critical value-driven questions are: (1) What are the values that led you to pursue your career? and (2) Are these the same values that keep you there? Some people might go into a career with passion and idealism, but then find that while it is soul-crushing, it is also lucrative. As much as they would like to make a career move, they sometimes feel lost. How else will they be able to support their lifestyle? Any other career would likely mean a serious pay cut. So while altruism may have gotten them there, money is the value that generally keeps them in the game.

What happens if your personal values are different from those of people in your profession? I recently interviewed an attorney who shared that as a junior lawyer, he was taught that he needed to put in 2500 billable hours a year over ten years, and this would help him make partner.

That equates to 48 billable hours a week and many more hours he can't bill for. And that is if he *never* took any time off! This is the culture, and if he didn't follow the norm, he'd be considered "subpar." Talk about pressure.

A mismatch in values is one of the reasons professionals burn out. Take a long hard look at why you do what you do, and if it isn't working for you, consider alternatives. Yes, sometimes these changes will require a change in lifestyle, at least in the short-term. But you have to look at what the cost is of staying in your profession.

STRESS AS A RESULT OF MISMATCHED VALUES

If you're burning out because of your values being out of sorts, you are at risk of experiencing chronic stress and developing stress-related problems. This can negatively affect your health in many ways, including a greater risk for developing 41 different autoimmune diseases (e.g., hypothyroidism, rheumatoid arthritis, psoriasis).[1] Researchers reported that men who had diabetes, heart disease, or a history of stroke and who worked in highly demanding jobs in which they had little control over their workload, were 68 percent more likely to experience premature death.[2]

Stress can also manifest cognitively. Do you know what it's like when you have so much on your mind that you can't turn the damn thing off? You try to get to sleep, but your brain is running a marathon. You review your day and worry about all that you have coming up the following morning. When you think about another to-do item, you don't want to forget it, so you spend hours rehearsing it in your head.

The next thing you know, it's time to wake up. You try to peel yourself off the sheets as you feel the dread of facing another day at the office. So while stress may keep you from getting proper sleep, ironically, when you don't sleep, you experience further symptoms like irritability and difficulty concentrating. Just when you needed to focus and get more done, you experience brain fog.

346

BALANCING YOUR VALUES

Values encompass different areas of your life. You have work-related values (autonomy, financial stability, or finding a sense of meaning), family-related values (spending quality time with loved ones, helping one another, and being a role-model for your children), and health-related values (feeling good physically, being in control of your emotions and behaviors, and experiencing peace of mind).

As you can guess, focusing on the various areas of your life is vitally important. You don't have to limit yourself to just one area. When you limit yourself, you might experience great success there but fail in all the remaining areas. If you're looking for an accurate measure of success, it might entail living a more balanced life. This is why we delve into values for the various life areas.

While you have your personal values, your workplace has values of its own. In today's day and age, the way to get ahead is to work more. When you prioritize your family, it creates conflict. You can no longer rely on your boss to remind you to go home at the end of the day. It is your job to be mindful of your time, of your commitments, and to make informed decisions that are value-driven. Otherwise, you'll experience guilt for having a life outside of work. You might believe that you should be working even when you're at home.

If you're chasing a paycheck, reflect on what's beyond the money. Is it family life, serving the community, or being a good friend? Remember that money is a means to an end. When you get too caught up in financial goals, you can forget that life is more than a contest and that you get the most value out of relationships, not material goods. You likely need less money than you think to live a happy and meaningful life. Money is a tool, but you have to be guided by a deeper vision of what that money can provide you with and be sure to live with integrity.

347

FINDING YOUR TRUE NORTH

Balance may not be what you care about most. What would be even better is making a positive impact on the world. What gives you the highest purpose considering your values?

_____

_____

_____

_____

Conclusion

To live an enlightened life is to live life to its fullest. In this state, you have peak experiences of optimal functioning and are self-actualized through creating a balanced, happy, and easy life. Enlightenment is also living with purpose whereby your decisions are aligned with your values. It's about transcending the basic needs of making a living and is instead about focusing on making living the point.

How You Can Reach Enlightenment

"If I really want to change my life, I might best begin by changing my mind."

– Pico Iyer

SO FAR, WE'VE said that enlightenment is about lightening your load so you can get to optimal performance. It results from brain training and is necessary to living your best life. Now that you know what it's all about and have some buy-in, let's uncover how you can get the results you want.

As I alluded to earlier, your brain can lead you astray. It can create meaning where there is none, interpret situations as threatening when they are simply colored by your personal lens, and lead to stress and burnout when it is working against you.

To best understand how you can overcome problematic thinking patterns and other cognitive obstacles, let me share with you what it takes to get unstuck.

Getting Unstuck

You have likely found yourself feeling frustrated and thinking, "I can't get out of this, no matter what I try." This happens when you see yourself doing the same thing over and over again and are unable to break out of a negative pattern.

There is a name for this. It's called self-sabotage. The name itself can be upsetting to people because it can be interpreted to mean that you're doing it to yourself. This is essentially what's happening, but it's unconscious for the most part. You are getting in your own way, but it's not your fault.

So what causes you to sabotage yourself, and what can you do to overcome this so you can live the life you actually want?

Self-sabotage is when you have an internal conflict. There is a part of you that wants something (e.g., more money, a promotion, a better relationship), but there is another part of you focused on self-preservation.

In fact, there are three obstacles that we contend with when we are stuck:

1. *Negative self-beliefs.* These are core beliefs you hold about yourself, other people, and the world. They are typically constructed in childhood or early life and create the lens through which you interpret events happening currently.

If you think to yourself that nothing you do is ever good enough, chances are you also don't believe you are good enough. If you can't seem to find the time to engage in self-care, you likely deem yourself unworthy. And if you are working too hard to avoid making a mistake, you likely see yourself as a failure.

350

When you link your self-worth with your productivity, you worry that every mistake you make will translate into a catastrophe. It's like putting all your chips on one number in the blackjack table rather than recognizing that, in reality, you have chips on multiple numbers, people don't expect you to be perfect, and they won't throw you out simply because you made one mistake.

IDENTIFYING LIMITING BELIEFS

Negative self-beliefs directly affect how you feel and how you behave. You may not be aware of what is driving your behaviors, so work backwards by looking at what you did, reflecting on why you did it, and which limiting belief might be a fit. Fill in the table below accordingly. In column 3, put A for "I am not enough," B for "I am unworthy," C for "I am unlovable," or if there is a different belief you hold, write it in yourself.

Sabotaging behavior	Why you did it	Limiting belief

---

2. *Fear.* When you have beliefs like "I am a loser" and are faced with a challenge that, if successfully overcome, can result in a promotion, you are immediately filled with a fear of failure. Your fears and your core beliefs go hand in hand.

If you let money, status, benefits, or other people's ideas sway you into a job that is wrong for you, no matter how hard you try, you are likely to experience burnout. You will more easily reach a state of exhaustion and overwhelm and feel too tired to engage in life outside of work. This might also be the case if you outgrow your job. Sometimes you keep

351

yourself stuck in a situation solely due to the fear of what will happen if you leave. This requires a perspective shift so you can see your situation from a different angle and then come back to take inspired action. Have compassion for yourself and recognize that you can make an intuitive choice rather than a fear-based one.

Instead of being afraid of the unknown, reflect on this scenario: You are walking through a forest. There are many paths you could take, and you don't know which one is right. You just have to pick one and see where it takes you. It might lead to a roadblock in which case, you'll turn around, get back to the fork in the road, and take a different path. The next time you get to the forest, you'll know not to go down the left-most path, but instead, go down the second path. You are learning as you go and can think about your mistakes as your guides.

If you have a goal and aren't doing anything about it because you're worried you'll be rejected or embarrassed, you are choosing to stay stuck in your current circumstances. Recognize the choices you are making and the ones you are overlooking.

Fears come in many flavors. In addition to a fear of failure and a fear of the unknown, the most popular fears include a fear of missing out and a fear of picking the wrong thing. The latter is what is known as an opportunity cost, and due to this fear, you are less likely to commit yourself to anything new. It's a sign that you don't trust yourself to make the right decision. You might be thinking, "Even if I made a decision, it might be the wrong one." Fear is an indication that you are in a state of conflict. There is a part of you that wants to find enrichment and meaning, and another part worried about the lack of security in making a decision that is not guaranteed to succeed.

LESSONS LEARNED

Take a look at your past experiences. What lessons have you learned?

_____

_____

Rather than regretting decisions that led to failure and not trusting yourself to make good decisions moving forward, consider how you can apply lessons from these experiences.

_____

_____

If what you want is success, keep in mind that people who take more risks are more successful.

_____

_____

Lastly, believing you are a failure sends a message to your brain that instills fear in you. When you are in this state, you might think that when you see evidence to the contrary, you'll change your belief, but it doesn't work that way. As Seth Godin put it, "Stop engaging with the false theory that the best way to stop feeling like a failure is to succeed."[1] You have to believe in your potential first (or at least that you are willing to try) and then take action to ever really have a chance.

3. _Emotional triggers._ When past negative events aren't properly processed, you may find yourself feeling triggered by situations that, in some way, remind you of the original trauma. These triggers can feel overwhelming and lead to the belief that you'll never get rid of them. They can also lead to worries about tackling them again in the future.

Anxiety is your way of planning in advance so that you won't be surprised by what happens. If you struggle with anxiety, you likely spend time imagining possible catastrophes in your mind. It's like packing a suitcase for a trip you don't know you're going to take. The truth is, the majority of what you worry about never comes to fruition and, focusing on the negative only robs you of the present moment.

The better solution is to be in the present at all times, believe in yourself enough to know that you can handle whatever comes your way, and follow your intuition.

Mindset

"There's a difference between having big problems and making your problems big."

– Margie Warrell

Even when you know what to do, if you have a limiting belief, you either won't take action, or you will end up sabotaging your efforts. To eliminate these inner obstacles, you must understand what your unconscious beliefs are.

You might be wondering, "How can I eliminate something I don't even know is there?" Great question. I've already mentioned two ways to go about this. The first is asking yourself why you behave as you do, examining common beliefs that people struggle with and seeing if any of these are true for you. The second is looking at your fears and deducing the underlying belief that leads to this fear. Ask yourself, "What must I believe that makes me afraid?"

For example, do you have a fear of change? If so, what do you believe will happen if things are different? This may be tied to other fears, such as a fear of failure and worry that you won't make it if you take a risk. It might be the idea that others around you may feel threatened by your newfound success, and to feel connected to them, you play small. You may not believe you deserve better circumstances or that you are capable of anything significant.

Perhaps you struggle with indecision. You have analysis paralysis when faced with too many choices. You wonder where to start, so you never take flight. Remember, you don't need a guarantee of future success. You just need to take it one step at a time. When you are in conversation with another person, you don't plan out every sentence you will say. You listen to what they are saying and bounce off of that in a natural rhythm. In the same way, focus on one action at a time and see where that takes you. Then you roll with what's in front of you. Trust yourself to find direction from within.

Your core beliefs develop early in life. One of the most common beliefs I've seen in my clients is the belief of personal inadequacy, which drives the focus on productivity. By ensuring that what you do is good enough, you get a temporary sense of relief. It's as if you hope your output will be an indication of your worth. The problem is, as soon as you finish working on Project A, you barely have any time to absorb your achievement. You are off to Project B, hence the unrelenting nature of this mindset and the propensity toward burnout. Remind yourself over and over that contrary to popular belief, your worth does not come from your work. It comes from your true nature. When you eliminate fear, you are more present and can allow your best work to come forth.

By understanding your beliefs and how they are or are not serving you, you can decide to change them. It might feel scary at first to do things differently, but as the saying goes, "If you always do what you always did, you will always get what you always got." Be bold. Be brave. Be you.

Do you ever tell yourself, "When I get a raise, then I'll be happy"? My client, Sally, worked in sales. During one of our sessions, she told me she wanted to close a deal she was working on, but had tremendous anxiety because she knew the customer was looking at her competition. She told me, "If I close this deal, I will be happy."

I explained to Sally that she doesn't have to wait to feel happy. She can choose to feel it in this moment regardless of whether she closes the sale or not. I then asked her some follow-up questions. Here's what I learned:

Sally had closed a sale earlier in the week. She felt happy for one hour afterward, but then became anxious again as her focus shifted to the next sale she needed to make.

Her closing rate was 25 percent, which meant that she was spending 100 percent of the time feeling anxious before closing any sale, then feeling disappointed 75 percent of the time when the sale didn't close, and even when she did close a sale, her happiness only lasted for a very short time.

If your happiness depends on circumstance, you are fooling yourself. This is a deficit model, where nothing is ever enough. The phenomenon of desires not being met that leads you to chase after a substitute is known in Buddhism as "hungry ghosts."

Focusing on money when what you want is happiness is a form of procrastination. You have less control over how much your boss will pay you than you do over how you feel. When you focus on the aspect of your life over which you have less control, you are likely to be less successful, which will then fill you with shame and self-doubt. You need to focus on finding satisfaction in what is in front of you rather than always living for tomorrow. Don't put your happiness on hold. Find joy in every moment.

One of the ways to adopt an abundance model is by practicing gratitude. Being grateful for what you have (even your challenges, failures, and difficulties) increases energy, reduces anxiety, improves sleep, and creates feelings of social connection.

To make the transition from a deficit model to an abundance model of thinking, you just need to change your viewpoint. Instead of "I have failed," tell yourself, "I can learn from my mistakes." Instead of "this is too hard for me," say, "I won't know until I try." Rather than becoming defensive or finding fault with others and saying, "Their advice doesn't help me," be open to influence and think instead, "I will try those ideas out."

To set yourself up for success, you need to program your mind in the direction of your goal. There are several ways you can do this, but here are five examples.

1. Every day, visualize the end-result. See yourself doing the work you dream of doing. Notice how you feel satisfied and fulfilled on the job. Notice how easily you get out of bed in the morning because you are filled with excitement about the day ahead.

2. Affirm your goal out loud. State what you are doing as if it's already accomplished, as in, "I am a successful chef working four nights a week at a beautiful Italian restaurant. I love innovating new recipes and getting the staff and the diners' enthusiastic feedback. My job gives me the flexibility to live a life of luxury and spend time with the people who are most important to me." Say this each day.

3. Communicate your goals to people who care about you and who can support you emotionally. Make your goal public to keep yourself accountable for your progress. If possible, work with someone else who is also striving for something new. When you communicate your accomplishments, your brain can recognize everything you have already done. This can help you keep moving forward with optimism.

4. Learn to prioritize what you spend your time on. Don't try to bite off more than you can chew. Focus on what is most crucial to help you make progress. Sometimes this means working directly on your goal, and sometimes it means going to sleep to recharge.

5. Be compassionate with yourself. Expecting everything to work out as you planned is unrealistic. We tend to overestimate how much

we can do and underestimate how long it will take us. Your plan won't be perfect. Your implementation will suffer on certain days. Regardless of what happens, it's a journey. You are making progress. Be kind and turn off any critical or judgmental voice that is comparing your performance to others or to an ideal.

Now that you know how to get unstuck and how to get your mind to work for you, we will dive into some practices you'll want to adopt into your daily life that can enlighten you.

Conclusion

Before you can attain an enlightened state, you need to remove any mindset barriers that keep you stuck. In particular, pay attention to negative beliefs you hold about yourself, to fears, and to emotional triggers, all of which create anxiety and take you out of the present moment. Instead, create an abundance mentality by focusing on gratitude, using power tools such as visualizations and mantras, obtaining social support, prioritizing your time wisely, and applying self-compassion.

Enlightenment Practices

THE BACKBONE OF THE 7E Solution to Burnout is the practices that lead to success. You already have a taste of some of them (e.g., mindfulness and meditation), but this section delves more deeply into how they can prevent burnout, how to put them into practice, and how they build on one another.

Mindfulness

"... steal, or still, the echo, so that you don't allow an event, however unpleasant or momentous, to claim any more time than it took for it to occur."

– Joseph Brodsky

Mindfulness is a skill that allows you to be present. It is having an awareness of where your mind is at any given moment and bringing it back to center. When you are mindful, you connect the dots between feelings of anxiety and being in the future (worrying about things that could go wrong). When you are aware, you also realize when you are stuck in the past (thinking about all the mistakes you've made, the misfortunes you've experienced, or the difficulties you've faced). Mindfulness can bring you back to the here-and-now whenever your mind has strayed. When you become the observer of your mind, you have the wherewithal to make a change.

There are five main obstacles to mindfulness. They are:

1. *Being on autopilot.* When you make decisions without any conscious effort, as happens when you engage in a habitual task like driving, you can easily drift out of the present moment. Because many of your limiting beliefs are unconscious, they often drive you to self-sabotage in an automatic way. And even when you are aware of habits you want to change, you might find it nearly impossible to do so because they are so ingrained.

2. *Dissociation.* When the circumstances you are facing are emotionally overwhelming, your mind might flee by re-focusing on something other than the task at hand. This can serve as a clue that something about the situation is an emotional trigger.

3. *Habits of mind.* If you have a habit of criticizing yourself, you may not even realize you're doing it. When you fall into such a habit, you can easily ruminate for minutes, hours, or even days about a mistake you made, which prevents you from being mindful.

4. *Attachment.* Everything is transient. When you become attached to the past, you fear change. When you become attached to how you want things to be in the future, you become anxious about them not working out. These attachments distract you from what's happening right now.

5. *Lack of training.* Like an untrained puppy, your mind naturally tends to run all over the place. If you want it to be still, you have to train it how to do so, which takes consistent practice over time. Mindfulness is this practice. It's about being aware of where your mind has wandered and redirecting it over and over again back to the present moment.

The key to success in many of the areas covered in this book is mindfulness. It increases your self-awareness and self-management, crucial aspects of Emotional Intelligence. It helps you pinpoint and minimize energy drains so you can increase personal power. It allows you to identify which tasks you find pleasurable and challenging so you can immerse yourself in them for optimal engagement and performance. It gives you a sense of when you need to recharge, so you don't run out of fuel, and alerts you when the effort-reward equation is out of balance so you don't lose motivation. As you're about to see, mindfulness is the key to overcoming burnout because of the way it counters the three biggest contributors to chronic stress: high demands, low control/resources, and low energy.

MINDFULNESS AND DEMANDS

Stress is based on the perception that the demands exceed your resources. When you focus on meeting demand after demand without taking time to replenish your energy, you can burn out. Therefore, high demands, low resources, and low energy often come together for the perfect storm.

When your work places a lot of demands on you, it can feel stressful if you think you don't have adequate time to finish your tasks, if you don't believe you are capable given your skill level, or if you lack the mental energy to focus.

Mindfulness is being aware of where you stand and is the first step toward taking the right action. It helps you discern what your stuck points are and gain control over your body and mind. Because stress is based on perception, when you utilize tools that bring you into the present moment, you get out of future thinking and can change your current state.

Through mindfulness, you slow your mind down. It allows you to dig deeper than merely focusing only on the external demands, on your negative thoughts about being unable to accomplish them, or on the lack of confidence you feel inside. You start to witness your breath and feel your body. You become aware of what might be scary and can challenge your thoughts to ensure they are accurate rather than fear-based.

Through positive self-talk, you can build up your resilience, remembering challenges from the past that you've overcome and changing your perception about what is possible. When you take the time to process information rather than react to it, you can assess whether the demands are solely external or whether you are adding your own demands for perfection. This can allow you to adjust your expectations so you feel capable and surer of yourself. Even if you need to take a step back before taking a step forward, by mindfully engaging in every moment, you are listening to your inner voice and honoring yourself.

It is said that we often overestimate what we can accomplish in one year but underestimate what we can achieve in three years. From my experience, I believe that we overestimate what we can achieve in a day, and when we burn out, we underestimate what we can accomplish in that same period.

I've worked with many high achieving clients who struggle with time management, partly because they underestimate how long tasks can take. They fail to account for events over which they lack control.

For example, if you know it takes you 30 minutes to drive to work, you may leave at 8:30 am to get to the office by 9 am. However, that doesn't account for traffic or the time it takes to find parking. In the same way, when you're working on a project, there are usually aspects that you depend on others for, and because they may take more time than you believed at first, it can delay progress on the goal. Even if you are the sole contributor to a project, you can't assume that you'll always be optimally focused and relaxed to get the job done in the time you think. That's why, as a rule of thumb, I encourage my clients to double the time they believe a task will take. It's always better to err on the side of having extra time between tasks than to be running late and stressing out. Having more time also allows you to recalibrate your energy before moving onto the next task.

Part of self-awareness is being mindful of your strengths and weaknesses. If you are given a task you deem to be beyond your skill level, consider whether this is indeed the case or rather a fear response to potential failure. If you truly lack the necessary skill, decide whether you are going to focus on professional development to fill in the gap or whether you are going to communicate about the inappropriateness of the assignment given your current knowledge and experience.

You already know that enjoyment increases task engagement. While it may not be realistic to expect that every aspect of your job will feel enjoyable, you can focus on the elements of the task that feel more pleasurable. Consider what about the work that you are doing provides you with an inherent reward, and zoom in on that aspect to alter your perception of the task.

Challenging your perceptions of yourself and what is possible is one part of job crafting. The other part is making decisions about how you conduct your work to make it more meaningful. Research conducted by University of Michigan professors points to four techniques that can help professionals in the service industry craft their job to have a more significant impact (see Figure 35.1).[1]

1. Go beyond your job's essential functions. If you are a nurse or doctor, this might include educating your patients on how to take care of their health. Lawyers might want to provide clients with recommended reading to protect themselves legally. Administrative assistants might look for ways to increase their skillset so they can perform a broader range of tasks or be more proficient in the tasks in which they already engage.

2. Tailor your services to your customers' needs. Your clients will have varying needs, and by tailoring your services to those needs, you have an opportunity to craft your job and create a human connection.

363

For instance, bookkeepers may take the role of a "financial therapist" and calm the nerves of their entrepreneurial clients. Chefs can alter recipes to address dietary restrictions. Therapists can customize their sessions depending on their client's goals and level of distress.

3. Avoid negative communication with customers. Often, professionals in the service industry become burned out because they deal with customers who are unpleasant, extremely needy, or unappreciative. While having good communication and negotiation skills are important to help you deal with such interactions, finding ways to avoid working with such individuals can be part of job crafting. If you've ever been to a restaurant that has a sign saying, "We reserve the right to refuse service," you've seen this principle in action. Consider how you can apply it to your industry.

4. Conduct your work in meaningful contexts. As a psychologist, I could choose to work in a hospital, a clinic, a foster care agency, a university, or a private practice. In deciding where you perform your job, think about the population you most want to serve.

By crafting your job to suit your needs and passions, you gain control of your experience at work. This can improve your self-image, your human connection, and your resilience. It is a way to increase your resourcefulness so you can cope with demands with less stress.

As you can see, job crafting is a way to alter your perceptions of your job as well as design your job to better fit your needs. To do so, you need to be aware of your needs, desires, strengths, and weaknesses. Mindfulness is what helps you increase that awareness.

Making Service Work Meaningful
Grant et al., 2007

Go beyond
the basics

Tailor your
services

Avoid draining
customers

Work in
meaningful contexts

Figure 35.1

MINDFULLY AND MEANINGFULLY MANAGING WORK DEMANDS

1. Is the task within your skill level? (Y/N) _____

   ❑ If you answered yes, skip to question 2.

   ❑ Is your reaction based on fear? (Y/N) _____

   ❑ If yes, focus on overcoming your fear.

   ❑ If no, do you plan on expanding your skill set? (Y/N) _____

   ❑ If yes, what resources do you need? _____.

   ❑ If no, ask to be given a more appropriate task.

2. Is the task pleasurable? (Y/N) _____

   ❑ If yes, skip to question 3.

   ❑ Identify one or more aspects of the job that is pleasurable or provides an inherent reward:

   _____

   _____

3. How can you go beyond your job's basic functions?

   _____

   _____

4. How can you tailor your services more to your customers?

   _____

   _____

5. How can you minimize negative communication with customers?

   ❑ Is the context in which you work meaningful? (Y/N) _____

   ❑ If yes, congratulations!

   ❑ If no, what other contexts can you work in that would be more meaningful?

   _____

   _____

MINDFULNESS AND CONTROL

When you deem a task to be stressful, you are evaluating your resource-fulness and stating that you fall short to meet the demands this task asks of you. Part of your framework in thinking about resources is your desire for control.

Throughout this book, you have seen the topic of control come up again and again. Control is an essential aspect of how you see yourself in the workplace. It's the reason people become perfectionists and are self-critical and judgmental of others. Let's take a look behind the scenes of how you might seek to gain control in ways that are sabotaging your intentions and how mindfulness can help you become more aligned with what you truly want.

As you know, perfectionism entails putting a ton of pressure on yourself to perform above and beyond expectations. So why would anyone in their right mind put such pressure on themselves? This behavior is in response to fear. If you are perfect, you reason, no one can criticize you. The hope is that your performance will speak for itself. And, if you are perfect, you can feel superior and even criticize others, which protects you from getting hurt. The problem is that needing a goal to be perfect is not only unattainable, therefore setting you up for failure, but in the process of aiming so high, you burn out.

Also, the downside of taking a perfectionistic approach is that it leads to loneliness.

For some people, perfectionism is born out of a desire to be orderly in the midst of chaos. Consider the story of Joey, who grew up in a family where he needed to compete for positive attention. He was one of five kids, and his parents, while they tried their best, were in over their heads. In an attempt to introduce some sanity into his home, Joey learned to be very neat, exacting, and orderly. This worked well to balance his otherwise chaotic environment.

As Joey grew up, his environment changed. He no longer lived with mom, dad, and his four siblings. After graduating college, Joey became romantically involved with Jenny. He had a good job and was making enough money to save up for his future.

But one thing stayed the same despite the changed circumstances: Joey was still a perfectionist. He worked hard at his job and in his home life with the same tenacity as he did when he was a kid. He carried around a belief that he wasn't good enough, which motivated him to strive harder. He was afraid of laziness and would overcompensate through his strong work ethic to prove to himself he was diligent.

On some days, Joey felt good about himself if he was able to attain his goals at work. He set the bar high so he could feel proud of his accomplishments. On such days, Joey found himself even feeling a sense of entitlement and superiority to his coworkers. On days when he couldn't meet the high bar he had set for himself, Joey struggled with low self-esteem as he wallowed in disappointment.

After a while of feeling in the dumps about himself, Joey developed a fear of failure. He didn't like how he felt when he failed. There was nothing glamorous about that state, so Joey did what he could to avoid it. He procrastinated on his tasks at work. In his mind, if the outcome didn't turn out as well as he wanted it to, he could save face by stating that he only gave it 10 percent of his efforts. It wasn't an accurate representation of his ability.

While Joey's justification tactics could help him avoid feeling bad about his failure, they didn't prevent it. When failure did show up, it reinforced Joey's belief that he is "a loser," which made him buckle down and set even higher standards for himself to prove his worth. But the fear did not subside, and the pattern of failure and avoidance continued.

Perfectionism is an overcompensation for a sense of helplessness and is an attempt to find control. If the end-result is that you feel worse about yourself because you've failed or exhausted yourself trying, you must find a better way. Ask yourself, "What would it be like to strive for excellence instead?" By taking your standards down a notch so that they are attainable and still very respectable, you have an opportunity to shine.

Rather than focusing on being perfect, aim to create a balance between doing good work and getting the job done. All too often, you might find yourself lagging because the outcome of what you are working on doesn't meet your standards. The goal is to get it done well and move on. You have other fish to fry, so don't get stuck on just one fish. Once you finish your task, take time to appreciate your efforts and to be happy with the outcome. In other words, don't focus too much on what other people might think of it. Instead, give yourself a seal of approval.

By incorporating self-compassion, reframing failures, and giving yourself credit for trying even when what you tried did not come out as well as you would have liked, you can overcome perfectionism and engage in your work in a way that allows you to stay in the game long-term and feel satisfied.

The good news is that by letting go of perfectionism, you will not only feel more satisfied in your work, but your relationships will benefit as well. According to one study, perfectionists were 33 percent less likely to have satisfying relationships.[2] So, to help your relationships at the office and beyond, give yourself permission not to know all the answers. Admit your mistakes and take responsibility for your failures. Let go of excuses and rationalizations. Don't become defensive when someone points out something that bothers them about you or your work. Take a deep breath and remind yourself that you are enough, and as a human, you aren't going to get it right all of the time. By reaching beyond your insecurities and opening yourself up to others, you can lead a more fulfilling life filled with connection rather than isolation.

As you've seen, the opposite of perfectionism is compassion. When you drop your critical self-statements and focus instead on self-assurance and on developing a growth mindset, you will feel better connected to yourself. This approach also provides you an opportunity to expand relationships with others, which, as we know, is what's most important in life at the end of the day.

Getting back to the issue of control, you want to seek control in healthy ways. True control comes from controlling your energy, your emotions, and your behaviors, which primarily come from being mindful. This means focusing on creating conditions that lead to optimal perform-ance and letting go of any attachment to the end-result. As Seth Godin says, "You're responsible for what you do, but you don't have authority and control over the outcome."[3]

In an attempt to be in control, you might try to control your feelings by fixing them, avoiding them, or distracting yourself–anything in order not to feel them. These approaches only lead your emotions to intensify. Even when you're not aware of your feelings, if they are left unprocessed, they live in your body. Ultimately, you feel less in control by avoiding your feelings than you would be facing them. Only when you are mindful of your emotions and can self-regulate are you truly in control where you can live without constant fear. Remaining unaware of how disconnected you are from yourself can lead to dysregulation, disorder, and disease.

When you have good self-management in this way, you can engage purposefully in your work and feel satisfied. In *Why We Work*, Barry Schwartz explained this notion. He correlated work satisfaction with engagement, challenge, autonomy, and "making a difference in the world."[4]

If you tend to focus a lot of your energy on what other people might think about you, in essence, you are giving away your power. You might let other people's perceptions of you sway your decisions, but this is a fruitless endeavor. You cannot control how other people see you and rarely can you truly know what they are thinking anyway. Be mindful of what you are focusing on and why.

Joey would benefit from understanding that his perfectionism was born as a way of coping when his environment was chaotic, but that it's no longer serving him. Instead of tying his self-worth to his productivity, he would need to work on the belief that he is good enough just the way he is without any qualifiers. Instead of setting himself up for failure by creating unattainable goals, Joey would benefit from creating goals he could accomplish given his time, qualifications, and everything else on his plate. By practicing self-compassion, he could stop being so hard on himself and thereby increase his motivation to work on his goals without fearing failure as much. But when failure rears its head, Joey could reframe it to mean that he is trying and learning along the way. He could give himself credit for his efforts and progress in his goals, no matter the immediate outcome.

By implementing the above changes, like Joey, you too could enjoy your work more. You would have less internal pressure to succeed, less harmful self-judgments, and be more aligned with your goals. You would like yourself more and feel more comfortable sharing your talents with the world.

MINDFULLY ATTAINING CONTROL AT WORK

Put a checkmark next to each strategy you are already using and an * next to the rest:

- ❑ Strive for excellent rather than perfect work
- ❑ Balance doing good work with getting the job done
- ❑ Appreciate your efforts no matter the outcome
- ❑ Substitute self-assurance and a growth mindset for critical self-statements
- ❑ Give yourself permission not to know all the answers

❑ Admit your mistakes

❑ Let go of excuses and rationalizations

❑ Remind yourself that you are enough

❑ Focus on what you can learn from each situation

❑ Restrain yourself from focusing on other people's perceptions of you

❑ Create attainable goals

Consider incorporating items with an * into your routine.

MINDFULNESS AT WORK

Mindfulness has been shown to decrease stress and anxiety, improve physical health, and increase Emotional Intelligence. Many companies are providing mindfulness classes to their employees and even starting their meetings with a meditation.

In his book *Mindful Work*, author David Gelles cites findings from a study done at the American insurance company, Aetna. There are high monetary costs to companies when their workers are stressed. To be accurate, Aetna found that it costs approximately $2000 more per year in healthcare for each employee who was highly stressed. In 2012, Aetna began implementing mindfulness programs and found that their healthcare costs went down by seven percent, the equivalent of over $6 million. And to put the icing on the cake, productivity went up by about $3000 per employee. No wonder companies like Apple, Google, Intel, and many more are taking notice and implementing their own workplace mindfulness practices.[5]

According to the Fiscal Times, 80 percent of executives at General Mills reported being able to "make better decisions" and 89 percent "said they became better listeners" after practicing mindfulness for seven weeks.[6]

Findings from internal research done at the legal firm Herbert Smith Freehills point to a 10 percent improvement in employee performance after a six-week meditation program due to increased focus, efficiency, communication skills, and work-life balance.[7]

Clearly, mindfulness is beneficial mentally, emotionally, and physically. That said, let's see how to optimize mindfulness further.

Meditation

Mindfulness results from training your mind to be still. To attain such control over yourself, you need a tool. Meditation is just what the doctor ordered.

Throughout this book, we've touched on meditation. You may have tried it in a yoga class or even adopted it as a practice. Whatever your understanding of this concept at this juncture, adopt a Beginner's Mind.

There are many forms of meditation, so not all meditation is created equal. We could argue that any kind of meditation is beneficial, but you need to properly align your goals with your tools to have the desired results.

Meditation can be guided or unguided. The beauty of guided meditation is that it is sometimes easier to keep your mind focused this way and is an excellent way for beginners to get acquainted with the nature of their mind.

Guided meditations can be used for relaxation, to increase awareness of bodily sensations, to connect you to spirit, and to help you visualize something beyond what you usually allow yourself to consider possible.

These are all wonderful ways to get into a positive space, but they don't necessarily train your brain to increase mindfulness. There is a meditation practice dedicated to this particular skill. If you want to increase your mindfulness muscle, practice a mindfulness-based meditation.

Your mind produces thousands of thoughts each day, and if you let it, ideas will endlessly stream in and out of your mind. The point of mindfulness meditation is to notice those thoughts rather than be swept up by them.

Imagine that you are a lifeguard. You are not in the water, but rather watching the actions of those below you. Similarly, when you are mindful, you are the observer of your thoughts. This is the first step. Once you notice thoughts taking up space in your mind, you consciously let them go. The goal is to focus on the space between the thoughts and, over time, to increase that space more and more.

Once you have accomplished this feat in meditation, you can start applying mindfulness outside of the practice. When you are going about your day at work, you can begin to notice your thoughts and refocus your mind. You can be more aware of what would typically distract you and bring yourself back to your work. You can notice more keenly how you feel when you are interacting with others around you and keep your emotions in check.

If you want to be muscular, you will have to pump iron regularly to maintain your results. Going to the gym once or twice will not suffice. Similarly, meditation is a practice. In order to maintain its benefits, you will need to develop a routine around it. Even if it's only for five minutes a day, this is an opportunity for you to be consistent.

In the book *Altered Traits*, Goldman and Davidson report on the changes to the brain that occur shortly after participants started practicing meditation. They found that the part of the brain where we process emotion (the amygdala) shows less reactivity to stress when people meditate. Also, participants' attention improved with practice. They were able to focus for more extended periods of time, their mind would wander less, and they improved their working memory, which allowed them to remember relevant information mid-task.[8]

374

To create an optimal meditation practice, focus on clearing out any clutter in your environment. Clutter blocks energy from flowing. If you've ever cleaned out your closet, you know how light you feel when there are fewer items around.

In addition to clearing physical clutter, make sure your financial affairs are in order. Pay off any outstanding bills. Focus on getting rid of any debts, so you can feel financially free. Because money is energy, by eliminating debt, you can attract more money into your life and have a stronger meditation as the energy flow is improved.

By stilling your body and staying consistent with your breath, you can focus your mind and reach the calm you seek, the peace you crave, and the joy you desire. You may have to mourn your losses, resolve your grief, and overcome your anger and disappointments to get there, but happiness is always in the heart beyond these emotions. Access the visual guide to a mindfulness meditation at www.BurnoutToResilience.com.

SETTING YOURSELF UP FOR SUCCESSFUL MEDITATION

- ❑ Declutter a space in your home for meditation

- ❑ Get your financial affairs in order

- ❑ Create a daily routine of meditating

- ❑ Keep track of your meditation sessions manually or through an app (e.g., Insight Timer) to keep your streak

- ❑ Focus on the space between your thoughts

- ❑ Each time you notice that your mind has wandered, bring it back without judgment

---

Selflessness

In addition to refocusing the mind, meditation is an opportunity to go beyond the self. Your beliefs about yourself and what is possible are often related to your personal history. If you grew up to believe that you don't matter, you'd be more likely to interpret situations at work to mean that you are unimportant. By bringing your old self into your current circumstances, you continue self-sabotaging patterns.

The self is also full of notions of how you compare to others. Often, this is how we decide about our self-importance. This can lead to arrogance on the one hand or a sense of insignificance on the other. When you derive your sense of self from what other people achieve or think, you are not only giving away your power, but you are more likely to engage in actions that you hope will gain you approval.

Your beliefs fuel your thoughts, which may leave you wondering, "How can I know if my inner voices are real?" They are a part of your experience, but are they part of the "self"? The keys to knowing your truth are to relinquish your need for admiration from others, follow your intuition, and listen to your body. Does the message you hear in your head resonate as truth, or is it a reaction to a circumstance or an embedded sense of insecurity?

Meditation helps you gain clarity and erase the self. It is your chance to take a step back and separate what you're bringing in from your personal history and what is coming from the job. It is a reminder to give others the benefit of the doubt rather than letting your generalized distrust of people get in the way. By letting go of the self, you can have honest conversations and get the perspective of someone who has been in the company longer or who has more experience to widen your lens.

Erasing the self means letting go of the stories you tell yourself about yourself and others. It is about mindfully identifying where your fears and desires lie and letting go of your attachments to them. If you are afraid to go against the grain because of what other people might think, release this fear. If you aspire to get recognition for your work, without which you feel resentful, this is a desire to let go of. Fears and desires only bring suffering. By practicing selflessness, you can be present and employ critical thinking rather than act impulsively, automatically, and mindlessly.

When you focus on desires, it brings up the fear of failure and the fear of missing out with worries such as, "What if I don't get this?" Should you be successful in attaining your goal, you might become fearful of losing it and wonder: "What if I can't hold onto what I've learned?" or "What will happen to my newfound success if I make a mistake moving forward?" Focusing on all of these "what if" scenarios takes you out of the present moment and you miss what is right in front of you. Instead of enjoying what you've accomplished, you're focused on potential disasters.

Take a step back to examine this pattern. From afar, you can see that it is not rational. If you were to live your life like this, you would never do anything. You would never get married because of the fear of divorce. You would never go to school because you might not pass an exam. You would never venture abroad because you might not find your way. This is the true form of missing out.

In meditation, notice your thoughts and whether they are tied to fear or desire and let them go. Remind yourself that you want to live in the here-and-now so you can appreciate life more fully and feel fulfilled by what is currently within rather than what might be without.

As with mindfulness, you can apply the skill of selflessness outside of meditation. This is when you focus on the greater good rather than on your ego. Often, my kids will storm into the kitchen begging for me to give them some task to do. They say they want to help. What they want, in fact, is to have an adventure. Their desire to partake in the food preparation is for their own sakes. It's not out of compassion for their

377

mother who is cooking. If what I really need is for them to do a task that is not very adventurous (like setting the table), their response is usually "I don't want to do that." As their mother, I can exemplify selflessness by giving them a task that I may not need help with, but that will entertain them. And when my kids engage in less exciting tasks to be truly helpful, they demonstrate their selflessness.

Being selfless is about wanting to do something that is not for yourself. Karma yoga is dedicated to making your work a spiritual practice whereby you selflessly give of yourself to your employer. Through this practice, you derive a sense of purpose beyond your desires. It's about making a contribution. It's about having an impact that is not about you.

In a recent study, researchers examined how kindness relates to goal attainment.[9] Because altruistic kindness is associated with intrinsic rewards and the emotional part of the brain, when participants gave altruistically without any external reward, they reaped the benefit of their action immediately. Their prize was intrinsic satisfaction. When participants exercised strategic kindness, there was a delay in incentive because this type of kindness correlates with extrinsic rewards. In other words, even when you are giving, if you are focused on what you will get in return, you will have to wait and see whether your actions get reciprocated or your reputation improves. But when you are selfless (or what these researchers referred to as "prosocial"), you end up with a greater reward because goal attainment starts immediately.[10]

By focusing on others, you tap into your giving spirit and, thereby, feel more connected. Your efforts have more significant meaning, which makes them more personally rewarding.

Sunshine was someone who worked in a deadline-driven environment. She would focus on getting as much done as she could before her deadline. Sometimes, however, she found that even with her most con-siderable efforts, she would not meet specific markers in time.

Instead of wasting time and energy trying anyway, she would help her coworkers get more accomplished in time for their deadline. Because she was generous with others, they would want to reciprocate the following quarter, which helped her reach greater heights than had she tried to accomplish her tasks alone. Not only that, she was well-liked, and this made her working environment pleasant and helped her feel easily motivated to go to work each day.

When you are selfless, even when you work long hours, you do not become drained. In the same way that optimal engagement allows you to work diligently without losing your energy, being selfless gives you a sense of lightness. That is because "the self" is very heavy.

Self-description holds you back. It tells you what you can and cannot do and is based on what you've learned from others. It's an illusion that makes you struggle and lose personal power. Release your personal history and self-description and find new possibilities within you.

When you immerse yourself in a task without the self, you go beyond thoughts and fears. You are pure action and allow intuition to guide you. This is a way to remain powerful.

Sometimes we think we have to do something to get to the next level. Enlightenment, which is the ultimate state of power, comes from doing nothing. By stilling the mind, you gain self-control, can shed the self, and be fully present.

Consider yourself a selfless warrior who can stop thought in meditation and stop any attack against you outside of meditation through the purity of your mind.

When someone else gets the promotion or attention you were seeking, be happy for them rather than bask in negativity about yourself.

Practice humility. Honor your opportunities. Take on new challenges, including delving into tasks that you don't like or are afraid of. This promotes growth and lets you reconstruct your story to be more fitting for where you are in that moment rather than staying stuck with the story of who you were.

CULTIVATING SELFLESSNESS

Use meditation as a means to go beyond the self. Identify one item at a time from the list below you want to release and focus on letting it go in your meditation:

❑ Admiration from others

❑ Stories about yourself

❑ Stories about others

❑ Fears

❑ Desires

Use these guidelines to maximize your practice:

❑ Discriminate between what is internal and what is external

❑ Give others the benefit of the doubt

❑ Employ critical thinking rather than act impulsively, automatically, and mindlessly

❑ Focus on the greater good rather than on your ego

❑ Make your work a spiritual practice

❑ Practice altruistic kindness without any external reward

❑ Allow your intuition to guide you

Heartfulness

Mindfulness is a way of gaining control over your inner world, and hopefully, by now, you see the benefits of practicing meditation and staying present. That said, there is a way to level up from there.

When you are mindful, you are focused on your thoughts. This is a good practice, as mentioned, but to be great, you will need to focus on the heart.

Heartfulness goes beyond conscious awareness. It's what leads you to be free because it's not about just observing what is happening, but rather about liberating you from limitation.

We saw how selflessness frees you from the confines of the ego, including fear and desire that ultimately lead to suffering. In a similar vein, heartfulness leads to transformation. It goes beyond your thoughts and into a deeper dimension that encompasses your values and true nature. When you are coming from the heart, you have compassion and a more positive frame of mind. On a day when you are struggling with work, heartfulness would allow you to take a step back and consider everything going on in your life. You could slow down rather than rush through every moment. This would center you with a greater appreciation for what you have.

Hamdi Ulukaya, the founder of America's biggest selling Greek yogurt, Chobani, exemplifies heartfulness. It all started when he went to see a yogurt factory that had been in existence for 80 years and was closing its doors. He saw how the workers whose families had been at the factory for generations were being given up on and became upset by this. He decided to purchase the factory, re-hire all the employees, and rebuild.

What made Ulukaya successful was his focus on community. He did not focus on the return on investment and how much money he could make. Instead, he focused on the people. He brought his heart into every decision, from training unskilled workers to employing refugees and immigrants in need of jobs. He focused on creating a thriving community with schools and soccer fields, and, in return, his company became wildly successful.[11]

Heartfulness is also about control and acceptance. Control is the result of mindfulness–being present and impeccable in your actions. This means having systems in place that lead you to be organized.

When you come home, you have a hook that you place your keys on so that you can easily find them the next morning when you are heading to work. In the same way that you keep your toothbrush on the bathroom counter so that you can effortlessly find it when you first wake up, you would find ways to organize your life and minimize unnecessary stress.

Acceptance is about letting go of things that are out of your control. Too often, we waste precious resources lamenting how events could have or should have gone. Recognize when you have control over a situation and do your best to show up fully, but when something is out of your control, let it go and accept the outcome.

By applying control and acceptance, you can be more heartful in your approach, more effective, and calmer even when life is hectic.

CULTIVATING HEARTFULNESS

Take a moment to recall what your intentions and vision for your career were when you first got started and write about this below:

_____

_____

Now reflect on the person you have become in the process:

_____

_____

What changes would you like to make to re-align yourself with the person you want to be?

_____

_____

Conclusion

There is no one antithesis to burnout, but there are essential skills and a mindset that can transform your experience. Your mind is key to this transformation because it is what brings about limitation. To conquer the mind, you need to establish and maintain a practice of mindfulness through meditation. You need to move beyond the ego to overcome fears and desires so you can be more in the moment. Ultimately, you want to bring your heart into everything you do because it establishes a connection from which you will derive meaning and pleasure.

You have the power to design your life, to live with purpose and intentionality so that at the end of your days, you can reflect back and feel contented and fulfilled.

Success comes in many forms. You have to reach beyond the materialistic world to find meaning. You find success when you are living authentically, when you can attain what you want beyond your basic needs, and when you surround yourself with other people. Take the advice of Albert Einstein (as quoted in LIFE Magazine): "Try not to become a man of success but rather try to become a man of value. He is considered successful in our day who gets more out of life than he puts in. But a man of value will give more than he receives."[12] The real reward is about who you become in the process.

When you are aware of something that is not uplifting you, it is an energy drain. You then have an opportunity to fix it. Rather than focusing on the problem, utilize your tools of meditation, mindfulness, compassion, selflessness, and heartfulness to make things better.

Instead of waiting for the perfect circumstance to present itself to you, focus on finding perfection in every condition.

Even when you have the best plan in the world and the greatest strategy to help you implement it, you can get stuck. Ironically enough, you are the reason for this stuckness. You get in your own way.

You do this by second-guessing your decisions, by going for instant gratification rather than thinking long-term, and by letting your past determine your future.

Enlightenment is going beyond the limitations of your mind based on your personal history and tapping, instead, into your limitless potential. By letting go of your attachments to the past, you free yourself to explore what is possible, attain greater heights, and lighten the load you carry. Just decide to be positive in the face of negativity, and you will be more powerful and experience more joy.

E#7: Empowering Exercise

While the empowerment blueprint is engagement, the enlightenment blueprint is non-engagement, or keeping still. There are reports of participants who practiced meditation and experienced improvement in focus and working memory after only two weeks.[1]

Now it's your turn. For the next two weeks, aim to spend 10 minutes or more in silent meditation daily. It is best to meditate first thing in the morning before you check your phone or email. With a clear mind after you get up (and possibly shower and drink a glass of water), sit down with a timer. Close your eyes and attempt to focus your mind. When you notice your thoughts drifting, simply bring your focus back to center without judgment. The more you see your mind wandering and bring it back, the stronger your mindfulness muscle becomes.

Fill in a daily entry for your start and end time as well as any observations about the practice itself (e.g., "I was able to bring my mind back twice today" or "I became aware of a pain in my body I didn't realize was there before").

Day	Start Time	End Time	Observations
1			
2			
3			
4			
5			
6			
7			
8			
9			

10			
11			
12			
13			
14			

Write below what changes you notice in your focus and working memory at the end of this two week trial:

_____

_____

_____

_____

_____

_____

_____

_____

If you found this helpful, consider maintaining meditation as a long-term practice.

CONCLUSION: From Burned Out to Fired Up

"I walk down the street. There is a deep hole in the sidewalk. I fall in. I am lost. I am helpless. It isn't my fault. It takes forever to find a way out. I walk down the same street. There is a deep hole in the sidewalk. I pretend I don't see it. I fall in again. I can't believe I'm in the same place, but it's still not my fault. It still takes a long time getting out. I walk down the street. There is a deep hole in the sidewalk. I see it is there, but I still fall in. It's a habit. My eyes are open. I know where I am. It is my fault. I get out immediately. I walk down the same street. There is a deep hole in the sidewalk. I walk around it. I walk down a different street."

-– The Parable of the Hole, Portia Nelson

The Seven Burnout Solutions

IF YOU'VE BEEN going through life in the same way and getting the same results, it is time to take responsibility and find a new way. This book provides you with seven different solutions to burnout (see Figure 36.1), each of which contains scores of additional resources and ideas. All the information you need about how to approach your circumstances differently is here. Now it's time to implement.

Figure 36.1

People burn out for different reasons depending on varying levels of demands and control, so it is necessary to start by identifying where you are on the engagement spectrum. To shift to optimal engagement and attain optimal performance, you'll need to take seven steps.

Step 1: Hone in on your Emotional Intelligence to better understand your needs. Upgrade your self-talk. Affirm that you are enough.

Focus on your strengths. And, of course, understand and control your emotions.

Step 2: Once you've identified your needs, Empower yourself. Prioritize what to focus on and get rid of any distractions or the idea that you have to get everything done. This helps the demands seem more reasonable and less stressful.

Empowerment is about being aware of what gives you power and what takes power away. Personal power is when you know that you can set your mind to doing something, find the fire within you to face the task even when it's hard, and come out the other side.

Step 3: Whatever you've deemed important enough to focus on, immerse yourself in that task for optimal Engagement. This is how you can enjoy your work without the pressure of being spread too thin. It's good to be immersed, but not so much that you drown.

For optimal performance, your fundamental need for autonomy must be met. While you may not have the independence to make every decision related to your work, autonomy can be seen as a willingness to engage in your assigned activities. It is a mindset declaration and a reminder that you always have a choice. Rather than feeling victimized by your tasks, state that you choose to be exactly where you are doing exactly what you are doing. And, when you decide that you are ready to choose differently, you can go forth with strength.

Engagement is also enhanced by both job resources (social support) and personal resources (hope, efficacy, resilience, and optimism).

Lastly, you need good time management skills, so that you can be both efficient and effective. Take inventory of what is getting in your way of engaging optimally and focus on building up your inner resources.

Step 4: As a result of engaging in tasks, you are likely to have more significant accomplishments. Let your mind mentally absorb your achievements to build up your Efficacy. Doing so will help you take authentic action, leading to the sense of pride you feel when you've achieved your goals and a sense of confidence in your ability to tackle additional tasks. It is that same sense of confidence that then fuels your courage to continually take risks and achieve more exceptional and challenging endeavors over time.

This is the action-focused protocol. However, to go higher, feel more fulfilled, live up to your potential, have a sense of purpose, and live the life you want to live, you need to incorporate three additional steps.

Step 5: As you are busying yourself with action, you need to be aware of your Energy, so you have sufficient fuel to keep going. The essential aspects of this step are to protect and recover your energy. Take breaks throughout each workday and take periodic vacations to unplug from work and recharge. Stop worrying about other people's perceptions of you. Your work ethic doesn't define you, and how hard you work does not define your work ethic. The quality of your work, more so than the number of hours you put in, makes the difference. If you are sluggish or exhausted, even if you sit in the office all day, you are not that valuable to anyone.

When you show up powerfully to work, you still need to prioritize self-care to recover any spent energy to stay afloat. Doing so requires setting healthy boundaries and having a strong sense of self-worth detached from productivity.

Step 6: Utilize your energy to engage in your work in a way that maximizes your Effort. This is about tapping into your motivations. If you are focused solely on external rewards, there is a chance that this job is a poor fit. Sure, you want to feel appreciated and well-compensated, but too often, we look for justifications for staying at a job we hate by asking for a raise or a promotion. Look for intrinsic rewards, like a sense of purpose, to drive you. Also, focus on manifestation and allowing the universe to help bring what you want to fruition, so you don't have to work so hard.

Step 7: The final burnout solution is Enlightenment. This is about getting the right mindset so you can lighten your mental load. This happens through a training of the mind using meditation and mindfulness practices.

Enlightenment is also about living a balanced life through selflessness and heartfulness. Rather than having your work burn you out, you need to have a burning ambition to engage in your work for the sake of the work itself, not for the results it will yield. When your ego is entrenched in your work, you have perfectionistic and unrealistic standards that can stress you out. You might worry about aspects over which you have no control, like whether you will get promoted. By engaging selflessly, you focus on overcoming challenges and delivering high-quality work.

Finally, when you bring your heart into everything you do, you are genuinely present, compassionate, and calm. As a result, you will more easily connect with others and draw people and success to you.

PUTTING IT ALL TOGETHER

Now that you've been exposed to each of the 7 burnout solutions, it's time to see how they can be applied together to your situation.

Doing Track:

Emotional Intelligence:

1. What are your unmet needs?

2. Choose an affirming self-statement:

3. How can you focus more on your strengths?

4. What will you do to control your emotions more?

Empowerment:

1. What are the most important tasks to prioritize?

2. What can you do to eliminate distractions?

3. How can you harness more of what gives you power?

4. How can you minimize energy drains?

Engagement:

1. How can you eliminate obstacles to optimal engagement?

2. What can you do to attain more social support?

3. How do you plan to increase personal resources (hope, efficacy, resilience, optimism)?

4. What changes can you implement to better manage your time?

Efficacy:

1. Identify an area where you lack efficacy:

2. What are some past accomplishments to consider?

3. What encouraging statement can you tell yourself given your past accomplishments that can build up your confidence in this identified area?

4. What small action can you take to have a small win?

PUTTING IT ALL TOGETHER

Non-Doing Track:

Energy:

Use the checklist below to manage, protect, and recover your energy:

- ❑ I take breaks throughout the day
- ❑ I take vacations at least once per year where I unplug from work
- ❑ I recognize that my productivity does not define my worth
- ❑ I have healthy boundaries in place that ensure I incorporate self-care

Effort:

- ❑ My job provides me with inner rewards
- ❑ I focus my mind on what I want rather than what I don't want
- ❑ I maintain a clutter-free work environment
- ❑ I fill my mind with positive thoughts and gratitude

Enlightenment:

- ❑ I train my mind through regular meditation and mindfulness practices
- ❑ I focus on overcoming challenges and delivering high-quality work
- ❑ I practice compassion with myself and others
- ❑ I keep bringing my focus back to the present

Making Sense of It All

The information presented as solutions to burnout can also be organized and understood energetically. There are energy centers in your body called dantians (according to Taoist tradition) or chakras (according to Indian tradition; see Figure 36.2). While there are seven main chakras along the spine, we will focus on the ones that align with the three dantians. These centers of energy correspond with the proposed solutions to burnout.

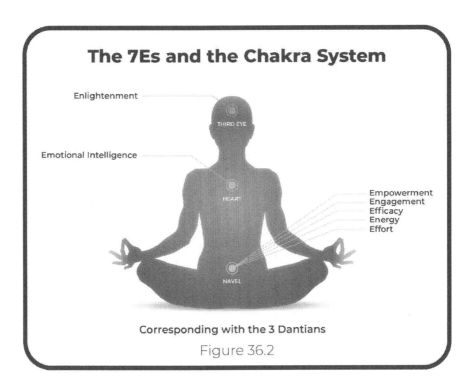

The 7Es and the Chakra System

Enlightenment

Emotional Intelligence

THIRD EYE

HEART

Empowerment
Engagement
Efficacy
Energy
Effort

NAVEL

Corresponding with the 3 Dantians

Figure 36.2

The lower dantian (navel chakra) is the center of personal power, which gives you access to your gut to make informed decisions.

We began this book by talking about Empowerment, Engagement, Efficacy, Energy, and Effort. These are all practices that strengthen you at the core, by which they augment the fire in your belly so that you can achieve what you desire.

Enlightenment and its associated practices are affiliated with the upper dantian (third eye chakra), the area between your eyebrows and slightly up. This chakra is your center of vision, perception, logic, and intuition. When this energy center is balanced, you are more prone to see the truth and access your intuitive knowing. This, too, can help you make good decisions.

In between the navel and third eye chakras lies the middle dantian (heart chakra). This area in the center of your chest is the area of love and compassion, which helps you connect with others. It accesses the relationship competencies of Emotional Intelligence to help you understand other people and engage with them. The heart chakra is also where you can practice self-love and find balance between giving and receiving. It is where all healing takes place, and it bridges your physical and spiritual life.

By focusing on these three meaningful energy centers, grounding and strengthening your core while also engaging the power of your mind will help you feel centered. Through the navel, third eye, and heart chakras, you develop power, wisdom, and balance, respectively. Balance lies in the heart. This is where you not only know and master yourself, but love yourself and your life.

When you utilize the 7E Solution to Burnout, you become *Extraordinary*.

A NOTE FROM THE AUTHOR

OVER THE COURSE of my career and through all of my personal development training, I learned some amazing tools, strategies, and mindsets for success. For a long time, I was on the receiving end of the information, consuming it like water to a thirsty soul. Eventually, however, I wanted to bring these powerful life hacks together in a meaningful way to benefit others.

Writing this book has been a gift through which I was able to put down on paper the essence of what has been impactful in my life and that of my clients', and share it with the world.

During the process of writing, I noticed myself going through the seven steps.

Emotional Intelligence: It was the awareness of my strengths and my desire to write that catapulted this project.

Empowerment: Over the past two and a half years, I often had to prioritize writing over other aspects of my business. I learned to minimize distractions and energy drains.

Engagement: I became ironically aware of how immersed I was in the writing. Hours would fly by, and when I would stop ever so briefly to check the time, I realized that I had forgotten to eat my lunch.

Efficacy: Although it has been the longest process I've ever committed myself to (even longer than my doctoral dissertation), my belief in my ability to finish the project never wavered. I started out by writing long weekly entries for my blog and then stitched them together to create this book.

Energy: I practice what I preach, and self-care has been an essential part of my journey that has helped move this book along. With few exceptions, I stuck to my wellness routines and paid close attention to my energy levels.

Effort: Looking back at all the work I've poured into this book can give the impression that it took tremendous effort—and it did, but it did not feel overwhelming. I employed the idea of working smartly and making the most of my time.

Enlightenment: Finally, I have reached the conclusion of this writing with a spring in my step, knowing that I have accomplished what I set out to do with the hope of enlightening those of you who need this book the most. From my heart to yours.

If it's your dream to thrive in your work and personal life, but burnout is getting you down, then set up a time to speak with me at: www.BookAChatWithSharon.com.

―――――――― 7E ――――――――

Remember to claim all the bonus materials from this book, which you can access at www.BurnoutToResilience.com:

- The accompanying workbook with all the book's exercises
- An infographic depicting the various ways burnout can manifest
- A guided breathing exercise to help you de-stress
- A gratitude template
- A guided loving-kindness meditation
- A grounding exercise called Taking Down the Flame
- A boundary-setting exercise to preserve and protect your energy
- A mindfulness meditation

ACKNOWLEDGEMENTS

IT WOULD BE FOOLISH to attribute the winnings of any trophy to only the athlete. It is their coach, parent, team, and role models that help shape their success. Similarly, I have the honor and privilege to acknowledge those who helped shape this book to become what it is today.

It would be remiss of me if I did not first name my husband—not because of his relationship to me, but because of his deep selflessness and understanding. Without missing a beat, anytime I explained that I needed to write, he would find ways to make it a possibility. He never questioned me or complained about my expressed needs. His unwavering support truly touches my heart.

I have been tremendously lucky to have such loving and supportive parents. They have been by my side throughout the writing of this book, supporting me even when they knew nothing of the book's contents. Thank you, dearly.

There is so much that I have learned from the challenges faced by my clients who were brave enough to share their journeys with me and entrusted me to the job of coaching them through the tough times.

Your stories are what, I believe, will help readers of this book better understand the concepts outlined. I thank you for allowing me to share them.

ACKNOWLEDGEMENTS

Every good coach needs a coach, and I have been so fortunate to work with and be inspired by Maryann Ehman and Michelle Kulp whose guidance and wisdom have lightened my load through the writing and publishing of this book, respectively.

I am also indebted to all the support staff that helped take this manuscript and liven it up, including my editors, Nicole Cosgrove and Karin Conn; and my designers, Gaudencio Jr. Canta, Una Salimovic, and Badsha Bulbul. I am grateful for your patience, talent, and creativity.

This book would not be as comprehensive a workbook as it is without the helpful recommendations of my friend Surya. Thank you for taking the time to read my manuscript and provide me with detailed suggestions of how to improve it. Your words of "make the reader work" resonated strongly.

Throughout these chapters, I have briefly mentioned Samvara's name. He is my spiritual teacher and many of these teachings are credited to him. Thank you for your wisdom and for broadening my understanding of what truly matters.

Lastly, I want to acknowledge you: the reader. It takes courage to admit you need help. Thank you for taking the time to read this. I hope this book transforms you out of burnout and leads you to live life the way it was meant to be lived.

ABOUT THE AUTHOR

DR. SHARON GROSSMAN is the founder of the Exhausted to Extraordinary™ Method, a 3-step method to unblock your mind, reshape your thinking, and return the joy to your work in 90 days. As a psychologist and success coach, Dr. Sharon works with 6-figure executives, entrepreneurs, and professionals in high-stress industries who are struggling with anxiety, overwhelm, and burnout. She shares tips and strategies as a keynote speaker and on her weekly podcasts, *Optimize Your Life* and *The Women in Medicine Badass Radioshow.*

Her educational successes are numerous. Dr. Sharon earned a Doctorate of Philosophy in Psychology from Fordham University. She has studied evidence-based interventions extensively including Cognitive Behavioral Therapy (CBT), Eye Movement Desensitization and Reprocessing (EMDR), and Emotional Freedom Technique (EFT), among other Energy Medicine techniques. Dr. Sharon is very committed to helping her clients and audiences utilize powerful tools to overcome life's challenges effectively. To this end, she incorporates mind-body strategies that optimally position your mind and energy, including meditation, mindfulness, and chakra healing and balancing.

Having worked in a variety of settings with clients facing a myriad of challenges, Dr. Sharon has acquired in-depth knowledge and extensive hands-on experience relating to a wide range of personal issues, including confidence, goal setting, and overcoming limiting beliefs.

Her coaching focuses on the whole person. To be truly successful, Dr. Sharon believes you have to be healthy, financially sound, have meaningful connections, and always strive for improvement. She skillfully addresses clients' career concerns such as productivity, stress management, conflict resolution, and leadership. As a mother of two small children, Dr. Sharon understands the challenges faced by working parents and the importance of incorporating self-care into every day. Known for her direct but compassionate and grounded nature, Dr. Sharon coaches her clients via video conferencing, online through her courses, and during specially designed workshops and retreats.

To further follow Dr. Sharon's work online, claim your spot in her FREE webinar: 3 Mindset Hacks High Achievers Need to Avoid Burnout, by going to www.drsharongrossman.com/webinar.

To reprogram your brain to work for you rather than against you, become a member of The Priming Lab.

Go to www.ThePrimingLab.com to become a member today.

Book Dr. Sharon as your Keynote Speaker and she will transform your audience with her high energy, inspirational stories, and empowering strategies.

Her sample speeches include:

Building Resilience to Avoid Burnout

Learn tools to manage and thrive in chronically stressful situations without burning out.

The Power of Mindfulness at Work

Learn how to develop mindfulness to deal effectively with the demands of work without burning out.

Calm Your Anxious Mind

Reduce your anxiety with simple tools so you can be more efficient and effective at work.

Work Smarter, Not Harder: Mastering the Art of Time Management

Get your work done more efficiently so you can have time to recover and come back even stronger.

Boost Your Confidence and Satisfaction At Work

Learn how to develop and utilize four personal resources to increase confidence on the job as well as job satisfaction.

The Compassionate and Strategic Approach to Overcoming Procrastination

Learn what leads to procrastination and how to overcome it through compassion.

How to Reverse a Negative Spiral: Nine Coping Strategies for Success

Learn about how your thinking contributes to your performance and how you can optimize the process.

How to Have Healthy Boundaries At Work

Learn how to set healthy boundaries with others to protect yourself from burnout.

NEXT STEPS

CHALLENGE YOURSELF

Take the 7-Day Burnout to Your Best Life Bootcamp:
www.7DayBurnoutChallenge.com

FREE BONUSES

Access additional helpful videos and downloads for free by visiting:
www.BurnoutToResilience.com

SHARE THE JOURNEY

Now that you've gone through the 7E Solution to Burnout, it's time to share it with your community. Gift the book to colleagues to qualify for FREE monthly coaching videos on topics ranging from conquering your fears to attaining mastery. Go to www.7ESolution.com for more information.

CONNECT WITH ME

Follow me on Facebook. Go to Facebook.com/CoachingBySharon.

Follow me on LinkedIn. Go to www.linkedin.com/in/sharongrossman and click FOLLOW.

For feedback, ideas, or inquiries about hiring me for your company's next event or professional conference, you can write to me at drsharongrossman.com/contact

Dr. Sharon Grossman

NOTES

THE STRESS-BURNOUT CONTINUUM

[1] Peter G. Nixon, "The Human Function Curve. With Special Reference to Cardiovascular Disorders: Part I," *Practitioner* 217, no. 1301 (1976): 765-70, https://www.ncbi.nlm.nih.gov/pubmed/995833.

[2] Suzanne C. Kobassa, Salvatore R. Maddi, and Sheila Courington, "Personality and Constitution as Mediators in the Stress-Illness Relationship," *Journal of Health and Social Behaviour* 22 (1981): 368- 78, https://www.ncbi.nlm.nih.gov/pubmed/7320474.

WHAT LEADS TO BURNOUT?

[1] Evangelia Demerouti et al., "The Job Demands-Resources Model of Burnout," *Journal of Applied Psychology* 86 (2001): 501, https://www.ncbi.nlm.nih.gov/pubmed/11419809.

[2] Lydia Saad, "The '40-Hour' Workweek Is Actually Longer – by Seven Hours," *Gallup*. August 29, 2014, https://news.gallup.com/poll/175286/hour-workweek-actually-longer-seven-hours.aspx.

[3] John Pencavel, "The Productivity of Working Hours," *IZA Discussion Paper Series*, no. 8129 (2014), http://ftp.iza.org/dp8129.pdf.

[4] Demerouti et al., "The Job Demands-Resources Model of Burnout," 499-512.

[5] Miron Zuckerman et al., "On the Importance of Self-Determination for Intrinsically Motivated Behaviour," *Personality and Social Psychology Bulletin 4*, no. 3 (1978): 443–446, https://www.researchgate.net/publication/258180784_On_the_Importance_of_Self-Determination_for_Intrinsically-Motivated_Behavior.

[6] Arnold B. Bakker and Evangelia Demerouti, "The Job Demands-Resources Model: State of the Art," *Journal of Managerial Psychology* 22, no. 3 (2007): 309-328, https://pdfs.semanticscholar.org/535b/dddb991b5ebe252e4030fd4c02c2368e9f14.pdf.

[7] Marcie A. Cavanaugh et al., "An Empirical Examination of Self- reported Work Stress Among U.S. Managers," *Journal of Applied Psychology* 85, no. 1 (2000): 65-74, https://www.ncbi.nlm.nih.gov/pubmed/10740957 .

[8] Haim H. Gaziel, "Determinants of Perceived Deficiency of Autonomy Among Elementary School Administrators," *Social, Behavior and Personality: An International Journal* 17, no. 1 (1989): 57- 66, https://www.sbp-journal.com/index.php/sbp/article/view/578.

[9] Edward L. Deci and Richard M. Ryan, "The Support of Autonomy and the Control of Behaviour," *Journal of Personality and Social Psychology* 53, no. 6 (1988): 1024, https://pdfs.semanticscholar.org/e2be/748cfba7a3500283a8d92e86c15121970172.pdf.

[10] Robert A. Karasek, "Job Demands, Job Decision Latitude, and Mental Strain: Implications for Job Redesign," *Administrative Science Quarterly* 24 (1979): 285, https://www.jstor.org/stable/pdf/2392498.pdf?seq=1.

[11] Dragan Mijakoski et al. , "Job Demands, Burnout, and Teamwork in Healthcare Professionals Working in a General Hospital that Was Analysed At Two Points in Time," *Open Access Macedonian Journal of Medical Sciences* 6, no. 4 (2018): 723-29, https://www.ncbi.nlm.nih.gov/pmc/articles/PMC5927511/ .

[12] Merriam-Webster, s.v. "High-achiever," https://www.merriam-webster.com/dictionary/high%20achiever .

[13] Richard S. Lazarus and Susan Folkman, *Stress, Appraisal, and Coping*. New York: Springer, 1984.

[14] Christina Maslach and Michael P. Leiter, The Truth About Burnout: How Organizations Cause Personal Stress and What to Do About It. San Francisco: Jossey-Bass, 1997.

[15] Robert L. Kahn, Organizational Stress: Studies in Role Conflict and Ambiguity. Oxford: John Wiley, 1964.

[16] Adeboye T. Ayinde and Aderami Obawole, "Pay Satisfaction and Role Ambiguity as Predictors of Burnout Among Osun State Civil Servants, Nigeria," *European Scientific Journal* 15, no. 8 (2019), https://www.academia.edu/38873344/Pay_Satisfaction_and_Role_Ambiguity_as_Predictors_of_Job_Burnout_Among_Osun_State_Civil_Servants_Nigeria?email_work_card=title .

[17] Lazarus and Folkman, Stress, Appraisal and Coping.

SYMPTOMS OF BURNOUT

[1] Steven Stack, "Suicide Risk Among Physicians: A Multivariate Analysis," *Archives of Suicide Research* 8, no. 3 (2004): 287-92, https://www.ncbi.nlm.nih.gov/pubmed/16081394.

[2] Brené Brown, *Rising Strong: How the Ability to Reset Transforms the Way We Live, Love, Parent, and Lead*. New York: Random House, 2017.

[3] Marc Van Veldoven and Sjaak Broersen, "Measurement Quality and Validity of the 'Need For Recovery Scale,'" *Occupational and Environmental Medicine* 60, no. 1 (2003): i4, doi: 10.1136/oem.60.suppl_1.i3.

[4] Robert A. Karasek, "Job Demands," 285.

[5] Ulrich Kraft, "Burned Out," *Scientific American Mind* 17, no. 3 (2006): 28–33, https://doi.org/10.1038/scientificamericanmind0606-28.

SELF AWARENESS

[1] The Myers-Briggs Company, "Myers-Briggs Type Indicator (MBTI)." Accessed September 19, 2019, https://www.themyersbriggs.com/en-US/Products-and-Services/Myers-Briggs.

[2] Abraham H. Maslow, "A Theory of Human Motivation," *Psychological Review* 50 (1943): 370-396, https://doi.org/10.1037/h0054346.

[3] R. Douglas Fields, *Why We Snap: Understanding the Rage Circuit in Your Brain*. New York: Baker & Taylor, 2016: 40-42.

[4] Webpage with date, no author: Wikipedia.. "List of Maladaptive Schemas." Wikipedia. https://en.m.wikipedia.org/wiki/List_of_maladaptive_schemas.

EMOTIONAL LITERACY

[1] Daniel J. Siegel: *The New Science of Personal Transformation*. New York: Bantam Books, 2010: 116.

EMOTIONAL MASTERY

[1] Malcolm Gladwell, *Outliers: A Story of Success*. New York: Back Bay Books, 2011.

[2] *Brené Brown: The Call to Courage.* Directed by Sandra Restrepo, 2019. United States: Netflix, https://www.netflix.com/title/81010166.

[3] Torrey, A. Creed, Jarrod Reisweber, and Aaron T. Beck, Cognitive *Therapy for Adolescents in School Settings.* New York: Guildford Press, 2011; Torrey Creed, "Using the Mnemonic 'Three Cs' with Children and Adolescents," *Beck Institute.* August 4, 2015, https:// beckinstitute.org/using-the-mnemonic-three-cs-with-children-and- adolescents/.

[4] Ilona Jerabek, "Self-Controlled vs. Emotionally Constipated: Study Reveals the Drawbacks of a Lack of Emotional Experience," *PR Web.* June 23, 2018, https://www.prweb.com/releases/2018/06/prweb15583282.htm.

ZONE OF OPTIMAL PERFORMANCE

[1] Eric Barker, Barking Up the Wrong Tree: The Surprising Science Behind Why Everything You Know About Success is (mostly) Wrong. New York: HarperOne, 2017.

EMPATHY

[1] Sergei Prokofiev, *Peter and the Wolf.* New York: Random House, 2004.

[2] Daniel H. Pink, Drive: The Surprising Truth About What Motivates Us. Edinburgh: Canongate Books, 2018: 143.

[3] Emma Seppälä and Marissa King, "Burnout at Work Isn't Just About Exhaustion. It's Also About Loneliness," *Harvard Business Review.* June 29, 2017, https://hbr.org/2017/06/burnout-at-work-isnt-just-about-exhaustion-its-also-about-loneliness .

[4] Caren Baruch-Feldman et al., "Sources of Social Support and Burnout, Job Satisfaction, and Productivity," *Journal of Occupational Health Psychology* 7, no. 1 (2002): 84–93, https://www.ncbi.nlm.nih.gov/pubmed/11827236

[5] Nurse Buff, "12 Ways Nurses Can Beat Compassion Fatigue." September 12, 2015, https://www.nursebuff.com/compassion- fatigue-in-nursing/.

RELATIONSHIP MANAGEMENT

[1] Marsha M. Linehan, *DBT Skills Training Manual*. New York: Guilford, 2017.

[2] Robert B. Cialdini, *Influence: The Psychology of Persuasion*. New York: Collins, 2007.

THE ESSENTIALS FOR EFFECTIVE COMMUNICATION

[1] William R. Miller and Stephen Rollnick, *Motivational Interviewing: Preparing People for Change*. New York: Guilford Press, 2002.

[2] William R. Miller, Cheryl A. Taylor, and JoAnne C. West, "Focused Versus Broad-Spectrum Behavior Therapy for Problem Drinkers," *Journal of Consulting and Clinical Psychology* 48, no. 5 (1980): 590–601, https://psycnet.apa.org/buy/1980-33187-001.

[3] The Dalai Lama and Paul Ekman, Emotional Awareness: Overcoming the Obstacles to Psychological Balance and Compassion: A Conversation Between the Dalai Lama and Paul Ekman. New York: Times Books, 2008.

PERSONAL POWER

[1] Justin Yang et al., "Association Between Push-up Exercise Capacity and Future Cardiovascular Events Among Active Adult Men," JAMA Network Open 2, no. 2 (2019), https://jamanetwork.com/journals/jamanetworkopen/fullarticle/2724778.

[2] Andrew Unterberger, "10 Reasons Peter Gabriel's 'Solsbury Hill' is One of the Greatest Songs of All Time," Billboard. February 25, 2017, https://www.billboard.com/articles/columns/rock/7702117/peter-gabriel-solsbury-hill-anniversary-greatest-song.

WAYS TO INCREASE POWER

[1] Alethia Luna, "6 Types of Energy Vampires That Emotionally Exhaust You," *Loner Wolf.* 13 December 2019, available at https://lonerwolf.com/types-energy-vampire/

BECOMING MORE YOURSELF

[1] Murray Bowen, *Family Therapy in Clinical Practice.* New York and London: Jason Aronson, 1978.

HIERARCHY OF NEEDS

[1] Abraham H. Maslow, "A Theory of Human Motivation," 370-396.

[2] Bronnie Ware, *The Top Five Regrets of the Dying: A Life Transformed by the Dearly Departing.* Alexandria: Hay House Australia, 2019.

[3] Candace B. Pert, *Molecules of Emotion.* New York: Scribner, 1997.

[4] Volney Streamer, *In Friendships Name.* New York: Brentanos, 1909:22.

[5] Tom Rath, *Vital Friends: The People You Can't Afford to Live Without.* Gallup Press, 2006.

[6] Mel Robbins, *Stop Saying You're Fine: The No-BS Guide to Getting What You Want.* New York: Three Rivers Press, 2012.

POOR ENGAGEMENT

[1] Christine Maslach, "Burned-Out," *Human Behavior* 5, no. 9 (1976): 16-22.

[2] Jim Harter, "Employee Engagement on the Rise in the U.S.," Gallup. August 26, 2018, https://news.gallup.com/poll/241649/employee-engagement-rise.aspx.

THREE DIMENSIONS OF OPTIMAL ENGAGEMENT

[1] Wilmar B. Schuafeli et al., "The Measurement of Engagement and Burnout: A Two Sample Confirmatory Factor Analytic Approach," *Journal of Happiness Studies* 3, no. 1 (2002): 71-92, https://link.springer.com/article/10.1023/A:1015630930326.

[2] Jari J. Hakanen, Maria C. W. Peters, and Wilmar B. Schaufeli, "Different Types of Employee Well-Being Across Time and Their Relationships With Job Crafting," *Journal of Occupational Health Psychology* 23, no. 2 (2018): 289-301, https://www.ncbi.nlm.nih.gov/pubmed/28191997.

[3] Mihaly Csikszentmihalyi, *Flow: The Psychology of Optimal Experience*. New York: Harper Row, 2009.

BEING ON FIRE

[1] Mihaly Csikszentmihalyi, *Flow*, 2009.

[2] Ibid.

[3] Mihaly Csikszentmihalyi, *Flow and the Foundations of Positive Psychology: The Collected Works of Mihaly Csikszentmihalyi*. Springer, 2016: 145.

JOB RESOURCES

[1] Wilmar B. Schaufeli, "Applying the Job Demands-Resources Model: A 'How To' Guide to Measuring and Tackling Work Engagement and Burnout." *Organizational Dynamics* 46, (2017): 121, https://www.wilmarschaufeli.nl/publications/Schaufeli/476.pdf.

[2] Ibid., 123.

[3] Jerzy Koniarek and Bohdan Dudek, "Social Support as a Buffer in the Stress-Burnout Relationship," *International Journal of Stress Management* 3, no. 2 (1996): 99-106, https://link.springer.com/article/10.1007%2FBF01857718.

[4] Lebena Varghese and Larissa K. Barber, "Are Your Employees Prone to Workplace Stress? Mentoring May Help," *APA Center for Organizational Excellence* 8, no. 9 (2014), http://www.mas.org.uk /uploads/artlib/are-your-employees-prone-to-workplace-stress- mentoring-may-help.pdf.

[5] Lillian T. Eby, Marcus Butts, and Angie Lockwood, "Predictors of Success in the Era of the Boundaryless Career," *Journal of Organizational Behavior* 24, no. 6 (2003): 689-708, doi:10.1002/job.214.

[6] William S. Marras et al., "The Influence of Psychosocial Stress, Gender, and Personality on Mechanical Loading of the Lumbar Spine," *Spine* 25, no. 23 (2000): 3045–3054, https://www.ncbi.nlm.nih.gov/pubmed/11145816.

[7] Christine Porath, "Why Being Respectful to Your Coworkers is Good For Business." *TED: Ideas Worth Spreading*. Video File. January 2018, https://www.ted.com/talks/christine_porath_why_being_ nice_to_your_coworkers_is_good_for_business/transcript?language=en.

[8] Ibid., Transcript 11:25.

[9] Lexy Adkins, "How Do Employees Asses Fairness?" *DeGarmo Group*. Accessed on November 8, 2019, http://www.degarmo.com/how-do-employees-assess-fairness; Expanded reading on the topic by E. C. Hollensbe, S. Khazanchi, and S. S. Masterson, "How Do I Assess If My Supervisor and Organization Are Fair: Identifying the Rules Underlying Entity-Based Justice Perceptions," *Academy of Management Journal* 51, no. 6 (2008): 1099-1116, https://doi.org/10.5465/amj.2008.35732600.

[10] Jim Collins, *Good to Great*. London: Random House Business, 2001.

PERSONAL RESOURCES

[1] Fred Luthans, Kyle W. Luthans, and Brett C. Luthans, "Positive Psychological Capital: Beyond Human and Social Capital," *Business Horizons* 47, no. 1 (2004): 45-50, https://doi.org/10.1016/j.bushor.2003.11.007.

2 Charles R. Snyder et al., "The Will and the Ways: Development and Validation of an Individual-Differences Measure of Hope," *Journal of Personality and Social Psychology* 60 (1991): 570-85, doi:10.1037//0022-3514.60.4.570.

3 Emotional Competency, "Hope." March 12, 2019, http://www.emotionalcompetency.com/hope.htm.

4 Jim C. Collins, *Good to Great,* 83-87.

5 Fred Luthans, Carolyn M. Youssef-Morgan, and Bruce J. Avolio, *Psychological Capital and Beyond.* Oxford University Press, 2015.

6 Albert Bandura, "Self-Efficacy Mechanism in Human Agency," *American Psychologist* 37, no. 2 (1982): 122-47, https://psycnet.apa.org/record/1982-25814-001.

7 Charles Darwin with David Quammen, *On the Origin of Species.* New York: Sterling Signature, 2011.

8 Carole Dweck, *Mindset.* London: Robinson, 2017.

9 Victor E. Frankl, *Man's Search for Meaning: An Introduction to Logotheraphy.* London: Hodder and Stoughton, 1962.

10 Philip Zimbardo and John Boyd, The Time Paradox: The New Psychology of Time That Will Change Your Life. London: Rider, 2009.

11 Nan Henderson and Mike M. Milstein, *Resiliency in Schools: Making It Happen for Students and Educators.* Thousand Oaks: Corwin Press, 2003.

12 K. M. Connor and J. R. T. Davidson, "Development of a New Resilience Scale: The Connor-Davidson Resilience Scale," *Depression and Anxiety* 18, no. 2 (2003): 76-82, doi: 10.1002/da.10113.

13 Aesop's Fable; [retold by Mark Schlichting]. *The Tortoise and the Hare.* Novato: Living Books, 1993.

[14] Brené Brown, *The Gifts of Imperfection: Let Go of Who You Think You're Supposed to Be and Embrace Who You Are.* Center City, MN: Hazelden, 2010: 63

[15] Lise Solberg Nes and S. C. Segerstrom, "Dispositional Optimism and Coping: A Meta-Analytic Review," *Personality and Social Psychology Review* 10, no. 3 (2006): 235–251, doi: 10.1207/s15327957pspr1003_3.

[16] Glenn Affleck, Howard Tennen, and Andrea Apter, "Optimism, Pessimism, and Daily Life With Chronic Illness," in E. C. Chang (Ed.), "Optimism & Pessimism: Implications for Theory, Research, and Practice," *American Psychological Association*, (2001): 147-68.

[17] Gabriele Prati and Luca Pietrantoni, "Optimism, Social Support, and Coping Strategies As Factors Contributing to Posttraumatic Growth: A Meta-Analysis," *Journal of Loss and Trauma* 14, no. 5 (2009): 364–388, https://doi.org/10.1080/15325020902724271.

[18] Nathan M. Radcliffe and William M. P. Klein, "Dispositional, Unrealistic, and Comparative Optimism: Differential Relations with the Knowledge and Processing of Risk Information and Beliefs About Personal Risk," *Personality and Social Psychology Bulletin* 28, no. 6 (2002): 836–846, https://doi.org/10.1177/0146167202289012.

[19] Leslie P. Kamen and Martin E. P. Seligman, "Explanatory Style and Health," *Current Psychology* 6, no. 3 (1987): 207–218, https://doi.org/10.1007/BF02686648.

[20] Richard E. Lucas, Ed Diener, and Eunkook Suh, "Discriminant Validity of Well-being Measures," *Journal of Personality and Social Psychology* 71, no. 3 (1996): 616-28, doi:10.1037//0022-3514.71.3.616.

[21] Michael E. Mccullough, Robert A. Emmons, and JoAnn Tsang, "The Grateful Disposition: A Conceptual and Empirical Topography," *Journal of Personality and Social Psychology* 82, no. 1 (2002): 112-27, doi: 10.1037//0022-3514.82.1.112; Sara B. Algoe and Jonathan Haidt, "Witnessing Excellence in Action: The 'Other- Praising' Emotions of Elevation, Gratitude, and Admiration," *The Journal of Positive Psychology* 4, no. 2 (2009): 105–127, doi: 10.1080/17439760802650519.

[22] Yik-man Wong et al., "Does Gratitude Writing Improve the Mental Health of Psychotherapy Clients? Evidence from a Randomized Controlled Trial," *Psychotherapy Research* 28, no. 2 (March 2016): 192–202, https://doi.org/10.1080/10503307.2016.1169332.

[23] Lung Hung Chen and Chiahuei Wu, "Gratitude Enhances Change in Athletes' Self-Esteem: The Moderating Role of Trust in Coach," *Journal of Applied Sport Psychology* 26, no. 3 (2014): 349-362, https://doi.org/10.1080/10413200.2014.889255.

[24] Patrick L. Hill, Mathias Allemand, and Brent W. Roberts, "Examining the Pathways Between Gratitude and Self-Rated Physical Health Across Adulthood," *Personality and Individual Differences* 54, no. 1 (2013): 92–96, doi: 10.1016/j.paid.2012.08.011.

[25] Alex M. Wood et al., "Gratitude Influences Sleep Through the Mechanism of Pre-Sleep Cognitions," *Journal of Psychosomatic Research* 66, no. 1 (2008): 43–48, doi: 10.1016/j.jpsychores.2008.09.002.

[26] Philip C. Watkins et al., "Gratitude and Happiness: Development of a Measure of Gratitude, and Relationship With Subjective Well-Being," *Social Behavior & Personality: An International Journal* 31 (2003): 431-52, doi: 10.2224/sbp.2003.31.5.431.

[27] Nathan DeWall et al., "A Grateful Heart is a Nonviolent Heart," *Social Psychological and Personality Science* 3, no. 2 (2011): 232–40, https://doi.org/10.1177/1948550611416675.

[28] Sara B. Algoe, B. L. Fredrickson, and S. L. Gable, "The Social Functions of the Emotion of Gratitude via Expression," *Emotion* 13, no. 4 (2013): 605–9, https://psycnet.apa.org/record/2008-07784-028.

[29] Sara B. Algoe, "Find, Remind, and Bind: The Functions of Gratitude in Everyday Relationships," *Social and Personality Psychology Compass 6*, no. 6 (2012): 455–69, http://cds.web.unc.edu/files/2015/03/Algoe_2012_find-remind-bind.pdf.

[30] Makenzie E. Tonelli and Amy B. Wachholtz, "Meditation-Based Treatment Yielding Immediate Relief for Meditation-Naïve Migraineurs," *Pain Management Nursing* 15, no.1 (2014): 36–40, doi: 10.1016/j.pmn.2012.04.002; Elizabeth A. Hoge et al., "Loving- Kindness Meditation Practice Associated with Longer Telomeres in Women," *Brain, Behavior, and Immunity* 32 (2013): 159–163, https://www.ncbi.nlm.nih.gov/pubmed/23602876.

[31] Harvard Health Publishing. "In Praise of Gratitude," November 2011. Updated June 5, 2019, https://www.health.harvard.edu/mind-and-mood/in-praise-of-gratitude.

TIME MANAGEMENT

[1] Stephen R. Covey, *The 7 Habits of Highly Effective People: Restoring the Character Ethic*. New York: Simon and Schuster, 1989.

[2] Eric Carle, *The Very Busy Spider*. New York: Philomel Books, 1984.

[3] Francesco Cirillo, *The Pomodoro Technique*. 2011-2019, https://francescocirillo.com/pages/pomodoro-technique.

[4] You can access the Rescuetime app at http://rescuetime.com

5 Michael J. A. Wohl, Timothy A. Pychyl, and Shannon H. Bennett, "I Forgive Myself, Now I Can Study: How Self-Forgiveness for Procrastinating Can Reduce Future Procrastination," *Personality and Individual Differences* 48, no. 7 (2010): 803–8, https://doi.org/10.1016/j. paid.2010.01.029.

E#4: EFFICACY

[1] Albert Bandura, *Self-efficacy: The Exercise of Control*. New York: Freeman, 1997.

SELF-EFFICACY SPIRALS

[1] Michael Masuch, "Vicious Circles in Organizations," *Administrative Science Quarterly* 30 (1985): 14-23, https://www.jstor.org/stable/2392809?seq=1; Karl E. Weick, *The Social Psychology of Organizing* (2nd ed.). New York: Addison-Wesley, 1979, 72-88.

HOW SPIRALS GET STARTED

[1] Dana H. Lindsley, Daniel J. Brass, and James B. Thomas, "Efficacy-Performance Spirals: A Multilevel Perspective," *The Academy of Management Review* 20, no. 3 (1995): 645, doi: 10.2307/258790.

WHAT KEEPS SPIRALS GOING

[1] Dana H. Lindsley et al., "Efficacy-Performance Spirals: A Multilevel Perspective," 645, doi: 10.2307/258790.

[2] J. L. Elkhorne, "Edison—The Fabulous Drone," 73, March 1967, Vol. XLVI, no. 3, p. 52, http://www.arimi.it/wp-content/73/03_March_1967.pdf

[3] Robert Rosenthal and Lenore Jacobson, "Pygmalion in the Classroom," *The Urban Review* 3, no. 1 (1968): 16-20, https://link.springer.com/article/10.1007/BF02322211.

HOW TO STOP A DOWNWARD SPIRAL

[1] Dana H. Lindsley et al., "Efficacy-Performance Spirals: A Multilevel Perspective," 645, doi: 10.2307/258790.

[2] Teresa M. Amabile and Steven J. Kramer, The Progress Principle Using Small Wins to Ignite Joy, Engagement, and Creativity at Work. Boston: Harvard Business Review Press, 2011.

REVERSING THE SPIRAL

[1] Lindsley et al., "Efficacy-Performance Spirals," 645.

MINDSET OBSTACLES TO SELF-CARE

[1] Thorpe, Matthew. "12 Science-Based Benefits of Meditation." *Healthline.* July 5, 2017, https://www.healthline.com/nutrition/12- benefits-of-meditation.

MANAGING YOUR ENERGY

[1] J. M. Ellenbogen, J. D. Payne, and R. Stickgold, "The Role of Sleep in Declarative Memory Consolidation: Passive, Permissive, Active or None?" *Current Opinion in Neurobiology* 16, no. 6 (2006): 716-22, doi: 10.1016/j.conb.2006.10.006.

[2] Harvard Health Publishing. "Benefits of Moderate Sun Exposure," September 2005. Updated January 20, 2017, https://www.health.harvard.edu/diseases-and-conditions/benefits-of-moderate-sun-exposure

[3] Michael A. Smith et al., "The Physical and Psychological Health Benefits of Positive Emotional Writing: Investigating the Moderating Role of Type D (Distressed) Personality," *British Journal of Health Psychology* 23, no. 4 (2018): 857-71, https://onlinelibrary.wiley.com/doi/full/10.1111/bjhp.12320.

[4] S. Leikas and V. J. Ilmarinen, "Happy Now, Tired Later? Extraverted and Conscientious Behavior Are Related to Immediate Mood Gains, But to Later Fatigue," *Journal of Personality* 85, no. 5 (2016): 603–15, doi: 10.1111/jopy.12264.

BOUNDARIES

[1] Shel Silverstein, *The Giving Tree*. New York: HarperCollins Publishers Inc., 1992: 27.

[2] "Dr. David Gruder Nonprofit Exchange." *YouTube*. Video File. February 27, 2017, https://www.youtube.com/watch?list= PLruEzkHGNTZ4bt2XgrpQFR6_GGrBKpsGm&time_continue=1184&v =1u3ls59du58.

[3] R. Skip Johnson. BDP Family: Facing Emotionally Intense Relationships. "Escaping Conflict and the Drama Triangle," January 3, 2018. Updated January 4, 2018, https://www.bpdfamily.com/content/karpman-drama-triangle.

TRANSITIONING OUT OF WORK-MODE

[1] U.S. Travel Association. "America's Vacation Behavior is Changing—and For the Better," 2018, https://www.ustravel.org/sites/default/files/media_root/document/2018_ Research_State%20of%20American%20Vacation%202018.pdf.

[2] Ibid., 5.

[3] U.S. Travel Association. "Paid Time-Off Trends in the U.S.," 2018, https://www.ustravel.org/sites/default/files/media_root/document/Paid% 20Time%20Off%20Trends%20Fact%20Sheet.pdf.

E#6: EFFORT

[1] *Oxford*, s.v. "Effort," https://www.lexico.com/en/definition/effort.

SMART EFFORT

[1] *Hidden Figures*. Directed by Theodore Melfi, 2016. United States: 20th Century Fox. Film.

[2] Greg Smith, "Why I Am Leaving Goldman Sachs," *The New York Times*, March 14, 2012, https://www.nytimes.com/2012/03/14/opinion/why-i-am-leaving-goldman-sachs.html.

[3] Christine Maslach, "Burned-Out," 16-22.

[4] Hely Innanen, Asko Tolvanen, and Katariina Salmela-Aro, "Burnout, Work Engagement and Workaholism Among Highly Educated Employees: Profiles, Antecedents and Outcomes," *Burnout Research* 1 (2014): 38-49, https://doi.org/10.1016/j.burn.2014.04.001.

[5] Leon Festinger and James M. Carlsmith, "Cognitive Consequences of Forced Compliance," *Journal of Abnormal and Social Psychology* 58 (1959): 2013-10, https://psycnet.apa.org/buy/1960-01158-001.

[6] Natasja van Vegchel, Jan de Jong, and Paul A. Landsbergis, "Occupational Stress in (Inter)action: The Interplay Between Job Demands and Job Resources," *Journal of Organizational Behaviour* 26, no. 5 (2005): 535-60, doi: 10.1002/job.327.

[7] Christina Maslach and Michael P. Leiter, *The Truth About Burnout.*

RIGHT EFFORT

[1] *Merriam-Webster*, s.v. "Eightfold Path," https://www.merriam-webster.com/dictionary/Eightfold%20Path.

[2] Mark Nathaniel Bing, "The Integrative Model of Personality Assessment for Achievement Motivation and Fear of Failure: Implications for the Prediction of Effort and Performance." PhD diss., University of Tennessee, 2002: 9, http://trace.tennessee.edu/cgi/viewcontent.cgi?article=3536&context=utk_graddiss.

[3] BBC. "Buddhism at a Glance," November 17, 2009, https://www.bbc.co.uk/religion/religions/buddhism/ataglance/glance.shtm.

[4] Samvara, "How to Do Buddhism, Satsang with Samvara." Lecture. Fort Mason Center, San Francisco, CA. October 27, 2018.

[5] Ibid.

[6] Ibid.

[7] Daniel Goleman and Richard J. Davidson, *Altered Traits: Science Reveals How Meditation Changes Your Mind, Brain, and Body*. New York, NY: Avery, 2018: 17.

[8] Daniel Duane, "El Capitan, My El Capitan," *The New York Times*, June 9, 2017, https://www.nytimes.com/2017/06/09/opinion/el-capitan-my-el-capitan.html.

[9] Samvara, "How to Do Buddhism, Satsang with Samvara." Lecture. Fort Mason Center, San Francisco, CA. October 27, 2018

WHAT IS ENLIGHTENMENT

[1] Aaron Antonovsky, *Health, Stress, and Coping*. San Francisco: Jossey- Bass Publishers, 1980.

WHY ENLIGHTENMENT IS IMPORTANT

[1] Maslow, "A Theory of Human Motivation," 370-396.

[2] Eric Barker, *Barking Up the Wrong Tree*, 2017.

PURPOSE

[1] Huan Song et al., "Association of Stress-Related Disorders With Subsequent Autoimmune Disease," *JAMA Network* 319, no. 23 (2018): 2388-400, doi:10.1001/jama.2018.7028; F. Fang et al., "The Autoimmune Spectrum of Myasthenia Gravis: A Swedish Population-Based Study," *Journal of Internal Medicine* 277, no. 5 (2014): 594–604, doi: 10.1111/joim.12310.

[2] Mika Kivimäki et al., "Work Stress and Risk of Death in Men and Women With and Without Cardiometabolic Disease: A Multicohort Study," *The Lancet Diabetes & Endocrinology* 6, no. 9 (2018): 705–13, https://www.thelancet.com/pdfs/journals/landia/PIIS2213-8587(18)30140-2.pdf .

HOW CAN YOU REACH ENLIGHTENMENT

[1] Seth Godin, "On Feeling Like a Failure," *Seth's Blog*. October 15, 2015, https://seths.blog/2015/10/on-feeling-like-a-failure/.

ENLIGHTENMENT PRACTICES

[1] Justin M. Berg, Jane E. Dutton, and Amy Wrzesniewski, "What is Job Crafting and Why Does it Matter?" Positive Organizational Scholarship, University of Michigan, 1 August, 2008, https://positiveorgs.bus.umich.edu/ wp-content/uploads/What-is-Job-Crafting-and-Why-Does-it-Matter1.pdf.

[2] Gordon L. Flett et al., "Perfectionism, Beliefs, and Adjustment in Dating Relationships," *Current Psychology* 20, no. 4 (2001): 289-311, http://citeseerx.ist.psu.edu/viewdoc/download?doi=10.1.1.582.448&rep=rep1&type=pdf.

[3] Seth Godin, "The Illusion of Control," *Seth's Blog*. August 5, 2015, https://seths.blog/2015/08/the-illusion-of-control/.

[4] Barry Schwartz, *Why We Work*. London: Simon & Schuster, 2015:1-2.

[5] David Gelles, *Mindful Work: How Meditation Is Changing Business from the Inside Out*. Boston: Eamon Dolon and Houghton Mifflin Harcourt, 2015.

[6] Laura Shin, "Secret Way to Boost the Corporate Bottom Line," The Fiscal Times. 25 September, 2012, http://www.thefiscaltimes.com/Articles/2012/09/25/Secret-Way-to-Boost-the-Corporate-Bottom-Line.

[7] John Hilton, "Why Mindfulness Works Wonders," *Learning and Development Professional*. February 17, 2016, https://www.thelawyermag.com/au/news/general/why-mindfulness-works-wonders/199457

[8] Goleman and Davidson, Altered Traits: Science Reveals How Meditation Changes Your Mind, Brain, and Body, 2018.

[9] Jo Cutler and Daniel Campbell-Meiklejohn, "A Comparative fMRI Meta-Analysis of Altruistic and Strategic Decision to Give," *NeuroImage* 184, no. 1 (2019): 227-41, https://www.ncbi.nlm.nih.gov/pubmed/30195947.

[10] Ibid, 227.

[11] Hamdi Ulukaya, "The Anti-CEO Playbook." TED: Ideas Worth Spreading. Video File. April 2019, https://www.ted.com/talks/hamdi_ulukaya_the_anti_ceo_playbook?language=en.

[12] William Miller, "Death of a Genius: His Fourth Dimension, Time, Overtakes Einstein, Subsection: Old Man's Advice to Youth:'Never Lose a Holy Curiosity'," *LIFE Magazine*, May 2, 1955: 64.

E#7: EMPOWERING EXERCISE

[1] Goleman and Davidson, *Altered Traits*, 2018.